Cross-Cultural Perspectives on Families, Work, and Change

The *Marriage & Family Review* series:

Cross-Cultural Perspectives on Families, Work, and Change

Katja Boh
Giovanni Sgritta
Marvin B. Sussman
Editors

The Haworth Press
New York • London

Cross-Cultural Perspectives on Families, Work, and Change has also been published as *Marriage and Family Review*, Volume 14, Numbers 1/2 1989.

The Haworth Press, Inc., 10 Alice Street, Binghamton, NY 13904-1580
EUROSPAN/Haworth, 3 Henrietta Street, London WC2E 8LU England

Library of Congress Cataloging-in-Publication Data

Cross-cultural perspectives on families, work, and change / Katja Boh, Giovanni Sgretta, Marvin
  B. Sussman, editors.
    p. cm.
Includes bibliographical references.
ISBN 0-86656-961-8
    1. Family—Cross-cultural studies. 2. Work and family—Cross cultural studies. I. Boh,
Katja, 1931- . II. Sgretta, Giovanni. III. Sussman, Marvin B.
HQ518.C74   1990
306.85—dc20
                                                         89-20092
                                                          CIP

Cross-Cultural Perspectives on Families, Work, and Change

CONTENTS

ABOUT THE EDITORS

Katja Boh, PhD, is a senior researcher at the Institute of Sociology in Ljubljana, Yugoslavia. She is the author of numerous papers, books, and monographs on health, rehabilitation, marital and family ties and relationships, women and work, gender roles, welfare, and retirement. Dr. Boh is an advocate of cross-cultural studies.

Giovanni Sgritta, PhD, is a professor in the Department of Scientific Demography, University of Rome, Italy. He has written over 100 publications on socialization, gender roles, political sociology, work and professional roles, and family studies.

Marvin B. Sussman, PhD, is Unidel Professor of Human Behavior Emeritus at the College of Human Resources, University of Delaware. A member of many professional organizations, he was awarded the 1980 Ernest W. Burgess Award of the National Council on Family Relations, as well as a life-long membership for services to the Groves Conference on Marriage and the Family in 1981. In 1983, he was elected to the prestigious academy of Groves for scholary contributions to the field. Dr. Sussman has published widely on areas dealing with family, community, rehabilitation, organizations, sociology of medicine, and aging. Dr. Sussman is the editor of *Marriage & Family Review.*

Preface

One constant, observers of societies count upon, is change. What is current today is tomorrow's history. Like a surfer on the highest wave on an unknown beach, societies worldwide are precariously perched. The rise to the extreme individuation of person and self has been a long, hard and successful climb, likened to climbing the giant wave. In the process of this climb the individual has shorn herself or himself of dependence on the group. The group exists for the benefit of the individual rather than the individual existing for the benefit of the group.

Societies are at the pinnacle of this surfer's wave or close to its summit. Societies like individuals, once they begin the downswing, will roar into churning waters full of problematics and pathologies created by the very wave itself, the wave which embodies the achievement of the individual regardless of social cost or consequences for the larger group. The roar down the underside of the great wave may land the surfer in the trough where there is ambiguity, uncertainty, malaise, and questioning. Is the achievement modality the correct ideology for humanity and does climbing the career ladder, for example, become tantamount or equivalent to epiphany, being in touch with a divine being? Success in the corporate board room can inflate the ego to such proportions that acts by such elites can be likened to manifestations of spiritual events.

Fortunately, encapsulated egos are easily pricked so that extremism for *self*, for *I*, is found only in limited situations. The question remains, however, what happens to the individual in his descent into the swirling waters which exemplify the social and political chaos of today's communities and societies? Do we have new paradigms, new ways of viewing reality so that the best components of the achievement (modern) society can be linked in supporting and nurturing ways with the best of traditional cultures and systems? The consequences of ascendent individualism necessitates the

xi

search and use of new paradigms which will meld the individual and group into a viable entity capable of providing for the wishes, needs, and aspirations of groups and their individual members.

One paradigm shift which is touching the mainsprings of all cultures and societies is the movement towards gender equity, sometimes referred to as the "gender revolution." The restructuring of relationships between the sexes has dramatically altered structures and practices of societal organizations and institutions in many societies, including the family. There are many other paradigm shifts such as the increasing acceptance of varied forms of families and life styles and efforts of service bureaucracies in a large number of countries to accommodate to this new reality.

This thematic collection is a sampler of substantive concerns studied by various investigators who live primarily in Europe. A careful reading of each respective story should trigger a memory from one's deep consciousness, a memory which recalls a similar story. Also these papers may stimulate the reader's concern to replicate a reprinted study in her or his own country or to begin cross-cultural work with one or more co-partners.

One conclusion from a reading of these papers is that societies vary in their experiencing transformation of historic structures, ideologies, and behaviors to new or modified ones. Special circumstances, cultural traditions, cataclysmic events, political ideologies, economic policies and market place conditions influence such transformations. This unevenness in transformational experience indicates the difficulties in attempting cross-cultural comparisons on any parameter of change. Yet these investigators have selected issues to illuminate ones for which they have a passion and vision. Thus, they have begun a much needed seeding for students to follow in the search for explanations of family and society change and the new paradigms, new ways of perceiving families in their critical roles over generation time.

The Concept of Family Strategy and Its Application to the Family-Work Complex: Some Theoretical and Methodological Problems

Chiara Saraceno

1. The concept of strategy involves at least four elements:

i. the existence of an intelligent actor able to evaluate and to choose;

ii. relationships of interdependent interaction, where the subjects are endowed with the ability to alter each others' behavior by their own moves;

iii. a given set of resources and constraints enabling choices to be made in the course of the interaction; and

iv. a temporal horizon, where time is not only a resource, or a constraint, i.e., relative to the allocation of time, but is the horizon within which the strategies unfold; the future, in which the possible outcomes of choices and decisions are assessed; the present, in which they are evaluated; the past, which provides the choices with form and informational content.

These are crucial dimensions in the understanding of family behavior. However, when applied to the family, they incur a number of theoretical and methodological problems.

The subject: it is here that most of the problems arise, with conse-

---

Chiara Saraceno is Professor, Universita di Trento, Italy.

quences that have repercussions for the other two dimensions. This is not so much a question of the rationality and freedom of the subject as presupposed by the concept of strategy. Rather, it is a problem of the definition of the term "subject" itself. What is at issue is to what extent it is possible to talk of the family as a subject endowed with its own intentionality, interests, rationality and needs distinct from those of its individual members. It seems to me that too little attention has been devoted to this problem, either when the existence of a single "family utility function" has been postulated, as in the authors of New Home Economics, or when attention focuses on the community dimension of the family. Apart from its empirical existence, the boundaries of which have to be established (i.e., with consideration to kinship ties) the family as an entity is also attributed with the property of "subjectivity." This property should be demonstrated. Policies which involve the family are actually directed towards individual members, even if these vary according to the task assigned to the family, or the recognized or claimed right of the family. Focus may be on the wife rather than the husband, the parents rather than the children, or male offspring rather than female offspring. As has been pointed out by Bianchi (1981) and I. De Sandre (1984), the family archetype evoked by many social policies, those adopted by the governing bodies of schools, for example, or those which advocate psychiatric reform or the humanization of social services, entails a particular kind of family order with particular patterns of affectivity. For example, a woman's husband rather than her mother may be with her as she gives birth, but a female relative, and not the father, may stay overnight with the small child in hospital. It also entails a distribution of family power. Different individual members of the family are, in fact, the possessor of different family rights and duties. In particular, as Marina Bianchi has remarked, so called social services for the family are services for women: either to help them with what are still seen to be their responsibilities and duties or to provide them with resources to utilize on behalf of their families. The rights of the family in the area of education are mostly those of the parents towards their children (see the issue of the right of families to decide and control the education of their own children).

The evocation of the family subject implicitly highlights its non-homogeneous, associative, even communitary nature. It is a collective, where its members not only share sometimes common, sometimes divergent and conflicting, interests but also have diversified and unequal access to resources, as well as to the definition of needs. It is this difficulty that has induced a number of social analysts to seek to avoid the term "family" altogether, insofar as it is too emotively loaded to lend itself to precise analysis.

The family as a specific social subject may be discussed, therefore, only with extreme caution. The term may be used to refer to a particular type of collective subject, whose identity and strategies are the result of complex mediations between what is perceived as belonging to "inside" the family and what is perceived as living "outside" the family. This involves a process where the structure of power and authority relationships, the diversity of access, and the availability of resources are important if not crucial factors in the constitution of the family subject itself. The single-career family, the family with two workers, the two-career family, the family that sends its children to work as soon as possible, the family that prolongs its children's economic dependence, the family that encourages independence and the family that encourages solidarity — these are families in possession of diverse resources and use different strategies to deal with the outside world. They are also families that are the outcome of the various strategies of their own members. The individual character of a family, both as an organization and in terms of its culture and images of family and family relationships, is a product of these diverse strategies.

One may, therefore, talk of family strategies as constitutive, productive of the family subject itself.

From these observations emerge the second of the elements that make strategic action possible. That is the interdependent interaction of the actors, both in terms of reciprocal relationships among the members of the family and of the family as an actor in its relations with other institutions. As has been observed by various authors, the model of strategic action, insofar as it is based on methodological individualism, presupposes single actors whose behavior is easily identifiable. However, this model becomes more complicated and less clear when it is applied to collective actors — that is, to families or institutions, e.g., services, businesses, groups. On the one hand, the strategies are as multiple and interwoven as are the forms of interdependence. On the other hand, the power of institutions is not deducible from a simple sum of individual force and actions, and consequently runs the risk of not being correctly understood.

The family as a collective subject, with its internal processes of mediation and differentiation and its asymmetrical potential for power and access to resources, is crucial to an understanding of family strategies with respect to resources, constraints and time. The available resources determine whether a strategy is possible, insofar as they provide or allow alternative behaviors. Resources are not only those embodied by so-called material resources, i.e., income, services, consumption goods, networks of relationships, etc., but are also cultural and symbolic in nature.

They involve family and individual identities, the family's or individual's self-image or self-knowledge and need, against which external material resources are weighed and evaluated. This means that not all so-called "resources" are seen as such by all individuals and families. For example, certain individuals or families prefer not to utilize certain resources, or prefer to appeal to friends rather than to kin for the satisfaction of certain needs. Also the same resource may have differing values for the various individuals and families that utilize it—and often for different members of the same family. Vice versa, not all constraints, the absence or inflexibility of a certain resource, are perceived as such or in the same way by different individuals or families.

Even if one must not disguise inequality as mere differences in values or culture, one must still concentrate attention on the diversity of family culture as an important factor in the elaboration of strategies. "Family cultures" are systems of definitions of needs, of priorities, and of relationships. These are elaborated by families through time and embody definite traditions handed down from one generation to another (and they interweave and combine with others whenever a couple starts a new family, which merges not just the individual histories of the spouses but the separate traditions of their families as well).

These traditions and family cultures, however, change through time; either because they continually combine and mix with others

as they pass down the male rather female lines of descent, or because exposure to different resources and constraints initiates
changes in behavior and evaluation. For these reasons, therefore, it
is not possible to talk of family traditions and culture as if they were
entirely static or immutable. Rather, close attention should be paid
to the ways in which these processes intermesh, to the complicated,
heterogeneous and sometimes contradictory stratification of familial experiences and cultures. The proponents of New Home Economics were aware of this when they included values in their model
for analysis of the family as a unit of rational decision (Becker
1981), although by doing so they impaired the simple and linear
rationality implicit in cost benefit analysis.

It is evident that the unfolding of family strategies happens
through the passing of time. To the extent that behavior is not seen
as mere reaction to stimuli or to external constraints, but rather as a
set of strategic actions, it entails a certain capacity for predicting the
consequences in terms of derived costs or benefits, or changes in
the behavior of others. Simultaneously, it entails a certain continuity with the past, in the form of an individual's memories and the
assessment of the experiences he or she has undergone. This means
that a capacity for strategic action also depends on a capacity for
conceiving time, in relation to the depth and breadth of one's experience of past and future, and to the degree of control that one believes one exerts over it.

It is well known that not all individuals or social groups share the
same awareness of temporal dimensions, or have the same capacities to exert control over time—either in daily life or throughout
their life span (e.g., Palmonari, Ricci Bitti, Sarchielli 1979). Neither do all individuals and social groups perceive their lives as being
punctuated in the same way by the same crucial events, divided up
into the same periods, etc. Comparative research into these dimensions is still scarce, especially in Italy and especially in terms of the
family. Nevertheless, short and long term strategies, immediate or
deferred gratification, the exchange of a service or satisfaction for
another to be repaid in the future, investments with non-immediate
returns, reciprocity of action rather than mere trade, all these involve the individual perception of the time span of one's own life
and of one's control over it. Also the diversity of attitude among

individuals, groups and families is related to the diverse cultures that they create or inherit, and also to the varying resources of planning and control over time that they have at their disposal. Consider, for example, the distinct cultures of time, and the differing strategies that derive from them, that separate city from country, or industrial workers from intellectuals.

Diversity in the perception and evaluation of time and of the crucial nature of timings and transitions, is characteristic of the same members of the family insofar as they do not belong to the same sex or the same age group. It is well documented by research that men and women are sensitive and affected by different timings and transitions in their life courses. The transitions that principally differentiate them are in fact those "common" milestones of family life such as marriage and the birth of children. If this differentiation actually exists, what is meant by elaborating a family strategy over life course time? Whose time-scale and whose point of view will be used in such evaluations?

Furthermore, recognition of this differentiation between the sexes, in terms of their perception of the transitions, dimensions and susceptibility to control of time requires more precise, less superficial attention to be focused on factors of social change. Not all phenomena have the same meaning for all groups and for both sexes. And the risk of analytical monocentrism in terms of social groups and sex, lies not only in the neglect of the experience of the forgotten sex or of unheeded social groups, but also in an inability to understand the range and significance of change. For example, only recently has contraception become a social issue of population structure and of social policy, and its cultural and social significance has become the object of scrutiny. For too long the family organization has been overlooked as the main agent of the process of the transformation of habits of hygiene, diet and sanitation: a process which underlies transformations in our life spans as well as of most of our daily routines (Ehrenreich and English 1978). To the extent that the effects of one's decisions or calculations are manifest only in the future, any analysis of costs and benefits should include not only an individual's perception of the future situation but also his individual and family preferences in the future. Thus, since in effect individuals and families change their interests through time, i.e., in the course of their lives, their strategies may be based on predictions of a future that they cannot control and which they tend to modify, with unforeseen effects. An operation of this sort is made even more complex by the passage from individual to collective actor in a family or other institution.

Age and generational differences as characteristic features of family relations complicate the questions of the perception and evaluation of time even further. They especially complicate family strategies in their dealing with time. From this point of view, an effective family strategy should consist primarily of an awareness that various life courses meet and interweave in the family (Elder 1975), each with its own timing and rhythms and with its own score to follow. For this reason, the various generations present in a family assess their own strategies and those of the family as a whole according to different temporal horizons. One of the great changes that has taken place in family life in our times has been the realization that individuals have the resources to differentiate their strategies and destinies from those of their families. Alternatively, family strategies can be interpreted as being investments and forecasts that vary according to the various life trajectories of individual family members variously privileging the working life of the man, the family life of the mother, the children's chance of finding employment, and so on. Research into the choices made concerning further education after compulsory schooling in Italy (Capecchi et al., 1983) shows, that these are not only differentiated by social class but also by sex. Families assess their children's futures differently and invest varying resources in them.

The diversity between generations, and between cohorts is also matched by a diversity among families, due to their being in different phases of their life courses and having different needs, experiences, resources and constraints.

The application of the term "strategy" to the family, therefore, embraces a series of conceptual and methodological difficulties which require further analysis. One of the benefits of a strategic approach to the family, however, is considering it as a dynamic and not purely reactive subject: one that is part of a network of relationships of interdependence rather than of simple, linear dependence. It is precisely this emphasis on the subjectivity of the family that requires greater attention to be paid to the plurality of members that compose it, as well as to the plurality of family experiences. I propose, therefore, to use it only as a working hypothesis, as an aid in the interpretation of this diversity of levels and experience and to the understanding of the intentionality of family members in their behavior.

It should also be pointed out that family strategies involve different dimensions and contents of experience. One may talk of strategies of fertility concerning the number and spacing of children; strategies of spending and consumption; strategies regarding the entry and exit of members from the labor market, and strategies for the utilization of services. These strategies are not always unequivocally connected one with the other; even less are they automatically deducible from one another. One task of analysis, therefore, is to identify these distinct strategies and, possibly, the ways in which they link together. It should examine the specific relationships of interdependent interaction in which these strategies are engaged, both within the family and between it and the system of constraints and resources that surrounds it. Included as part of this system are the institutional, and not purely individual dimensions of both resources and constraints.

2. *The topic of family strategies from the point of view of work and its transformations necessitates a reduction of the field of observation.* Work — what work, done by whom, when, for whom, in exchange for what, in terms of what needs — the division of labor, access to work, the availability of work and the need for work is a privileged area of so-called family strategies. They provide the context both for the strategies that embody family relations and for the strategies that differentiate between families or, vice versa, make them similar (see also Saraceno 1988).

Focusing on the work-family nexus also illumines the varieties of work performed. One is "family production" (Balbo 1981, Del Boca 1982, Ingrosso 1979, 1984): a formulation which reveals family work as comprising (a) the work involved in patching together, coordinating, supplementing and adjusting available resources, i.e., as a "resources of resources," and, (b) the work involved in the production of the family itself, of its culture, unity, definition of itself and its needs (Saraceno 1980, Bimbi 1985).

A related issue is the complexity of paid work itself in the variety of labor markets and in the formal and informal economies, as well as the changeable behavior of labor supply, dependent on family organization and constraints.

Research in Italy, using the concept of social and economic formation has demonstrated that families living in diverse social-economic areas have access to differing systems of resources and, are also confronted by differing constraints (Bagnasco 1977, Balbo 1976, 1977, M. Paci et al. 1980, Saraceno 1982, Capecchi 1982, Bimbi and Pristinger 1985).

Regarding the work we have called family production, numerous studies have found family work to be specific, complex and by no means residual. This work is entirely internal to contemporary society, characterized by a particular level of technological development, by special patterns of the organization and segmentation of time and the division of labor.

Family work is the result of two processes of modernization. The first has given origin to "house-work" — as distinct from productive work. Family production, in fact, is distinguished from production *tout court* and has its own contents and intentionality. This type of work gives social identity not only to a specific family figure — the housewife, but also to a specific family strategy. In order to maximize the well-being of the family, one person dedicates herself full time during the entire adult life span to serving the family. The task of producing income belongs primarily to another person. Crucial to the definition of this strategy is the availability of resources for domesticity, but also the availability or resources for family and individual needs distinct from those of simple survival and reproduction. The original impulse behind the differentiation of interests within the family is to be found precisely in this identification of family needs. As a consequence, the production of a family identity can no longer be taken for granted but must itself become the object of work and intentionality.

The second process of modernization has increased the range of housework to include utilizing, recomposing and supplementing resources external to the family. Simultaneously, it involves mediation and elaboration of the constraints that these same resources impose, insofar as they contribute to the definition of needs. What is now called family work emerges from this process as being itself composed of various activities and as requiring different areas of responsibility in a continual process of transformation. The concept of family work is no longer adequate for the understanding of this highly-articulated differentiation; except for preserving the important referential term "family," understood both as the object of work and as the members who plan, allocate and carry out this work.

Attempts have already been made to draw up a lexicon that more closely accounts for this highly complex and articulated nature of family work; one that can deal not only with activities and needs but also with family members and their relationships. Thus various terms have been formulated — service work, care, self help — which seek to capture its various dimensions and the various types of relationship in which this work takes place (Balbo 1985).

There is no doubt that research indicates that the modes and strategies of the allocation and investment in family work are still dictated by a division of labor between the sexes. This assumes the features of a definite gender system, as demonstrated by recent survey research which reported that in Italy women are massively present in caring activities directed towards both their own families and kin and friends (ISTAT 1985, Sgritta 1985). Also confirmed by international surveys is the provision of aid and informal medical assistance to family members and kin (Grunow 1985, Riedmuller 1985, Pitrou 1985).

Simply to talk of "traditional" behaviors would be misleading. This would fail to capture the constraints and the social prescriptions that underlie this division of labor, and therefore the specific nature of the contemporary family with its internal patterns of relationships, its nexus with society as a whole. Also it would fail to capture how this particular sex/gender system differs from those of other social systems. The technological transformation of family work, the utilization of services for a series of family needs, new patterns of consumption and widespread school attendance have brought radical changes to the situation of the housewife regarding of standards of adequacy and the distribution of time. These changes have involved and affected cohorts of women who have reached adulthood today, sometimes breaking the linear flow of communication and transmission. Also set in motion are new forms of intergenerational transmission of information and learning and establishing new boundaries and forms of continuity between generations and between sexes.

For these reasons the analysis of family behaviors of adult women is particularly insightful regarding changes in customs, patterns of adequacy, and also strategic action regarding the satisfaction of individual and family needs. The life structure of the contemporary adult woman that has been called "dual presence" (Balbo, 1977, Bimbi 1985) reflects this mesh of adaptation and choice, constraints and opportunities. What should be emphasized is that this is not a question of setting a relatively new role or activity — paid labor — alongside an old one. It is a redefinition of the form and content — of family work and, more generally, of the work of reproduction.

Moreover, these new resources and constraints for family work and for the definition of its object also constitute new criteria and forms of diversification among families at the level of class and rank, and to a significant extent, at the regional and local level.

These differences arise out of the interweaving of various dimensions. Some involve demographic variables: the numerical composition of the family, the phase of the family life cycle and the presence or not of an extended kinship network. These variables, either provide resources for family strategies or constraints, depending on the direction of needs and the flow of solidarity. For example, the above-mentioned ISTAT survey shows that middle age families, who therefore still have children to care for, are among the most dedicated providers of assistance to families with older adults. Further confirmation is provided by the greater flow of inter-family assistance towards those living alone, mostly old people. Finally, the ISTAT survey shows how the flow of inter-family help, the strength of the sustaining network, varies according to geographical area. In areas of high urbanization and in higher social class families the network extends beyond the kinship group (see Sgritta 1986).

These demographic family variables combine with those that concern (a) income, (b) market resources, and (c) public (services) resources. Together, this set of variables establishes the framework of possible resources for family and individual well-being and strategies for achieving it. It should be pointed out that the ISTAT survey implicitly disproves the hypothesis that the absence of market or public services may be compensated for by informal networks of solidarity. On the contrary, it appears that where the social context external to the family is lacking in infrastructures and supply of services, there is a corresponding diminution in the network of informal assistance. Lower-income groups living in less-urbanized area and/or the Italian *Mezzogiorno* resort more frequently to informal assistance since they have scarce resource in terms of income and services, they limit their exchanges within a network of close family relatives, almost entirely excluding friends, solidarity groups or other forms of voluntary assistance. Thus, they are more constrained in their options, in the definition of their needs and in their movement within the network of social relationship. From this point of view, albeit a "strategic choice," family, kinship, even community solidarity may be a more or less constrained option, according to social circumstances. In this regard, the fine research carried out by C. Stack (1974) into solidarity networks in a black urban ghetto in the U.S. found that there are few chances of escaping from poverty without running the risk of breaking the solidarity network. Escape almost inevitably means risking the loss of one's guarantees of survival. Here, an interpretation of behavior in terms of strategies, although it may shed light on the ingenuity of the actors and on the complex dynamics that are set in motion, may overlook those dynamics that more specifically involve institutions or collective actors, e.g., the welfare system and the labor market. Too often the inability to escape from the poverty trap is blamed exclusively on the inefficacy of individual micro-strategies.

The lack of socially provided resources such as social security and social services is certainly a constraint on family options and strategies. But the way these resources are provided may represent a still different kind of constraint. Research has documented for instance the massive constraints imposed by the system of social services on the individual in the form of schedules, rules and conditions of access, and the definition of needs (Martinotti 1982, Bianchi 1981, Saraceno 1984). On the other hand, to treat them indiscriminately as constraints, as it is somewhat fashionable in Italy now, would be just as misleading as to treat them solely in terms of pure resources, as was the fashion until the early 1970s. It is much more fruitful to investigate to what extent, and in what kinds of combination with other resources such as income, kinship networks and time they make it possible not just to carry out relatively efficient, relatively shrewd adjustments, but also to draw up autonomous definitions of needs and standards and definitions proposed. How far can given resources be adapted and bent to suit the requirements of the individual family when they are put together in various packages of resources? To what extent do they grant degrees of autonomy to individual family members, and thus empower them to acquire resources on their own behalf in order to participate in the processes of the construction of the family itself?

The same arguments can be developed, as we shall see, concerning the resources of the informal economy. These too can either be seen as alternative, or substitute or even supplementary resources. In the same way, they can also be seen as constraints on particular members of the family.

It is the package of resources as a whole, their flexibility, compatibility, possible equivalence, articulation and variety that enables the drawing up of real strategies to deal with the modes of working and of reproduction.

From this point of view, it should be remembered that work for the market itself may interfere with the work of family production, since it is both a resource and a constraint for it, by virtue of the income it provides and its distinct timing and schedules.

Too little investigation has been carried out in Italy into the varying organization of time, the division of labor, and conditions regulating the use of services among families who have to cope not only with various incomes but also with differing daily working routines and work careers—something that was the subject of research by Young and Wilmott in England a few years ago (1974). Recent research conducted on a limited and relatively homogeneous geographical area (in the Emilia Romagna region) has demonstrated the variety of family organization—not only regarding the organization of her time by the adult woman, but also the use of services, the scansions and rhythms of the daily routine of the family, deriving from different working conditions such as those to be found in factory work or in the tourist-hotel sector (Balbo 1986).

3. *An analysis of family strategies regarding work in general, and not just family work, provides important data for the understanding of the dynamic of labor supply and its characteristics.* Firstly the family may be viewed as a constraint on a certain quota of the labor force, especially adult female labor. This is not solely a question of seeing adult married women as a marginal quota of the labor force: it is one of seeing female "dual work" — in the family and in the paid labor force — as a fundamental component in family organization. In different ways and symbolic outcomes (as far as they apply to individual and family identities), which vary according to family traditions, the local labor market and the overall system of services, this dual work of the adult women acts as an important family strategy in coping with needs of care and income. However, there is still much analytical work to be done on dual presence/dual work structures, individual life courses and family strategies in the various social classes, geographical areas and cohorts of age.

A second analytical avenue is in the opposite direction. It considers the family organization in terms of the division of labor and composition/distribution of resources not as a constraint, but as a resource for certain members of the labor force. This avenue is still relatively unexplored and what work has been done has been related only to various "weak" or underprivileged groups: the young, the old and women. The family is seen as a resource insofar as it combines different incomes and resources so that a low or partial income from work (or a pension) by an individual member may be integrated with other incomes, or costs of reproduction may be shared with others. Moreover, if a young person, or even an old person, does not have to pay to have his clothes washed or his cooking or cleaning done, or if they have someone to deal with certain bureaucratic matters for them, they can make their earnings go further. Analogously, if a married woman with children is able to count on the family work of another member of the family she has more time to be active in the labor market.

Less attention has been devoted to the family as a resource for the "strong" or privileged members of the labor market. Since the early years of industrialization the factory worker has been closely mirrored by the family worker, the housewife. This nexus between the supply of "strong" work and a particular organization of the family around domestic labor has not weakened at all, but has only been made more complex.

A third avenue for analysis is viewing the family as the site and organizing centre of the informal economy, not only on the labor supply side of labor, but also on the side of production. Of course, analysis solely from the standpoint of the family is not sufficient to investigate in depth all the varieties of the informal economy (see Capecchi and Pesce 1983, Redclift and Mingione 1985). The research mentioned previously on the Marche region demonstrated how work in the informal economy, apart from family work, plays a role in family strategies: work in the home without insurance coverage, part-time work in the family micro-company, or work with output for self-consumption, e.g., in agriculture or building one's own house (see also Pahl 1983). On the one hand, analysis of the way in which these various forms of work in the informal economy provide resources and sources of direct and indirect income makes a major contribution to knowledge of the overall income levels of the family, and to a differentiation in access and availability of resources that is normally neglected (Gershuny 1978, 1983; Pahl, 1983, 1984), the *Exchange et Project* group in France demonstrate that access to informal economy resources, in particular as far as self-production is concerned, reducing expenses may also reduce the amount of income to be procured in the labor market. In this manner, moving away from a metropolitan area and its services to an area with resources for the informal economy may indeed have its compensatory effects in economic terms. Access to forms of informal economy may greatly differentiate between the qualities of life and possibilities for decent survival of families equally placed in the formal economy. On the other hand, the existence of official and guaranteed incomes in the family may provide greater security to those members of the family who function in the informal or non-guaranteed labor market.

However, this kind of analysis reveals a series of problems regarding the actors of these strategies and the definition of needs and the degrees of freedom in both defining them and satisfying them.

In fact, most often found in the informal economy, both in the market informal economy and the informal economy for self-consumption, are certain members of the family — women, old people and young people. Here are also found those families with minor access to the resources of the formal economy — in terms of the labor market and services. For certain groups and individuals, their reliance, whole or partial, on the resources of the informal economy may be a life style choice. For other groups it rather appears an "obligatory choice," given the lack of alternatives. This is true for a large portion of the population of the Italian Mezzogiorno, for many women and older men, for many young looking for their first job.

These remarks bring me back to my opening observations concerning the fruitfulness of the strategic approach for the understanding of family action. Certainly, at a descriptive level, despite the problems of identifying the subject, this approach appears to be most fruitful insofar as it avoids the short sighted *a priori* deduction of family behaviors from institutional expectations and brings to light the various and not always consistent processes that underlie them. However, analysis that limits itself to describing this continuous activity of adjustment, transference, manipulation of resources to meet without simultaneously investigating the diverse nature of the resources available to various groups, power relationships in which interdependent interactions take place, therefore also institutional as well as inter-individual dynamics, runs the risk of only providing a unidimensional photograph; one which reveals variety but hides the inequality among families and within families.

REFERENCES

Bagnasco, Arnaldo. *Le tre Italie*, Il Mulino, Bologna, 1977.

Balbo, Laura. *Stato di famiglia*, Etas Libri, Milano, 1976.

Balbo, Laura. Un caso di capitalismo assistenziale: la società italiana, *Inchiesta*, 7, 1977.

Becchi Collidà, Ada. *Politiche sociali e garanzie del reddito*, Il Mulino, Bologna, 1979.

Becker, Gary. *A Treatise on the Family*, Harvard University Press, Cambridge (Mass.), 1981.

Bianchi, Marina. *I servizi sociali*, De Donato, Bari, 1981.

Bimbi, Franca. La doppia presenza: diffusione di un modello e trasformazioni dell'identità, in *Profili sovrapposti*, F. Bimbi e F. Pristinger (eds.). F. Angeli, Milano, 1985.

Capecchi, Vittorio. Famiglia operaia e cultura borghese, in Capecchi et al., *Famiglia operaia, mutamento culturale, 150 ore*, Il Mulino, Bologna, 1982.

Capecchi Vittorio, Pesce Adele. Se la diversità è un valore, *Inchiesta*, 59-60, 1983.

Capecchi, Vittorio et al. *Prima e dopo il diploma*, Il Mulino, Bologna, 1983.

David, Patrizia and Vicarelli Giovanna (eds.). *L'azienda famiglia*, Laterza, Bari, 1983.

De Sandre, Italo. Famiglia, strategie e politiche sociali, *Inchiesta*, 6, 1984.

Elder, Glen Jr. Age Differentiation and the Life Course, *Annual Review of Sociology*, 1, 1975.

Elder, Glen Jr. Family History and the Life Course, in *Transitions. The Family and the Life Course in Historical Perspective*, a cura di T. Hareven, The Academic Press, New York, 1978.

Enhrenreich, Barbara and Deirdre English. *For Her Own Good*, Pantheon Books, New York, 1979.

Gershuny, Jonathan. *After Industrial Society*, MacMillan, London, 1978.

Gershuny, Jonathan. *Social Innovation and the Division of Labour*, Oxford University Press, Oxford, 1983.

Grunow, Dieter. Lavoro e aiuto sanitario autonomo quotidiano nelle famiglie e nelle reti sociali. Un'indagine nella RTF, *Inchiesta*, 67-68, 1985.

Ingrosso, Marco. *Produzione sociale e lavoro domestico*, F. Angeli, Milano, 1979.

Ingrosso, Marco. *Strategie familiari e servizi sociali*, F. Angeli, Milano, 1984.

ISTAT, *Indagine sulle strutture e comportamenti familiari*, Roma, 1985.

Martinotti, Guido (ed.). *Progetto Torino: La città difficile*, F. Angeli, Milano, 1982.

Paci, Massimo et al. *Famiglia e mercato del lavoro in una economia periferica*, F. Angeli, Milano, 1980.

Pahl, Raymond E. Strategie del lavoro domestico ed economia informale, *Inchiesta*, 59-60, 1983. 1984 *Divisions of Labour*, Basil Blackwell, Oxford, 1984.

Palmonari A., Carugati F., Ricci Bitti P., and Sarchielli G., *Identità imperfette*, Il Mulino, Bologna, 1979.

Pitrou, Agnes. La famiglia contemporanea e le solidarietà familiari: collegamenti e ostacoli per la promozione di nuove pratiche, *Inchiesta*, 67-68, 1985.

Redclift, Manneke and Mingone Enzo. *Beyond Employment*, Basil Blackwell, London, 1985.

Riedmuller, Barbara. L'azione pubblica verso la famiglia e la salute, *Inchiesta*, 67-68, 1985.

Sachs, Ignacy. La crisi, il progresso tecnico e l'economia sommersa, *Inchiesta*, 59-60, 1983.

Saraceno, Chiara. Introduzione to *Il lavoro mal diviso*, C. Saraceno (ed.), De Donato, Bari, 1981.

Saraceno, Chiara. Modelli di famiglia, in AA. VV., Ritratto di famiglia degli anni ottanta, Laterza, Bari, 1982.

Saraceno, Chiara. The social construction of childhood, in Social Problems, February, 1984.

Saraceno, Chiara. *Sociologia della famiglia*, Il Mulino, Bologna, 1988.

Sgritta, Giovanni. La struttura delle relazioni interfamiliari, Atti del Convegno *La famiglia in Italia*, Roma, ISTAT, 1985.

Stack, Carol. *All Our Kin*, Harper, New York, 1974.

Young, Michael, and Wilmott Peter. *The Symmetrical Family*, Routledge and Kegan Paul, London, 1974.

The Impact of Social Policies
on the Italian Family of the Seventies

Rossana Trifiletti

PREMISE:
DOES A FAMILY POLICY EXIST IN ITALY?

Italy is similar to countries found in the typology of Kamerman and Kahn who possess an "implicit and reluctant family policy" (1978, p.329). Recently Italy has adopted "classic" measures of family welfare such as: (1) a recent change in family allowances establishes much higher awards for low income levels; (2) the first report of the Poverty Investigating Commission, which focuses on family size as a cause of poverty, proposes a strategy involving coordination of tax policy and income transfers (Presidency of Cabinet Council, 1987, pp.43-46); and (3) recent provisions adjusting the tax system provide more equitable legal protection to every member of family-owned small enterprises in case of the need for a division of the business (Law N.17, dated 2/17/85).

Involved are measures which, in their disparity, suggest that legislators today have a much greater awareness of possible impact of economic and social conditions on the family institution and of the need to carefully calibrate the means of action of the policy established by law.

Does this signify the need for a more comprehensive family policy capable of coordinating the social welfare sector, already generally recognized in other advanced Welfare States? (Donati, 1981). Another basic issue is whether a policy for the Italian family

Rossana Trifiletti is a researcher in the Department of Political Science and Sociology of the "Cesare Alfieri" Faculty of Political Sciences at the University of Florence, Italy, and is also on the editorial staff of the periodical *Inchiesta*.

really existed previously. Over the past two decades the temptation is to link a series of increased individual liberties in the family to a spate of legislative and judicial actions which, beginning at the end of the 60s profoundly influenced national mores and life-style. Examples are the 1965 Supreme Court decision revising legislation pertaining to adultery; the 1971 decision allowing dissemination of birth control information and the providing for the welfare of working mothers; the 1967 law rewriting adoption laws; the 1968 law instituting kindergarten in the public school system; the 1971 law establishing a national day care center system; the 1975 law setting up free public family planning clinics; the 1977 law guaranteeing sexual equality in the workplace: all of which taken together represent an impressive series of measures in various areas in little more than a decade. This suggests a coherent program of modernization and secularization of those phases of social life regarding the family. In addition, in the same period two of the most widely-known and decisive political conflict took place, revolving around the hotly-debated laws permitting divorce (1971) and legalizing abortion (1978); and the binding national referenda called (unsuccessfully) to abrogate the same. Above all, in 1975 a systematic reform of the family code was passed which gained recognition as being in certain respects among the most advanced in Europe (Cinciari Rodano 1983) and which would seem to represent the culminating moment of this putative program.

The position I am taking in this paper is that there has not been a family policy in the past and that it is unlikely there will be one in the foreseeable future. Even if we adopt the pragmatic viewpoint of a family policy of a "particularistic" type (De Bie 1978, p.6), it is no easy matter to reconstruct a unified decision-making process, even one characterized by piecemeal incrementalism (Lindbloom and Braybrooke 1963). if it is true that "family policy may be defined as the result of an awareness of objectives affecting family which leads to social organized action" (De Bie 1978, p.8), two essential characteristics would seem to be lacking in the Italian experience: the prerequisite of purposiveness (Heclo 1972, p.84) and some interest in the tutelage or transformation of the family; such as might have provided the basis for a policy with non-generic objectives, but which was never brought into existence.

With reference to Gronseth's classical definition of family policy as "a more or less well-defined and coherent theory and practice having as its aim the influencing of the structure and function of family units" (Dumon 1981, p.47), one has the impression that Italy is a case of the practice without the theory. Even the revision of family law which has an appearance of careful planning, incorporates contradictory logics (Donati 1976, pp.163 ss.) and is characterized more by the exigencies of normative compatibility than by any reforming intent.

Thus, the Italian tardiness to act on this matter, can be largely explained in terms of the underlying structural factors: the understandable diffidence of the Left towards issues traditionally associated with demographic policies (Lory 1978, p.71) and the Catholic Church, the existence of more pressing problems relating to uneven socio-economic development (De Bie 1978, p.25). Another "cultural" element should, however, not be underestimated: that of the apparent "invisibility" of the family in the current debate. As Chiara Saraceno has observed, the so-called "rediscovery" of the family in the mid Seventies (Saraceno 1981, p.45) is symptomatic of the sudden realization that the Italian family was still a vital, functioning institution and of the ideological blinders which had over hastily decreed the demise of the family, due to scant empirical knowledge of the subject.

An explanation is called for concerning the fact that while of the advanced nations Italy has among the lowest divorce, cohabitation and illegitimacy rates and the highest incidences of extended families among advanced nations, yet when a politician, journalist or moralist pontificates on the family, it is regarding its supposed crisis and near demise.

Many observers have noted that the need for a family policy begins with the realization of the non-weakening of the family institution (Kamerman and Kahn 1978, p.10; Peters 1978, p.57) supported of descriptive surveys on the normality of various family forms (Fogarty 1981; Sussman 1971b). This would seem to confirm Dumon's thesis that family policy changes not as a function of real needs, but by the perceived views of politicians and governing bodies (Dumon 1981, p.43). It can be inferred that by intervening on the family as a generic—or even undefined—object, some consequences may be unintended.

The visibility and legitimization of family policy are empirically linked to its actual effectiveness (Kamerman and Kahn 1982, p.369). Regarding Italian family reforms, the changes that took place frequently differed from those envisioned, especially where included in their formulation were principles which, although sacrosanct, revealed a complete lack in awareness of the actual impact they were likely to have.

In writing the history of their effects, such reforms could be seen in a pattern diametrically opposed to that which was generally expected.

I will now look at the case of Law N.1431 dated 6/5/67 regarding adoption to illustrate the point. The adoption provision, at the time, was viewed as being highly innovative and progressive. It introduced the principle that affective ties to the adoptive family must take precedence over those of the natural family, even to the extent of granting judicial authority to dissolve the child's relationship with the biological parents.

At the time of the passage of this legislation it represented a huge advance in terms of self realization with respect to the previous compulsory norms of unsatisfactory family ties. This interpretation proved to be naive in the following respects: (1) it assigned to the family courts a role which would create organizational problems; (2) it failed to foresee that a cohort of children unsuitable for adoption would be destined for institutionalization; and (3) it could not predict the unfair effect of confirming the marginal status of certain underprivileged social classes for which adoption would have taken the place of needed rehabilitative measures (Sacchetti 1974, pp.894-896; Sgritta 1984b, pp.226-236; Donati and Nicoletti 1974).

This example suggests that legislative activity in general was based on a highly generic image of what is a good or bad family, without any reference to social background.

If therefore, as it appears, Italy is about to, or will in the future, embark upon a family policy—because of the family's new visibility[1]—it will have to draw lessons from its own experience and that of others, in order to fashion for itself tools of analysis sophisticated enough to:

1. avoid the mistaken assumption that the good intentions of legislators are automatically transformed into implemented policy;
2. work with a realistic image of the family or rather of *families* and their mode of operation.

These two points are worth examining in more detail.

TOWARD A THEORETICAL FRAMEWORK: FAMILY POLICY AND SOCIAL POLICY ANALYSIS

It is an error, however, to think that it is possible to apply directly the reflections and practical experiences of other countries in the area of family social policy to a country with such striking social differentiation such as Italy. The effort toward achieving a comprehensive family policy—something which in reality has probably never been realized anywhere (Buric 1978, p.29)—might well prove to create a dangerous myth in a context so highly diversified geographically and historically such as Italy.

At present the practice has come to the fore in studies regarding family policy to place in typological opposition the more integrated, visible and systematic policies of the European countries with the less-articulated policies of the United States which center more on the individual than on the family unit.

It is evident that the Italian situation presents many affinities to that of the United States, including a long-term interest in a policy of redistribution in vertical as well as horizontal directions (Aldous and Dumon 1978; Lory 1978). Similarities exist in terms of a three-tier legislative and administrative structure. The United States has been one of the more important places where, as a consequence of disenchantment with the social programs of the 60s (Pressman and Wildavski 1973), an interdisciplinary approach in the study of social policy has arisen, especially with regard to implementation. This has been defined as the "missing link" between policy and administration, between the moment of legislative decision-making and the ability to have an actual impact (Hargrove 1975). The fruitfulness of the new paradigm coupled with an ample availability of funding has caused the analysis of the workings of Federal programs, their monitoring and the formal evaluation of their results, to become a widespread practice, fostering the development of appropriate, highly complex techniques.

Therefore, it is legitimate to ask what contribution toward the study of effects on the family may be gleaned from such accumulated experience. Two specific approaches have arisen, *family evaluation research* and *family impact analysis*.

The first represents a fairly routine application of evaluation research techniques to programs which may affect the family. Studies on this type tend to couple sophisticated methodology to quasi-experimental designs with recognized weakness in theoretical concepts (Chen and Rossi 1981; 1973): a practice which is particularly unsuited to the subject of the family.

In particular, given the need for measurable results from phenomena studied, the consequences may be "slipshod" operations in providing scores obtained from batteries of tests involving very young children; the exact weight at birth of babies "at risk" (Keherer and Wolin 1979); or blood pressure readings as a measure of anxiety in teenage mothers (Wildmarer et al. 1980). Most studies seem to skirt the issues, either reaching provisional conclusions due to the inadequacy of existing data bases, as in the debate on child care (White et al. 1973; Boles 1980; Kirst et al. 1980),[2] or arriving at a statement of the non evaluability of relevant factors, which are often precisely those variables of a familial nature that most merit further study, as in the case of home assistance (Weissert et al. 1980; Weissert 1981; Chiswick 1976).

But if family evaluation research limits itself to measuring the effects of programs that involve families *with respect to their stated goals*, much greater expectations were aroused by the second approach, family impact analysis. This is a procedure to foresee unanticipated consequences of the impact of proposed social policies in terms of family variables (Kamerman 1976; Jo Bane 1978; Giele 1979). Even if research appears to be in a preliminary phase of elaboration of formalized models, some empirical research does exist that can be located within the confines of this approach (Nye and McDonald 1979).

The hypothesis has been advanced (Lerman 1973; Turem and Arnow 1973) that transfer payments under Aid to Families with Dependent Children, one of the earliest such programs in the United States, might have a disintegrative effect on the recipient families. Since eligibility was limited to single-parent families, it was asked whether this might constitute an incentive to separation, desertion by the father and illegitimate birth, with the obvious perverse effect of encouraging disruptive behaviors in the very families whose welfare was meant to be safeguarded to the benefit of underprivileged children (Blaydon and Stack 1977). A lot of studies have been accumulated (Ross and Sawhill 1978; Bradbury 1977) which deal with the problem from different cross-sectional or temporal series approaches, using census reports, longitudinal survey data (Bahr 1979), and income maintenance experiments (Hannan et al. 1977). Such studies have on occasion employed diverse methodologies, from a simple crossing of variables to econometric models (Honig 1974; Minarik and Goldfarb 1976) and multivariate analysis: the focus of attention ranged from the illegitimate birthrate (Janowitz 1976), to the number of households headed by women (Ross and Sawhill 1975; Boles 1976); from the incidence of separation or desertion (Greenfield and Falk 1973), to the percentage of divorcees who remarry (Bahr 1979). The difficulty in compiling such results in unified form is readily understandable.

In any event, aside from the unfortunate case of two studies based on identical data yielding dissimilar results by a different procedure of regression (Ross and Sawhill 1978, p.109), a possible synthesis is that the results are neither conclusive nor in open contradiction. The only overall conclusion that can be drawn is that the negative effects produced on the family by Welfare support, if such exist, are of limited scope. Hypothetically they contribute to precipitate family crises that otherwise would have been kept hidden due to the necessity of maintaining the family together, with resulting emotional costs that can only be estimated. In other words, an "independence effect" on women more than real institutional dissolution, just as, conversely, other types of nonselective income transfers would *not* be capable of providing stabilizing effects. By far the most important conclusion that can be drawn is that the income transfer program "affects households composition incentives through *interactions* with preexisting incentives" (Mayo, 1976, p.402, italics added). The possibility of finding correlations depends on one's ability to refine one's analysis and therefore on the choice of other variables to keep under control. The mechanism investigated is part of such a tight network of interrelationships that no identifiable quantitative relation can give the subjective state of the persons directly involved in facing the alternative of breaking or not breaking up a family understandably under stress.

Although this type of research often points to useful details,[3] a basic question is if one's investigation were aimed in a qualitative direction would this be more productive than piling up correlations which have so limited meaning and value. Even authors sympathetic to the family policy approach view realistically the divarication deriving between "broad maps of relevant policies on the one hand and highly specific formulas for measuring narrow policy impact on the other" (Giele 1979, p.298) and make clear that both approaches we are examining derive from the matrix of a rational policy model (Zimmerman 1979).

This last observation is crucial since it is symbolized by the need to construct recognizable approaches, codified as well as by an official name, a precise delimitation of methods and aims and further defined as being "relatively value-free" (Nye and McDonald 1979, p.479; Zimmerman 1979, p.494). This seems the main direction of study of family policy in the United States[4] and conforms to a strictly rationalist model for policy process.

This is neither the only nor the most interesting approach to the policies in question, and thus a progressive divarication between family policy and social policy analysis is now manifest. The last, beginning with the pioneering studies of Pressman and Wildavski (1973) and Bardach (1975) links now to other European approaches involving comparative studies (Heclo Heidenheimer and Teich Adams 1975) and the sociology of organizations and bureaucracies (Ham and Hill 1986). These point to redesigning the process of policy-making to one of limited rationality or of "enlarged" rationality (Boudon 1985).

It is easy to share Sgritta's contention that the qualitative leap in family studies (in Italy and elsewhere) is due to "a tendency toward the progressively more *problematic nature of the disciplinary divisions* of family research" (1984a, p.303). It would be useful and desirable to consider an interdisciplinary approach of this type. While the theoretical short circuit has come about in a productive way in the area of History, Economy and Demography, one could contemplate a fruitful breaking down of barriers of non formal Political Science.

We are not completely helpless when faced with the problem of complexity and of family in complex societies. Italian family sociology needs to rethink the family/state relationship in two ways (Saraceno 1984, p.2): while we now accept as proven that Italian families vary regionally in type and ways of functioning, we are still too rigid in our descriptions of the State as the interlocutor of these families. From this standpoint I view the contribution in terms of realism and down-to-earth thinking that is needed in a study of the impact of social policies on the family (cf. Sussman 1971a).

In the same way the particular features of the Italian family are such as to require a method of study where the starting point is no longer that provided by the naive vision of legal norms, as if the intent of the legislators could be translated without problems of feasibility into social practice (Majone 1975). To consider the law in Italy which extends the possibility of maternity leave to the father as well as to the mother, as a family policy measure capable of having an effect on role division, would be very misleading if not preceded by serious quantitative research. Such research would have to establish first how many people really take advantage of this policy and, second, by serious qualitative methods, how fathers react to it. If this is not done we would find ourselves facing the same sort of difficulties as would occur due to non-consideration of obstacles to application in the actual phase, or the structural conditions of the job market.

The course to follow in investigating the possibility of family policies in Italy, leads in the direction opposite to the way it has developed in the United States, from analysis *for* policies to analysis *of* policies (Gordon et al. 1977). The course should converge with the empirical and short-term studies being pursued regarding the Italian Welfare State (Ascoli 1984; Ferrera 1985; Ascoli and Dente 1985; *contra* Donati 1986).

There are lessons to be learned from public policy analysis which help to avoid the danger of fragmentation. For instance, the portrayal of the process in terms of "policy communities," based on a network of relatively stable interactions among politicians and administrators who share a common subculture (Heclo 1978) and who contribute to the formulation and implementation of each given policy considerably more on the basis of shared characteristics than as representatives of special interests, recaptures its diachronic dimension, the multiplicity of subjects involved and the centrality of single issues (Godwin and Ingram 1980). In addition it is adapted to substantive issues (Heidenheimer 1975) and to discerning the relationships between the phase of formulation and the phase of implementation (Mayntz 1980). It holds a vision that does not take social demand as preexistent, but rather as destined to be formed in the context of policy-making (Brinton Milward 1980; Godard and Pendaries 1984). The chance that initial outcomes may be dispersive and involve analytic descriptions and a great number of case studies (Heclo 1972) is a risk worth taking.

SOCIAL POLICY AND FAMILY CHANGE: SOME SUGGESTIONS FROM ITALIAN EMPIRICAL RESEARCH OF THE SEVENTIES

The direction suggested as the most fitting for channeling research in Italy is confirmed by emerging elements from empirical research in recent years. If one poses the question of the impact of social policies, we are immediately forced to come to terms with the incontrovertible fact of diversification. Implementation of virtually all social service policies varies quantitatively and qualitatively on a local basis. Such policies interact with subcultural and regional socio-economic realities that present preexistent particular attributes and ways of functioning (Bagnasco 1977; Bagnasco and Pini 1981; Trigilia 1981).

The first useful action is analysis of individual social programs. The need for subnational comparative studies likewise becomes evident.

From this standpoint the two theoretical frameworks most frequently employed in Italy for the interpretation of societal impact of social policies are of little use. They are too all-embracing. Donati, on the one hand assumes a perverse type of modernization of the family, with a concomitant deresponsabilizing due to social practices invading the private sphere, thus overloading the family with expectations and increasing its dependency on the State (1981a, pp.44-82; 1981b, pp.79-82). Ergas on the other hand doesn't concern herself specifically with the family, but stakes out a point of view reminiscent of the model of Fox Piven and Cloward in which social policies are a mere governmental expedient, in that they are designed to silence certain social pressure groups (1986, pp.82-110).

More useful and progressive is the theoretical framework recently proposed by Laura Balbo (1984a; 1984b) which suggests that the outcome of the reformist political cycle has been the growth of "widespread intelligence" and the increasing capacity of the family to operate in the context of ever more complex institutional and extra-institutional relationships.

Also in international debate on family policy we find two opposing images in the renewed interest in the family institution. One credits such interest to the mature development of the universalistic Welfare State which oversees the need for better coordination of social policies with greater awareness of the interlocutor, and extends the idea and practice of insuring against social risk (Kamerman and Kahn 1975; Cohen and Connery 1967; Giele 1979, *spec*. p.280). The other view is that interest in family policy is derived from the halt in the development of the Welfare State, with the resulting cuts in social services and delegating back to the family responsibilities and attributes previously assumed (Flora 1981; Tallman 1979; Aymone 1984).

Both the foregoing ideas underplay what appears to be the salient finding of research in the 70s and 80s: that the family behaves as an active entity, not only *not* disorganized and overburdened, but rather as a protagonist with autonomous aims, capable of choosing among the myriad of possible interactions and of giving meaning to the sum of choices as witnessed by recurrent use of the term "family strategy" (Sussman and Shanas 1979; Sussman 1971a; 1971b;

1974; Sussman and Steinmetz 1987; Saraceno 1985, p.330; De Sandre 1984a; 1986). Beyond the justified optimism over the change in outlook embodied in this key term, the danger is that the naivetè thrown out the window will come back through the door in the guise of the notion that modernization must perforce be homogenizing (Bagnasco 1985).

For instance, it is well known that in the south of Italy the policies of widespread income transfer of modest amounts — below the minimum income maintenance level — have combined with a situation of subsistence agriculture to keep alive an illegal underground job market (Boccella 1978; Becchi Collidà 1979). This "combination of breadcrumbs" has its focal point in the family. But to employ the identical term "strategy" here can be misleading if we fail to take into account its precarious nature, the preponderant weight of self-employment and the resultant compression of income and consumption in the underprivileged classes (Mingione 1983, pp.215-236) and the low quality of life of all social strata in this region (Siebert-Zahar 1984, pp.39-47). I do not mean to deny that this, too, is a form of strategy — perhaps a very ancient one in Italy, since certain types of family also in the past have had the ability to resist proletarianization (Barbagli 1984) — but only to emphasize that this has not the same meaning for individuals. It is highly distorting to identify the incidence of nuclearization as a measure of the disruptive impact of social policies, especially using national aggregate data; this process should be broken down into its components. Nuclearization is more pronounced in some geographical areas (in part due to demographic factors) and slower to take hold in others. There is also a "fictitious" nuclearization whose measure is provided by the notable discrepancy between the number of *de facto* families and the number of officially recorded families (Golini 1985).

There is the interesting phenomenon of non-nuclearization which differentiates Italy from the other complex societies. The national figure, estimated at around 11% for extended families (Sgritta 1985), presents problems of comparison with statistics of earlier times and therefore is difficult to interpret. The results of sociological surveys are more explicit. It remains to be explained why in some areas in Italy most favored in terms of social services and of "service culture" (Bianchi 1981), and not only in areas where small business is prevalent (Paci 1980), but in urban contexts with a mature tertiary sector such as in Central Italy (Vicarelli 1982; Trifiletti and Turi 1983; Balbo et al. 1985) and in the Veneto region (Bimbi and Pristinger 1985) one finds an incidence of extended families that ranges from 10% to almost 20% in some cases. These figures are anything but irrelevant when one takes into account that the extended family is only one stage of the life cycle, and as such perhaps a relatively normal one in certain contexts.

The need is to seriously study diachronically family strategies in response to the impact of various policies, no longer based on estimated differences in conduct between one part of the country and another, but starting with the relevant variables emerging from the comparison, once having *discounted* for contextual differences.

In order to reach an understanding of the life-style of varied types of family we must not overlook the crucial nexus with services — not in terms of percentage of users, but in terms of cultural images and legitimization exchanged. Consider that the extended families are found in the same age groups in which the work load of married women is heaviest. In Italy, unlike other countries, withdrawal from the job market is still frequently irreversible and is attributable more to the burden of family responsibility than to the birth of a first child. This points to the problem of rendering the use of diverse services compatible. Wherever there is coincidence it would be highly misleading to place these families in the normal category of dual worker.

AN EXAMPLE:
A FEW REMARKS ON DAY CARE POLICY

A particularly appropriate illustration is the day care policy of the last decade, because it involves perhaps the only law having an impact on the family, whose enactment was preceded by a hot cultural debate on the bill and revendicated by a social movement opposed to the traditional image of family. The movement was headed by an organization devoted to the betterment of women, the *Unione Donne Italiane* (U.D.I., the women's organization close to the Communist Party), which early raised the issue as a matter of high profile reform "for a new type of family" (U.D.I. 1965). The day care reform bill seemed the closest thing to a family policy measure that had ever been seen in Italy. In an apparently inexplicable way one of its most visible results is that today the theme of family has disappeared from the lexicon of those operating in the sector in the political and cultural debates intended to improve and reform this service. Family is being replaced by the key terms "educational service" and "needs of children," in the very years of the rediscovery of the family by sociologists.

It would be impossible to understand such a turnabout without going back to the specificities of the formulation process when two openly conflicting visions — that of residual and that of institutional welfare policy — collided in the form of two separate bills, one sponsored by the labour union movement and the other resulting from popular initiative sponsored by the U.D.I. The fact that the Italian Parliament gave preference to the latter, probably also as a result of the political climate around 1968 (Ferrera 1985), must be reread taking into account that this was *not* a matter of scattering and wearing down a social movement; the communist women's movement was already in crisis on its own account (Viviani and Michetti 1983), it had enjoyed considerably greater strength for some years previously, but had succeeded in imposing the day care issue to the political agenda. Legislators were not really operating on the basis of "an awareness of objectives affecting the family," as previously defined. Rather, they were interested in formulating a symbolic policy, as typically occurs in highly fragmented decision-making situations, where it is deemed preferable to choose policies which can achieve unanimous consensus with little implication to real effects (Regonini 1985).[5] In fact, the machinery for putting the law into effect, despite an apparent ability and willingness to fund at the national level, in effect mortgaged its future by providing for three-tier implementation (State, regions and local communities) at a time when such practice was in its very initial phase.

It is for this reason that even today all over Italy there is an unequal distribution of this service. The implementation process has given very different meanings to the policy, so that we find such contrasts as the Region of Sicily with just four day care centers in operation (with funding of over 58 thousand millions of liras), whereas the Emilia-Romagna Region has 197 in operation, with a funding of 35 thousand millions of liras in assigned funds and another 83 thousand millions of liras in locally raised funds (Regional Data 1983). It is clear, therefore, that only where a policy community of professional administrators and culturally-aware individuals has formed and linked up with progressive politicians to promote policies ideologically compatible with their own values, and where an issue subculture has evolved, has it been possible not only to resolve problems contingent to implementation, but to create the very demand for services.

CONCLUSION

In the face of indications of a growing interest in Italy in the family policy issue and practice, the question is raised herein as to why, to date, this approach has been neither widespread nor really useful in reading the transformation of legislation regarding the family. The answer suggested is that in Italy there are difficulties to confront with the topic of family policy, because of scant empirical knowledge of the family realities, but still more because of cultural prejudices which prevent to make use of existent knowledge. Theoretical and methodological contribution of two american approaches, family evaluation research and family impact analysis, are briefly examined, setting aside the hypothesis of the practicability of the same in the study of the Italian situation.

In light of indications suggested by the most recent Italian research findings the question is posed of whether it wouldn't be more promising in the case of Italy to assimilate the lesson offered by studies of public policy analysis, because it seems the most apt to take into account the specificities of a very complex and fragmented decision-making process.

NOTES

1. Something which could be facilitated at this point in Italy by the availability of a substantial national descriptive survey (ISTAT 1985).
2. For a more comprehensive view of the debate above and beyond studies of evaluation compare: Rothman 1973; Kamerman and Kahn 1979; Kushman 1979; Woolsley 1977; Bruce Briggs 1977; Kamerman and Kahn 1981.

3. In those ambits in which the operationalism of the variables is less arbitrary and numeration makes sense, as for instance in the case of the divorce rate following a change in legislation (Mazur et al. 1977); or else when numerical operationalism is *not* attempted, such as in the interesting study by Kreisman and Jay (1975) that documents the central-ity of the feminine role in family adjustment to the period-ical return of a mentally-ill member, long before de-institutionalization became the norm.

4. At least in the two approaches examined here, but the same can be said of another approach, intended to be more comprehensive, of the "research for family policy" proposed by Nye and McDonald; this would supposedly combine both praxes of evaluation and of family impact, as is demonstrated by the assumption of the possibility to express in rational terms the cost/benefits of purely relational and personal aspects of types of supposedly problematic family structures.

5. Compare the support of such groups as C.i.f, A.c.l.i., the Christian Democratic Women's Movement, etc.

BIBLIOGRAPHY

Aldous, J. e Dumon, W. European and United States perspective on family policy: a summing up, in Aldous, J. e Dumon, W. (eds.) *The politics and programs of family policy*, Leuven University Press, 1978.

Ascoli, U. *Welfare state all'italiana*, Bari, Laterza, 1984.

Ascoli, U. Tendenze del sistema di welfare in Italia, relazione al convegno Innovazione e regolazione sociale nelle società contemporanee, Trento 7/10 ottobre 1985.

Ascoli, U. e Dente, B. Recenti tendenze del Welfare State in Italia, in *Stato e Mercato*, 14, 283-291, 1985.

Aymone, T. Politiche sociali a un bivio: l'esperienza della sinistra italiana nelle amministrazioni locali, in *Inchiesta*, 66, 16-23, 1984.

Bagnasco, A. *Le tre Italie*, Bologna, Il Mulino, 1977.

Bagnasco, A. Intervento al seminario "Modelli di culture dei servizi: ricerche su organizzaaione familiare e sistema dei servizi" Bologna 3/1 1985.

Bagnasco, A. e Pini, R. *Economia e struttura sociale*, Quaderni della Fondazione Giangiacomo Feltrinelli, n.14, 1981.

Bahr, S.J. The effects of welfare on marital stability and remarriage, in *Journal of Marriage and the Family*, 3, 553-560, 1979.

Balbo, L. Famiglia e stato nella società contemporanea, in *Stato e Mercato*, 10, 3-32, 1984a.

Balbo, L. Immersione piena, intelligenza diffusa, in *Inchiesta*, 66, 2-7, 1984b.

Balbo, L. Cacioppo, M. May, M.P. *Struttura urbana, sistemi di orari, bisogni*, rapporto preliminare, Bologna, 1985.

Barbagli, M. *Sotto lo stesso tetto*, Bologna, Il Mulino, 1984.

Bardach, E. *The implementation game*, Cambridge, M.I.T. Press, 1975.

Becchi Collidà, A. *Politiche del lavoro e garanzia del reddito in Italia*, Bologna, Il Mulino, 1979.

Bianchi, M. *I servizi sociali*, Bari, De Donato, 1981.

Bimbi, F. e Pristinger, F. *Profili sovrapposti*, Milano, Angeli, 1985.

Blaydon, C.C. e Stack, C.B. Income support policies and the family, in *Daedalus*, 106, 147-161, 1977.

Boccella, N. Transferimenti alle famiglie e struttura sociale del Mezzogiorno: un quadro d'insieme, in Becchi Collidà, A. (ed.) *Sussidi, lavoro, Mezzogiorno*, Milano, Angeli, 1978.

Boles, J.K. The politics of child care, in *Social Service Review*, sep. 334-362, 1980.

Boudon, R. L'acteur social est-il si irrational et si conformiste qu'on le dit?, in *L'individu*, 22-24, oct, 1985.

Bradbury, K. Bishop, J. Burdett, P. Garfinkel, I Middleton, R. Skidmore, F. and Walter, E. *The effect of welfare reform alternatives for the family*, University of Wisconsin Institute for Research on Poverty, 1977.

Brinton Milward, H. Policy entrepreneurship and bureaucratic demand creation, in Ingram, H.M. e Mann, D.E. (eds.) *Why policies succeed or fail?*, Beverly Hills, Sage, 1980.

Bruce Briggs, B. Child care: the fiscal time bomb, in *The Public Interest*, 49, 87-102, 1977.

Buric, O. Scientific basis for family policy, in *The scientific bases of family policy*, Icofa, Louvain, 1978.

Chen, H.T. e Rossi, P.H. The multi-goal theory-driven approach to evaluation, in *Social Forces*, 59, 106-122, 1981.

Chen, H.T. and Rossi, P.H. Evaluating with sense. The theory-driven approach, in *Evaluation Review*, 3, 283-302, 1983.

Chiswick, B.B. The demand for nursing home care: an analysis of the substitution between institutional and noninstitutional care, in *The Journal of Human Resources*, 3, 295-316, 1976.

CISF *La politica familiare in Europa. Prospettive per gli anni '80*, Milano, Angeli, 1981.

Cohen, N.E. e Connery, M.F. Government policy and the family, in *Journal of Marriage and the Family*, 1, 6-17, 1967.

De Bie, P. The rationale and social context of family policy in western Europe, in Aldous, e Dumon, W. (eds.), 1978.

Del Boca, D. Strategie familiari e interessi individuali, in Martinotti, G. (ed.) *La città difficile*, Milano, Angeli, 1982.

Dente, B. *Governare la frammentazione*, Bologna, Il Mulino, 1985.

De Sandre, I. Famiglia, strategie e politiche sociali, in *Inchiesta*, 64, 3-10, 1984.

De Sandre, I. Vita quotidiana, strategie familiari, struttura delle risorse: una esplorazione concettuale, in Bimbi, F. e Capecchi, V. *Strutture e strategie della vita quotidiana*, Milano, Angeli, 1986.

Donati, P.P. Forme familiari e nuovo diritto di famiglia: una riflessione sociologica, in *Studi di sociologia*, 2/3, 113-167, 1976.

Donati, P.P. Introduzione: interrelazioni fra le varie dimensioni della politica familiare: è possibile un approccio unificante?, in CISF, 15-40. 1981a.

Donati, P.P. *Famiglia e politiche sociali*, Milano, Angeli, 1981b.

Donati, P.P. "Le politiche sociali negli 'Stati del benessere'," in P. Donati (ed.) *Le frontiere della politica sociale*, Milano, Angeli. 1986.

Donati, P.P. e Nicoletti, G. Famiglia, adozione e servizi sociali, in *La Ricerca Sociale*, 73, 43-72, 1974.

Dumon, W. La famiglia e la politica familiare in evoluzione nella società degli anni '80, in CISF, 43-52, 1981.

Ergas, Y. *Nelle maglie della politica*, Milano, Angeli, spec. 82-110, 1986.

Ferrera, M. *Il welfare state in Italia*, Bologna, Il Mulino, 1985.

Flora, P. Solution or source of crises? The welfare state in historical perspective, in W. J. Mommsen *The emergence of the welfare in Britain and Germany*, London, Croom Helm, 343-389, 1981.

Fogarty, M.P. Come nasce una politica familiare: il caso della Gran Bretagna, in CISF, 142-159, 1981.

Giele, J.Z. Social policy and the family, in *Annual Review of Sociology*, 5, 275-302, 1979.

Godard, F. e Pendaries, J.R. La domanda sociale come prodotto politico-istituzionale. Il ruolo dell'amministrazione locale, in P.L. Crosta *La produzione sociale del piano*, Milano, Angeli, 1984.

Godwin, R.K. e Ingram, H.M. Single issues: their impact on politics, in Ingram, H.M. e Mann, D.H. (eds.) *Why policies succeed or fail?*, in Beverly Hills, 279-299, 1980.

Golini, A. La famiglia in Italia. Tendenze recenti, immagine, esigenze di ricerca, intervento al covegno "La famiglia in Italia," Roma 29-30 ottobre 1985.

Gordon, I. Lewis, J. e Young, K. Perspectives on policy analysis, in *Public Administration Bulletin*, 25, 125-137, 1977.

Greenfield, L. e Falk, M. Welfare grants reduction and family breakup among the working poor, in *Public Welfare*, 31, 26-31, 1973.

Ham, C. e Hill, M. *Introduzione all'analisi delle politiche pubbliche*, Bologna, Il Mulino, 1986.

Hannan, M.T. et al. Income and marital events: evidence from an income maintenance experiment, in *American Journal of Sociology*, 82, 1186-1211, 1977.

Hargrove, E.C. *The missing link*, Washington, The Urban Institute, 1975.

Heclo, H. Review Article: Policy analysis, in *British Journal of Political Science*, 2, 1972.

Heclo, H. Issue nNetwork and the executive establishment, in King, A. (ed.) *The new political american system*, Washington, American Enterprise Institute, 87-124, 1978.

Heidenheimer, A.J. Heclo, H. e Adams, C.T. *Comparative public policy*, New York, St. Martin's Press, 1975.

Heidenheimer, A.J. Introduction, in Heidenheimer, A.J. Heclo, H. e Adams, C.T. *Comparative public policy*, New York, St Martin's Press, 1975.

Hirschorn, L. Social policy and the life cycle, in *Social Service Review*, 3, 434-450, 1977.

Honig, M. AFDC income, recipient rates and family dissolution, in *Journal of Human Resources*, 3, 303-321, 1974.

ISTAT *Indagine sulle strutture e i comportamenti familiari*, Roma, ISTAT, 1985.

Janowitz, B. The impact of AFDC on illegitimate birth rates, in *Journal of Marriage and the Family*, 38, 485-493, 1976.

Jo Bane, M. Toward a description and evaluation of United States family policy, in Aldous, J. e Dumon, W., 155-190, 1978.

Kamerman, S. *Developing a family impact statement*, New York, Foundation for Child Development, 1976.

Kamerman, S. e Kahn, H. *Not for poor alone*, Philadelphia, Temple University Press, 1975.

Kamerman, S. & Kahn, H. *Family policy, government and families in fourteen countries*, New York, Columbia University Press, 1978.

Kamerman, S. & Kahn, H. The day care debate: a wider view, in *The Public Interest*, 54, 76-93, 1979.

Kamerman, S. & Kahn, H. *Child care, family benefits and working parents*, New York, Columbia University Press, 1981.

Kamerman, S. & Kahn, H. Income Transfers, work and the economic well-being of families with children, in *International Social Security Review*, 3, 345-382, 1982.

Keherer, B.H. e Wolin, C.M. Impact of income maintenance on low birth weight: evidence from the gary experiment, in *The Journal of Human Resources*, 4, 434-462, 1979.

Kirst, M.W. Garms, W e Opperman, T. State services for children: an exploration of who benefits, who governs, in *Public Policy*, 2, 185-206, 1980.

Kreisman, D.E. e Joy, V.D. The family as reactor to mental illness of a relative, in Guttentag, M. e Struening, E.L. *Handbook of evaluation research*, Beverly Hills, Sage, 1975.

Kushman, J.E. A public choice model of day care center services, in *Social Science Quarterly*, 60, 295-308, 1979.

Lerman, R.I. The family, poverty and welfare programs, in *Studies in Public Welfare*, 12, Washington, GPO, 1973.

Lindbloom, C. e Braybrooke, D. *A strategy of decision*, London, Collier, 1963.

Lory, B. Changes in european family policy, in Aldous, J e Dumon, W., 69-122, 1978.

Majone, G. The feasibility of social policies, in *Policy Sciences*, 6, 49-69, 1975.

Mayntz, R. (hrsg.) *Implementation politischer programme*, Königstein, Athenäum, 1980.

Mayo, S.K. The household composition effect of income transfer programs, in *Public policy*, 3, 395-422, 1976.

Mazur-Hart, S.F. e Berman, J.J. Changing from fault to no-fault divorce: an interrupted time series analysis, in *Journal of Applied Psychology*, 4, 300-312, 1977.

Minarik, J.J. e Goldfarb, R.S. AFDC income, recipient rates and family dissolution: a skeptical comment, in *Journal of Human Resources*, 1, 243-249, 1976.

Mingione, E. *Urbanizzazione, classi sociali e lavoro informale*, Milano, Angeli, 1983.

Moen, P. e Goodwin, L. The evolution and implementation of family welfare policy, in *Policy Studies Journal*, 1, 632-652, 1980.

Moles, J.K. The politics of child care,' in *Social Service Review*, 3, 344-362, 1980.

Nye, F.I. e McDonald, G.W. Family policy research: emergent models and some theoretical issues, in *Journal of Marriage and the Family*, 3, 473-486, 1979.

Paci, M. *Famiglia e mercato del lavoro in un'economia periferica*, Milano, Angeli, 1980.

Peters, J.B.M. An evaluation of the effects of family policy in europe, in Aldous, J. e Dumon, W., 39-62, 1978.

Presidenza del Consiglio dei Ministri. *La povertà in Italia*. Rapporto conclusivo della Commissione di studio instituita presso la Presidenza del Consiglio dei ministri, Roma, Poligrafico dello Stato, 37-56, 1985.

Pressman, J. e Wildavski, A. *Implementation*, Berkeley, University of California Press, 1973.

Regonini, G. Le politiche sociali in Italia: metodi di analisi, in *Revista Italiana di Scienza Politica*, 3, 335-378, 1985.

Ross, H.L. e Sawhill, I.V. *Time of transition: the growth of families headed by women*, Washington, The Urban Institute, 1975.

Ross, H.L. & Sawhill, I.V. Welfare policy and the family, in *Public Policy*, 1, 89-115, 1978.

Rothman, S.M. Other people's children. The day care experience in america, in *Public Interest*, 30, 11-27, 1973.

Sacchetti, L. la famiglia tra cattolici e marxisti, in *Il Mulino*, 236, 892-909, 1974.

Saraceno, C. Modelli di famiglia, in AA.VV. *Ritratto di famiglia deli anni '80*, Bari, Laterza, 1981.

Saraceno, C. Il rapporto famiglia-Stato e i contributi di analisi "dalla parte delle donne," in *Inchiesta*, 65, 26-32 e pp.1-2, 1984.

Saraceno, C. La sociologia della famiglia tra crisi delle teorie ed innovazione tematica, in *Quaderni di Sociologia*, 4-5, 307-334, 1985.

Sgritta, G. Studi sulla famiglia in Italia, *Rassegna Italiana di Sociologia*, 2, 125-140, 1984a.

Sgritta, G. *Emarqinazione dipendenza e politica sociale*, Milano, Angeli, pp.211-236, 1984b.

Sgritta, G. La struttura delle relazioni interfamiliari, relazione al convegno "La famiglia in Italia," Roma, 29/30 ottobre, 1985.

Siebert-Zahar, R. *Le ali di un elefante*, Milano, Angeli, 1984.

Sussman, M.B. Family systems in the 1970's: analysis, policies and programs, in *The Annals of the American Academy of Political and Social sciences*, 396, jul., 40-56, 1971a.

Sussman, M.B. *Changing families in a changing society*, Washington D.C., U.S. Government Printing Office, 1971b.

Sussman, M.B. Issues and developments in family sociology in the 1970s, *Current Sociology*, 27-65, 1974.

Sussman, M.B. Shanas, E. *Family, bureaucracy and the elderly*, Durham, Duke University Press, 1979.

Sussman, M.B. Steinmetz S.K. *Handbook of marriage and the family*, New York, Plenum Press, 1987.

Tallman, I. Implementation of a national family policy: the role of the social scientist, in *Journal of Marriage and the Family*, 3, 469-472, 1979.

Trifiletti, R. e Turi, P. Immagini, interpretazioni e attese della famiglia di fronte al nido: una ricerca in Toscana e in Umbria, in *Il bambino di fronte ad una famiglia e ad una società che cambiano*, Bergamo, Juvenilia, 1983.

Trigilia, C. *Le subculture politiche territoriali*, Quaderni della Fondazione Giangiacomo Feltrinelli, 16, 1981.

Turem, e Arnow, M. *Welfare policy and family splitting*, Washington, The Urban Institute, 1973.

U.D.I. Per una famiglia ed una società nuove, Roma, U.D.I. 1965.

Vicarelli, G. Strategie familiari nel sistema delle garanzie, in *Inchiesta* 56, 34-43, 1982.

Viviani, L. Michetti, M. e Repetto, M. *U.D.I., laboratorio di politica delle donne*, Roma, Cooperativa Libera Stampa, 1984.

Weissert, W.G. Toward a continuum of care for the elderly: a note of caution in *Public Policy*, 3, 331-340, 1981.

Weissert, W.G. Wan, T Livieratos, B e Katz, S. Effects and costs of day care services for the chronically ill: a randomized experiment, in Freeman, E.H. e Solomon, M. *Evaluation Studies Annual*, vol.6, Beverly Hills, Sage, 301-318, 1980.

White, S.H. et al. *Federal programs for young children: review and recommendations* Washington D.C., Department of Health Education and Welfare, 1973.

Wildmarer, S.M. Stringer, S. Ignatieff, E. e Field, T.M. Teenage, lower class, black mothers and their preterm infant, in *Child Development*, 2, 426-436, 1980.

Woolsley, S.H. Pied piper politics and the child care debate, *Daedalus*, 106, 127-146, 1977.

Zimmerman, S.L. Policy, social policy and family policy: concepts, concerns and analytic tools, in *Journal of Marriage and the Family*, 3, 507-518, 1979.

A More Symmetrical Family —
A Greater Demand for Public Care?

Kari Waerness

SUMMARY. An analysis of different meanings of the concept "caring" is used to argue that the changes in the gender division of labor and the growth of the welfare state services which have taken place in Norwegian Society in recent years, has made informal care more of a complement rather than an alternative to public care services.

Both theoretical considerations and empirical studies are used to argue that to some extent more symmetrical family relations may lead to a greater demand for public care services.

Caring has become a central issue both in social policy and the social sciences in recent years. There are different reasons behind the growing political interest in the issue, especially in "informal care." It is important that social scientists acknowledge the lack of ready-made conceptual frameworks for analyzing all the different activities and relations which in everyday life are called "caring" or "care." Our traditional sociological dichotomies such as private/public, home/work, leisure/labor, fail to confront experiences like caring which transcend such divisions.

Feminists during recent years have made great efforts to overcome this deficiency in our scientific apparatus. Feminism has not, however, transformed the conceptual frameworks of the social sciences. The conventional categories of the social sciences still cannot offer us any sophisticated understanding of the changes in infor-

Kari Waerness is Professor, Department of Sociology, University of Bergen, Hans Holmboesgt, Bergen, Norway.

Thanks to Pal Farsund for language corrections.

41

mal care and the demand for public care which are related to the so-called "crisis of the welfare state."

Finding the conceptual frameworks from the academic disciplines inadequate for analyses of caring, many writers have used a dictionary as a starting point (Graham 1983; Noddings 1984; Waerness 1982; 1984a,b). In broad terms, caring is a concept encompassing that range of human experiences which have to do with feeling, concern and taking charge of the well-being of others. Graham (1983) argues on the line with Rousseau that caring is experienced as "a labour of love."

Noddings (1984) argues that the reason why moral philosophy does not provide a thorough understanding of the moral problems of caring, is that moral issues have mainly been discussed in the language of the father, i.e., in terms such as justification, fairness and equity. Noddings offers an alternative view, an ethic of caring, rooted in receptivity, relatedness and responsiveness. To analyze what it means to care and be cared for she takes relation as ontologically basic, that human encounter and affective response is a basic fact of human existence. Without answering the empirical question, to what extent her alternative approach in everyday life is more typical for women than for men, she still characterizes this approach as a feminine one.

This feminine approach also may explain why women often have been judged as inferior to men in the moral domain (Gilligan 1982). It seems that women more often than men do not approach moral problems as problems of principle, reasoning and judgment, but rather through a consideration of the concrete elements of specific situations and a regard for themselves as caring individuals. In order to cope with the problems within the context of caring, a mode of thinking which is contextual and narrative rather than formal and abstract is required (Waerness 1984b). One may argue that a tension exists between the morality of rights and the morality of caring as Thomas Aquinas expressed it — justice untempered with mercy is brutality and mercy uncontrolled by justice is the mother of dissolution (quoted in Schumacher 1980:142). There is good reason to assume that the changes in the gender division of labor and the growth of welfare institutions outside the family have made this tension both stronger and more visible.

As long as a greater part of the caring activities is a task for family and kin, and the traditional gender division of labor is accepted, this tension can be kept in balance. When the division of labor between the state and the family in reproduction becomes more ambiguous and women claim the same citizenship rights as men, caring becomes visible as a social problem and thereby an important issue for the social sciences. The fact that the Norwegian Prime Minister in his New Year's Evening address to the Norwegian population in 1985 explicitly stated the necessity of men taking more "caring responsibility," can be interpreted as an indicator of how closely the caring problematique today is linked to changes in the gender division of labor. So even if important aspects of caring belong to "what we know but cannot tell," it probably is worthwhile to attempt to capture in scientific terms what Wittgenstein advised "we must pass over in silence." As a central issue in social policy, caring is related both to identities and activities. On the one hand, the experience of caring is intimately bound up with the way we define ourselves and our social relations. On the other, caring is an integral process by which the society reproduces itself and maintains the physical and mental health of its population.

Caring is expected to take place in relations and situations which differ enormously with respect to intensity, time span and formality. From the view of the caregiver there is, however, an important aspect which is common without regard to the situational conditions and type of relationship in which caring takes place. Caring is normatively characterized by a move away from self. Our motivation in caring is directed toward the welfare, protection, and enhancement of the cared-for. Whenever I care, I should ideally be able to present reasons for my action, or inaction, which would persuade a reasonable disinterested observer that I have acted on behalf of the cared-for. This does not mean that all observers would have behaved as I did. On the contrary, they may have seen other alternatives as better or preferable.

We, therefore, cannot judge "right" or "wrong" in caring by a simple application of principles developed in situations of sameness. This fact leads to special difficulties in using conventional methods of social science to give empirical estimates of quantitative and qualitative changes in different kinds of caring. We have to be careful not to judge every increase in the demand for public care services as signs of decrease in informal care or the other way around. We should be even more careful to judge whether the growth of public care services is due to changes in people's morality, rather than to a decrease in the capacity for informal care or to an increase in needs.

What follows is a categorization of different relationships which are called "caring relations." This categorization makes it visible that more symmetrical family relations today most probably will lead to a greater rather than a lesser demand for public care services. Then I will use findings from a national survey on the Norwegian urban population in the age group 25-64[1] to discuss the importance of different social relations with respect to access to confidants and helpers in different problem situations and how this is about to change. A central focus in this discussion is on gender differences in giving and receiving care and how these differences eventually are influenced by women's increasing employment.

CARING IN SYMMETRICAL
AND ASYMMETRICAL RELATIONS

Caring takes place in relationships which vary much in regard to reciprocity and likeness between the caregiver and the cared-for. Reciprocity implies equality; what you do for me I return to you in equal measure. We can depend on each other a lot or a little, but we depend on each other equally. Caring relations based on reciprocity and equality most often are characterized as friendship relations. Norms of reciprocity and equality in such relations presuppose a certain degree of similarity: I have roughly the same things to offer and the same needs as you have. Of course there can be wide variations in what friends receive and give during shorter periods of time, but if a great difference continues the balance is lost and inequality begins to characterize the relationship. Once inequality enters the relationship there is a strong potential for break-up.

The norms of reciprocity, equality and similarity imply strong limitations on how much and what kinds of caring may be exchanged within friendship relations. The special needs for care due to illness, disability or other kinds of problems which result in decreasing capacity to manage on one's own in everyday life, can, therefore, only to a very limited degree be met within what most people in modern society would characterize as "friendship relations." This is not to say that help and support from friends are not important in such situations. On the contrary, intimate friendship relations may be more important than family relations to avoid deterioration of morale during illness, bereavement and old age (Arling 1976; Bell 1981). But there probably are strong limitations to friends working as housemaids or nurses. Or, if a person has to rely on friends or close kin for considerable help with the household chores, it may become difficult or impossible also to burden them with the emotional problems caused by serious illness and disablement. In order not to make the relations too imbalanced this may imply that urgent needs for emotional care cannot be met. The norms of friendship, therefore, means that informal care from friends can substitute minimally the traditional caring functions of the family or be an alternative to public care services in illness and disablement.

Friendship appears to have the greatest significance as emotional support in times of crises, more so for women than for men. The differences between male and female friendship relations in many western societies, demonstrated by sociological research (Bell 1981), imply that friendship is more important as emotional help and support for women than for men. The stress on intimacy and revelation in female friendships, and sociability and coolness in the friendship relations between men, imply that men have to rely more on their spouses for satisfying needs of intimacy. Since marriage has become a more fragile institution, men should probably benefit much from entering into more intimate friendship relations than they traditionally have done. For such a change to take place would, however, entail giving up many of the value commitments to notions of traditional masculinity in Western culture.

An important difference between *asymmetrical* caring relations is whether it is the caregiver or the cared-for who hold the superior position. Mother/child, teacher/pupil, doctor/patient are examples of relationships where the cared-for is in a subordinate position. The extent of inequality may vary and change with time, but the dependent situation of the cared-for, which is inherent in such relations, always means subordination. The asymmetry inherent in the parent/child relation means that for adult children to meet their parents' dependency needs in old age implies something quite different than to give in return "the same" as the parents gave to them in infancy and childhood.

Being depended on by one's elderly parent on the one hand and by one's young child on the other has different inner meanings. Also from the perspective of the older person the role reversal implied in dependency on one's child does not seem to be the kind of care which at least a substantial part of the disabled elderly women prefer. Studies have shown that what Rosenmayr and Kockeis (1965) named "intimacy, but at a distance" seems to be the kind of relation a growing number of elderly people prefer to have with their children. (Shanas 1979; Brody 1985; Daatland 1983; Nordhus 1981; Widding Isaksen 1984). That parents today are less "parental" and authoritarian and more of a companion probably has consequences for what kinds of stress and strains different dependency needs in old age entail. Older women seek emotional support from their children more than anything else. Economic aid, shared households, and personal care services have become less acceptable (Brody et al. 1984). This can be the result of changes in the norms regulating parent/child relations. Earlier this relation was more based on parental authority; today it is based more on companionship.

The fact that parent/child relations are genderized, and that most of the care of frail elderly parents is provided by daughters, means that today's changes in women's roles probably changes the family as a caring institution in old age more fundamentally than we hitherto have realized or at least been willing to admit. Even if sons sustain bonds of affection, perform some gender-defined tasks and become the "responsible relatives," the burdensome care, including intimate physical care, very seldom is performed by sons. There are good reasons to assume that many of the daughters who perform the most demanding care for impaired parents are in subordinate or dependent positions in relation to the cared-for (Brody 1985). Women's greater economic independence of the family and access to non-stigmatizing social services probably have changed elderly disabled people's preference for daughters as the main providers of household services and nursing. The fact that impaired elderly Norwegian women seem to prefer companionship rather than institutionalized obligations as the basis of the parent/child relationship in adulthood, may also explain why care from daughters is preferred as complement rather than as an alternative to public care services. (Aure 1984; Nordhus 1981; Widding Isaksen 1984). Shortage of public care services in relation to increasing needs often creates greater dependence on daughters than both mothers and daughters find acceptable according to norms, and results in a lot of emotional strain and symptoms of mental illness.

Long-term parent care today, in contrast to earlier times, has become a normative experience — expectable, though usually unexpected (Brody 1985). It can overlay many different ages and stages in different people and different families, it can be a time-extended process, and it can compete for time and attention with other very different obligations. This means there can be no set of behavioral norms for parental care on which old age policy in the modern welfare state can be based. Models describing parent care as a developmental stage of life called "filial maturity" — a transitional stage before old age — such as suggested in social gerontology (Blenkner 1965), therefore does not seem to be an adequate or fruitful conceptualization.

The greater part of the active and personalized manifestation of care for the ill and disabled comprises tasks which adult people normally do for themselves — the tasks of tending. In our society motherhood has been, and still seems to be, the dominating model for tending regardless of the setting where it takes place (Ungerson 1983). This model creates problems and tensions within many forms of tending, not as model for skills and aptitudes, but as a model for the relationship between the caregiver and the cared-for.

The infantilization implied in the model, may insult and hurt many disabled people, and the role adjustment also creates complex emotional problems. Impaired mothers who are looked after by their daughters may resent giving up their maternal power and the exchange of "mothering" may in itself be problematic. The use of the model may create tensions and difficulties both within institutions and at home. But for many old people tending through mothering by strangers in their home, or even in an institution, may be more acceptable than by close kin who at one time have been lovers, siblings or children. Mothering may also be more acceptable to men than to women, since tending as mothering, in many respects, bears similar characteristics to the human servicing element of domestic labor conventionally carried out by wives (Evers 1981).

Ungerson (1983) argues that the motherhood model of tending raises a lot of issues pertinent to the question of the possibility of maintenance or change of the so-called "caring capacity of the community" without preserving the gender division of labor in caring. The physical care of the ill and disabled is a crucial issue in this connection. To get a more thorough understanding of the difficulties of changing the gender division of labor in caring, she suggests to analyze the taboo systems that may exist. She uses the word "taboo" instead of "norm" to convey the idea that the transgression of the system is perceived as polluting and dangerous. That nappy changing seems to be a central issue in establishing the boundaries of fathers' willingness to help in child-care (Oakley 1974), and that women seem to have a virtual monopoly on dealing with incontinence and other human excreta, is ascribed to a system of taboos in modern society. Ungerson (1983) argues that when we here are dealing with a system of taboos, it is unlikely that men can be responsible for tending incontinent people. If they did, they would threaten their own personal order and that of the people they care for.

Ungerson also finds the system of taboos circumventing incest relevant to tending. A great deal of tending inevitably involves touching genitalia. Where the tending is carried out by close kin of the opposite sex, we can assume that the incest taboos are of great importance. Many caregivers break down this taboo system under the force of circumstances. We can however assume that many such caring relations imply exceptionally trying circumstances both for the caregiver and the cared-for, and that fears of incest in most cases are left unarticulated and largely unrecognized.

To develop a better understanding of the difficult problems of tending due to the motherhood model, a system of taboos and norms in relation to nudity should be of vital importance, if only to increase the sensibility and understanding of the professionals responsible for and dependent on the maintenance of good informal care at home. There remains, however, a great problem of how to do social research in a domain which involves the uncovering of largely unarticulated social rules and the recognition of hidden and unrecognized feelings.

While I assume that more companion-like and less authoritarian parent/child relations will increase the preference for formal household and nursing services in old age and disablement, it seems more difficult to predict what might be the consequence of more symmetrical roles in marriage. Wives' traditional caring for their husbands constitutes a caring relation where the cared-for holds the superior position. In such caring relations the dependency of the cared-for on the caregiver is not openly recognized. On the contrary, it is the caregiver's dependency on the cared-for which mainly defines the relation. This means that the provision of personal services by wives is taken for granted and often can be more a question of what they are "forced" to do as a result of their subordinate position than of what they want to do as a result of their concern for the husband's well-being. More symmetrical conjugal relations, including a more equal sharing of the domestic tasks, should imply that couples can manage better in everyday life also when ill-health and disability strikes the wife. Today, men's incompetence in household work often leads to great strain for disabled wives, even when husbands in such situations "care as best they can," and results in a greater need for home help services than would otherwise be the case (Nygaard 1982). A greater capacity in household tasks also should increase men's possibilities to manage on their own in case of widowhood.

On the other hand, more equal conjugal roles also may lead to an increase in the demand for public care services from married people. If wives' caring for their husbands no longer can be taken for granted, the nearly universal expectation that wives will take on everything necessary when husbands become ill or disabled has to change. The establishment of the so-called "association of carers" in many western countries, including Norway, in recent years may be seen as an indication of changing norms related to wifely care in situations of heavy illness or impairment of the husband. These associations argue that wives of disabled men compose a group of carers that is widely ignored, and that great improvement in the provision of respite service for this group is necessary (Oliver 1983). For younger wives increased employment will imply more demand for services when husbands become disabled. For older women more consideration of their own health state will have the same effect. More symmetrical conjugal relations will also probably lead to more disabled husbands not wanting their wives always present, always free to assist and always willing to subjugate their own needs and wishes to the husbands.

As a conclusion to these considerations on the probable future development of informal caring, I will argue the following: More companionlike and symmetrical relations between parents and adult children and between spouses will lead to more rather than to less demand for non-stigmatizing public care services like home help and home nursing. At the same time these relations may become of greater importance for emotional well-being in situations of illness, disablement and bereavement. Emotional isolation and morale in such situations may be better handled in friendship rather than in asymmetric caring relations.

Without great changes in our living arrangements, i.e., a great increase rather than decrease in single-person households in the adult and healthy population, we, therefore, can assume that the demand for public home care services will continue to increase. This will at least be the case if not stigmatizing or charges become rationing devices.

The most important way in which caring friends may reduce the need for formal health and social services, is probably as a preventive "service." To the extent that integration in informal networks of friends prevents illness and disablement, or increases people's own capacity to manage the activities of everyday life, it also may reduce the demand for health and social services. When illness or disablement occurs, symmetric informal caring function more as a supplement to formal care and to some extent as a condition for acquiring non-stigmatizing public care services.

CONFIDANTS AND HELPERS IN DIFFERENT PROBLEM SITUATIONS

In the discussion of "the crisis of the welfare state," the increasing use of professional help to solve or cope with personal and family problems is differently evaluated. Many have argued that the increase in the demand for professional services in such situations indicates that more people lack confidants, or that the growth of professional services leads to the loss of the spontaneity and the ability to help each other. Others have argued that the use and knowledge of professional help indicates a higher level of competence than relying on informal social networks.

Even if it seems self-evident that sole reliance on professional help may indicate social isolation, to think in terms of *either* informal *or* professional help is much too simplified. Concerning emotional problems, the provision of help and care is not a zero-sum activity in that more informal help unambiguously leads to less professional help or the other way around. Professional services may function both as complements, supplements and substitutes to informal care in situations of emotional strain and crisis.

These possible different and complicated relations between informal and professional care heavily limit the value of survey methods in analyzing what access to confidants and informal helpers imply with respect to demands for professional help. Another serious limitation in the use of survey methods in studying the importance of informal relations are that the most isolated and lonely probably are heavily underrepresented, and that the categories which we force on our respondents may have systematically different inner meanings to different groups. We have to bear these limitations in mind in trying to capture more intimate and private aspects of people's lives.

A main assumption underlying the design of the survey from which I present some results was that the changes in women's roles during the last decades are both a cause and a consequence of important changes in family and friendship relations. I will focus on what these data can convey about changing trends in women's and men's relations to family and friends, as sources for intimacy and emotional support, and what kind of helpers men and women prefer in different hypothetical problem situations.

Table 1 shows that for a small majority of the sample family and home have greater significance than relations and activities in worklife or leisure time. The difference between men and women is not great, but in the expected direction. Comparing the different

TABLE 1. The most important life sphere according to age and gender. Percentages. (Urban Norwegian population in the age group 25-64, 1983)

	Men					Women				
	Age 25 - 30 %	Age 31 - 40 %	Age 41 - 50 %	Age 51 - 64 %	All %	Age 25 - 30 %	Age 31 - 40 %	Age 41 - 50 %	Age 51 - 64 %	All %
Family/home life	30	49	67	74	53	54	67	59	64	60
Work or studies	46	31	9	0	24	26	10	15	10	16
Leisure time interests	12	6	12	8	9	1	5	3	7	4
Do not know/ difficult to say/ no answer	12	15	14	18	14	20	17	23	20	20
	101	99	100	100	100	101	99	100	101	100
(N)	(69)	(68)	(44)	(62)	(243)	(86)	(58)	(39)	(74)	(257)

age-groups, one finds that men's preference for family life increases with age. This is not true for women. The discrimination analyses in Table 2 suggest that aging and marriage means more for men's than for women's family and homecenteredness, while for women the most determining factor is whether or not they have younger children.

This difference seems to confirm that the Durkheimian assumption of the conjugal bond being the most important family bond for men whereas the mother/child bond is most important for women. This still has some validity in Norwegian society. The discrepancy as to *when* in the life course family versus work or studies is most important may grow into a more important source of conflict in marriage as the employment of women increases.

Men's greater reliance on spouses/cohabitants to satisfy their needs for intimacy is confirmed in this survey as shown in Table 3a and b.

The difference between the younger and the older as to whether they have a confidant other than the spouse is greater among men than among women. This may indicate that men in the future will become more self-revealing outside the conjugal relation in old age. This difference may, however, also be explained by changing norms during the life course. The proportion of *female* confidants other than the spouse is higher rather than lower in the younger age group. There is no indication of *male* friendship relations becoming more important for meeting men's needs for intimacy.

The gender difference in the meaning of friendship is indicated in the answers to the questions on friendship relations at the workplace, as shown in Table 4 and 5.

The difference between male and female employees as to whether they have personal friends among their workmates is not great, but in favor of men. Women, however, more often have friends of both sexes and more often get help from workmates when they have personal problems. Since there is no great difference between younger and older men in revealing personal problems to workmates, there is nothing indicating that men's informal networks at work are becoming more important in meeting needs for intimacy.

There is, however, some evidence, although weak, that marital

TABLE 2. Canonical discriminant function for men and women on groups defined by family/home being most important in life or not. (Urban Norwegian population in the age group 25-64, 1983).

Variables[1]	Men Stand. can. discr. function coeffisients	Women Stand. can. discr. function coeffisients
Age	.38	.19
Marital status	- .59	- .20
Employment	.06	.28
General education	- .12	- .26
Vocational education	.03	- .30
Children	.49	.65
	Canonical correlation	Canonical correlation
	.61	.68
	Wilk's Lambda	Wilk's Lambda
	.626	.534
	significance	significance
	.0000	.0000
N	(243)	(257)

1) The variables are defined in the following way:

Age: In years

Marital status: Married   = 1
                     All others   = 2

Employment: Full-time employed, self-employed,
                     student   = 1
                     All others   = 2

General education: Primary school   = 1
                     Continuation school   = 2
                     Lower secondary school   = 3
                     Higher secondary school   = 4

Vocational education: Number of years

Children: No children
                     Youngest child > 20 years   = 1
                     10 - 19 years   = 2
                      0 - 9 years   = 3

This analysis shows that to be married is the most important factor for men in defining family life as most important, followed by having (younger) children and being older. For women having (younger) children is most important, and education and employment is more determining for not giving priority to family life than being younger and non-married.

status is more a determinant for men than for women regarding whether or not people are helped with personal problems at work. This is shown in Table 6.

This table confirms the assumption that other confidants are an alternative rather than a supplement to the spouse to a greater extent for men than for women. This gender difference is related to different norms for help-seeking behaviour in conjugal crises. The findings presented in Table 7 confirms this assumption.

If the reply "problems should be kept in the family" is used as an indicator of the privatisation of the marriage relation, then conjugal

TABLE 3a. Confidants according to sex and age. Percentages. (Urban Norwegian population in the age group 25-64, 1983) (More answers possible)

	25-40 years		41-65 years		All	
	Men	Women	Men	Women	Men	Women
	%	%	%	%	%	%
No confidant / or don't know	17	8	23	13	19	11
Spouse / cohabitant	54	61	60	46	56	52
Female relatives[1]	15	30	9	32	12	31
Male relatives	9	11	8	15	9	12
Female friends	15	30	4	20	10	26
Male friends	20	8	11	8	16	8
Professionals	2	3	2	3	2	3
N	(137)	(144)	(106)	(113)	(243)	(257)
Percentage of the married/ cohabitating who has the spouse as a confidant	80	79	75	66	77	71

1) Among the female relatives mother is the most important in the youngest age group (mentioned by 17 per cent of the women, 9 per cent of the men. In the oldest age groups daughter is the most important for women (mentioned by 15 per cent) while no special family relation comes out as most important for men.

TABLE 3b. Percentages having at least one confidant according to marital status and gender. (Urban Norwegian population in the age group 25-64, 1983)

Marital status:	Men	Women	All	(N)
	%	%	%	
Non-married	70	88	79	(134)
Married/cohabitating	85	90	88	(366)
All	81	90	86	(500)
(N)	(243)	(257)	(500)	

crises are viewed as private matters more by men than by women. If one assumes that the norms of the individual in this field are relatively stable during adulthood, the difference between the age groups can be interpreted as a weakening of the privatisation of marriage both among women and men. At the same time men still seem to be more privatised than women.

Among women both education and employment decrease privatisation. Employed and well-educated women more often than full-time housewives will talk to friends rather than keep such problems inside the family.[2] Multivariate statistical analyses indicate that higher socioeconomic status and living in bigger cities promote more use of informal networks rather than keeping the problem inside the family both for men and women.[3] As for the use of professional help, the statistical analyses show no significant difference between different socioeconomic groups.

There is no support in these data for the assumption that professionals are taking over as *first* helpers in conjugal crises. The main trend in urban Norway is that the use of *both* family and friendship networks are replacing the norm of keeping marital problems within the family. This trend may be interpreted as a weakening of the conjugal bond or the loyalty between spouses. Those who claim that such problems should be kept within the family, more seldom than others have the spouse as a confidant or a confidant altogether.[4] This may imply that the norm of not relating to others about marital problems is connected to a lifestyle of being more reserved with respect to relating about emotional problems in general. It seems as

TABLE 4. Personal friends among workmates according to age and gender among the employed. Percentages. (Urban Norwegian population in the age group 25-64, 1983)

	Age 25 - 30 M %	Age 25 - 30 W %	Age 31 - 40 M %	Age 31 - 40 W %	Age 41 - 50 M %	Age 41 - 50 W %	Age 50 - 64 M %	Age 50 - 64 W %	All M %	All W %
No friends among workmates	25	24	33	34	25	40	40	40	31	34
Only friends of own gender	51	26	26	22	48	17	40	31	40	24
Both male and female friends	20	32	38	35	13	37	17	14	22	31
Only friends of opposite gender	3	10	2	3	3	0	0	2	2	4
Don't know / no answer	0	8	1	5	10	7	4	12	3	8
	99	100	100	99	99	101	101	99	100	101
N	(59)	(50)	(61)	(42)	(40)	(32)	(45)	(43)	(205)	(167)

57

TABLE 5. Got help from workmates when having personal problems according to age and gender. Percentages. (Urban Norwegian population in the age group 25-64, 1983)

	Age 25 - 40		Age 41 - 65		All
	Men %	Women %	Men %	Women %	%
Often or sometimes	28	42	27	51	35
Never	21	13	23	9	17
Don't have such problems or don't discuss them at the work-place	47	38	41	33	41
Don't know / no answer	4	6	9	6	7
	100	99	100	99	100
N	(120)	(92)	(83)	(75)	(370)

though this lifestyle is on return especially among women. If this is the case, it may explain why the use of professional help in emotional crises is increasing, without a corresponding decrease in access to informal help and support. The strength of the intergenerational bonds, especially between mothers and daughters, which is indicated by the replies on confidants and helpers, may be surprising initially in view of rapid change in norms of family and sexual behaviors which have taken place in the last decades. While the generations undoubtedly have conflicting norms and values, it does not seem to have much influence on the confidence between parents and adult children and especially between mothers and daughters. The importance of family confidants and helpers for the divorced and for cohabitants also indicates that the weakening of the conjugal bond so far does not seem to have reduced the importance of the emotional bonds between the generations in the family.[5]

The relative importance of the parent/child relation compared to other informal relations is greater when it comes to economic problems as shown in Table 8.

The asymmetry between the generations becomes clear. Parents are far more important helpers for the younger generation than

TABLE 6. Got help from workmates when having personal problems according to marital status and gender. Percentages. (Urban Norwegian population in the age group 25-64, 1983)

	Unmarried		Married/ cohabitating		Previously married		All	
	Men %	Women %	Men %	Women %	Men %	Women %	M %	W %
Often or sometimes	31	43	25	43	44	68	27	44
Never	17	14	22	11	31	5	21	11
Don't have such problems or don't discuss them at the work place	45	35	47	39	19	15	45	36
Don't know/ no answer	6	7	6	7	6	12	6	7
(N)	99 (35)	99 (28)	100 (152)	100 (119)	100 (16)	100 (19)	99 (203)	100 (166)

59

TABLE 7. Preferred first helpers when encountering problems in co-life with spouse/cohabitant according to age and gender. Percentages. (Urban Norwegian population in the age group 25-64, 1983)

	Age groups.									
	25 - 30		31 - 40		41 - 50		50 - 64		All	
	Men	Women	Men	Women	Men	Women	Men	Women	Men	Women
	%	%	%	%	%	%	%	%	%	%
Parents / parents in law	35	25	22	30	6	17	2	2	17	20
Children, moved from home	-	-	-	-	0	7	13	38	4	11
Other relatives	8	20	4	11	31	30	6	11	12	18
Friends/workmates	25	31	31	30	19	33	13	11	22	28
Professional helpers	6	11	7	11	25	10	6	9	10	10
Problems should be kept in the family	17	6	28	9	31	23	37	19	28	13
	100	100	100	100	100	100	100	100	100	100
	(48)	(65)	(45)	(47)	(32)	(30)	(52)	(47)	(177)	(189)

60

TABLE 8. Preferred helpers when encountering economic problems according to age and gender. Percentages. (Urban Norwegian population in the age group 25-64, 1983)

Age groups

	25 – 30		31 – 40		41 – 50		51 – 64		All	
	Men %	Women %	Men %	Women %	Men %	Women %	Men %	Women %	Men %	Women %
Parents/ parents in law	38	46	27	43	9	28	2	3	20	30
Children moved from home	-	-	-	-	2	3	8	18	3	5
Other relatives	1	4	3	3	7	3	7	5	3	5
Friends/workmates	8	8	13	5	7	8	7	3	8	6
Social welfare office	1	4	3	5	9	3	5	11	4	6
Bank	25	14	22	12	25	21	29	20	27	16
Employer	7	1	12	2	7	8	13	1	10	2
Would prefer to handle it on my own	15	17	18	21	25	18	29	27	19	21
No answer	5	6	2	9	9	8	0	12	6	9
	100	100	100	100	100	100	100	100	100	100
(N)	(69)	(86)	(68)	(58)	(144)	(39)	(62)	(74)	(243)	(257)

grown-up children are for the older. Rather than interpreting this as solely a consequence of parents being more altruistic in relation to grown-up children than vice versa, it seems reasonable to assume that this difference mainly is due to middle aged and older generations being economically more well-off than the younger. The difference in the proportions of the age-groups who can solve their economic problems with the support of banks or employers is one indicator.

Elderly women's greater reliance on children in economic problem situations as compared to men, is as much an indication of their weak integration in worklife as a sign of their greater integration into the family network. As Table 8 indicates, the social welfare services has not become an attractive alternative for solving economic problems. The stigma connected to means-tested economic aid still seems to work as an effective rationing device, implying that informal help functioning as alternative to welfare state service is closely related to whether the service is defined as a citizen right.

In handling difficult problems concerning their own teenage children, professional helpers seem to be more often preferred by urban Norwegian parents than family or friends, as shown in Table 9.

Multivariate statistical analyses provide no significant results as to how education and socioeconomic status influence this preference. This result indicates that there is no great difference between the socioeconomic groups regarding their confidence in the welfare state services. The great reliance on professional helpers can be interpreted as an indicator of what Lasch (1977) has conceptualized as "the proletarization of parenthood." On the other hand, what better alternative may parents have, if they are to be rational, than to rely on professional help? Certainly the most serious problems of the children and teenagers of today in many ways seem very different from those of their parents' and grandparents'. The idea of our society as a post-figurative society (Mead 1978) implies that the experiences of the older generations are of limited relevance in order to cope with the most difficult problems of the younger. It, therefore, does not seem reasonable to use the answers of this question as an indicator of integration in informal caring networks.

TABLE 9. Preferred helpers if having teen-age children neglecting themselves. Percentages. (Urban Norwegian population in the age group 25-64, 1983)

	Age 25 - 40		Age 41 - 65		All	
	Men %	Women %	Men %	Women %	Men %	Women %
Parents/parents-in-law	23	21	5	8	13	14
Other relatives	2	3	11	11	7	7
Friends/workmates	17	12	10	11	13	12
Professional helpers	32	40	42	35	38	37
Problems should be kept in the family	13	12	21	18	18	16
No answer	13	12	11	16	11	14
	100	100	100	99	100	100
(N)	(60)	(91)	(92)	(97)	(152)	(188)

CONCLUSIONS

On the basis of theoretical considerations and on some empirical findings, to assume that the growth of the demand for public care services is due to a great decrease in family and other kind of informal caring, is much too simplified. On the other hand, it is more reasonable to assume that the meaning and content of family care is changing as family relations are becoming based more on companionship than on parents' and husbands' authority. The development of rights and opportunities for achievement in modern society have made such changes possible, and at the same time has made marriage and family a more fragile, though not necessarily a less satisfying institution. It should, therefore, be acknowledged that many of the problems which the public care system is facing nowadays, not only is a result of inefficiency and injustice, but also a consequence of its promotion of social rights, and social consciousness of these rights. The modern welfare state now has citizens who need public care serviced not only because they have become passively dependent on the state.

Rather, through the action of the state, however imperfect, and certainly due to the action of political interest groups which have pushed for more welfare state services, more people have acquired the possibility of richer personal and private lives. The history of the modern welfare state and its citizens lies in the oscillation between these two polar opposites: the state's initiatives which can be unjust, inefficient, controlling and overly homogenizing, but at the same time catalyzing a new consciousness of needs.

The continually shifting boundaries between private and public responsibilities, has implied continually shifting definitions of the kind of caring women are expected to provide as family members and as paid service workers. Women today seem to be the protagonists of the so-called "culture of services" (Saraceno 1981). This differentiates them from their predecessors, both in the dependency on out-of the family service structures, and in their ability to articulate their own and family members' needs and demands.

Greater economic insecurity and relatively smaller access to non-stigmatizing social services may reintroduce greater asymmetry in relations between parents and children and husbands and wives. To suggest that this will have positive consequences in creating more informal caring is to foster a dangerous illusion. I think that more varying responsibility on the part of men ought to start with an acknowledgement of the present day public care system's dependence on women's traditional caring services, which cannot be preserved without preserving women's subordinate position in the family. For social research the challenge still exists to develop better conceptual and methodological tools in order to provide more adequate and systematic knowledge on how to develop and change the public care system to make it fit with more symmetrical roles in the family.

NOTES

1. The survey was conducted in May-June 1983 as a part of the European Comparative research project *Changing Family Patterns in Europe*, coordinated by the European Coordination Centre for Research and Documentation in the Social Sciences, Vienna.

2. Of the full-time-employed or studying-women, 41 percent said they would turn to a friend and 8 percent said the problems should be kept in the family. The corresponding numbers for the part-time employed or full-time housewives were 20 and 19 percent, respectively.

3. A canonical discriminant analysis was tried in order to find what variables would explain the difference between the group who answered problems should be kept inside the family and the rest of the sample. The canonical correlation was small and the result was not very significant, but this group turned out to have a little less education and income, to live more often in smaller cities and to have less socioeconomic status than the rest. Trying the same kind of analysis on discriminating between the ones who would choose professional help and the rest, no differences according to the same background variables were found.

4. Among all married women 90 percent have a confidant; among the group who would keep the problem inside the family only 74 percent. The corresponding numbers for married men are 85 and 77 percent, respectively.

5. Among all the divorced 50 percent mention a family member as a confidant, 42 percent a friend, 13 percent professionals while 16 percent have no confidant. Among the cohabitants (of which most are younger people) 23 percent would use parents/parents-in-law as the first helper in a crisis with their cohabitant, 10 percent will use other relatives, while 39 percent would use friends and 17 percent would keep the problems inside the family. Also among the cohabitants there are the same differences between the sexes as to the willingness to talk to others about such problems. Twenty-nine percent of the cohabiting men against 4 percent of the women would keep the problem inside the family.

REFERENCES

Arling, G. The elderly widow and her family, neighbours and friends. *Journal of Marriage and Family*. Nov.: 767-768, 1976.

Aure, A. B. *Det er det daglige det kjem an på*. Eldreomsorgen i et klientperspektiv. Thesis. Department of Sociology, University of Bergen, Norway, 1984.

Bell, R. *Worlds of friendship*. London: Sage, 1981.

Blenkner, M. Social Work and Family Relations in Later Life with Some Thoughts on Filial Maturity, in E. Shanas and F.G. Streib (eds). *Social structure and the family: Generational relations*. Englewood Cliffs, N.J.: Prentice-Hall, 1965.

Brody, E. M. et al. *Women who provide parent care: Characteristics of those who work and those who do not*. Paper presented at the 37th Annual Meeting of the Gerontological Society of America, San Antonio TX, November, 1984.

Brody, E.M. Parent care as normative stress, in *The Gerontologist*. 25, 1: 19-29, 1985.

Daatland, S. O. Eldreomsorgen i en småby: De offentlige tjenester og familiens rolle. *Tidsskrift for Samfunnsforskning*, nr. 2: 155-173, 1983.

Evers, H. Care or custody? The experiences of women patients in long stay geriatric wards, in G. Williams and B. Hutter (eds). *Controlling women – The normal and deviant*. London: Croom Helm, 1981.

Gilligan, C. *In a different voice*. Cambridge, Massachusetts: Harvard University Press, 1982.

Graham, H. Caring: A labour of love, in Janet Finch and Dulcie Groves (eds): *A labour of love women, work and caring*. London: Routledge and Kegan Paul, 1983.

Lasch, C. *Haven in a heartless world. The family besieged*. New York: Basic Books Inc., 1977.

Mead, M. *Culture and commitment. The new relations between the generations in the 70's*. New York, 1978.

Noddings, N. *Caring a feminine approach to ethic and moral education*. New York/London: University of California Press, 1984.

Nordhus, I. H. *Gammel og avhengig?* Thesis. Department of Psychology, University of Bergen, Norway, 1981.

Nygard, L. *Omsorgsressurser hos nære pårørande*. Trondheim: Report 2/82, Norsk Institutt for sykehusforskning, 1982.

Oakley, A. *The sociology of housework*. New York: Pantheon Books, 1974.

Oliver, J. "The Caring Wife" in Eva Garmanikov et al. (eds). *The public and the private*. London: Heinemann Ltd, 1983.

Raddum, I. 1985. *Kreftpasient i velferdsstaten*. Thesis. Department of Sociology, University of Bergen, Norway.

Rosenmayr, L., and Køckeis, E. Propositions for a sociological theory of aging and the family, *International Social Science Journal*: 410-426, 1965.

Saraceno, C. *State interventions, the social sphere and private life chances for a progressive change of the family's role or just a roll-back?* Contribution to Expert meeting on Can there be a new welfare state: Social policy options toward shaping an uncertain future. Baden Austria Sept. 25-Oct. 1, Eurosocial R120, 1983.

Schumacher, E.F. *Good work*. London: Abacus, 1980.

Shanas, E. Social myth as hypothesis: the case of the family relations of the elderly. *The Gerontologist*, 19, 1: 3-9, 1979.

Ungerson, C. Women's caring: skills, tasks and taboos in Eva Garmanikov et al. (eds.) *The public and the private*. London: Heinemann Ltd, 1984.

Widding Isaksen, A.E. *Omsorg i grenseland*. Thesis. Centre for Womens Studies. University of Bergen, Norway, 1984.

Waerness, K. Caregiving as women's work in the welfare state in Harriet Holter (ed) *Patriarchy in a welfare society*. Oslo: University Press, 1984a.

Waerness, K. The rationality of caring, in *Economic and industrial democracy*. Sage 5: 185-211, 1984b.

The Other Side of Employed Parents' Life in Slovenia

Nevenka Černigoj-Sadar

SUMMARY. In this article are described some basic patterns of employed parents' life and the social and psychological factors which prevent changing their prevailing ways of life.

Most parents with children up to the age of 15 (more than ninety percent) are regularly employed. In terms of formal financial resources not all dual-earner families are above the social security level. Parents try to improve their living conditions in the following ways: all household work is done by family members (mainly mothers), they do different kinds of paid informal work and resolve their housing problems by building on their own with the help of relatives and bank credits. During all stages of life women are more burdened with informal work than men. Activities connected with the mass media and/or activities which have utilitarian value are the main preoccupations of parents in their free time.

Most parents have no choice concerning their employment status and even the possibilities of choosing among various free time activities are quite limited.

THE RESOURCES OF FORMAL PAID WORK

The developmental trend in Europe indicates that "men and women's adulthood today increasingly involves being economically active as well as being a parent" (Rapoport and Sierakowski, 1982). In Slovenia since the Second World War, the economically active population working in the agricultural sector has rapidly diminished in favor of employment in other sectors of the economy. Along with this, women's participation in the labor force has introduced considerable changes into family life. The family has lost its central position in satisfying the needs of family members. The in-

Nevenka Černigoj-Sadar is Senior Researcher at the Institute for Sociology and Lecturer of Psychology at the University Edvard Kardelj in Ljubljana.

stitutions outside the family have altered the possibilities available and the ways of satisfying the needs of family members. Paid work outside home and family life are becoming parallel life priorities for which people may have different motivations. It is difficult to find out which is decisive because egalitarian socialist ideology is often combined with the principle of economic necessity. Individual motivations are intertwined.

In the present article some data are presented which were obtained on the basis of several empirical research projects carried out at the Institute for Sociology in Ljubljana.[1] The discussion will be concerned mainly with basic patterns of employed parents' life and the factors which prevent changing their prevailing ways of life. In the survey "Quality of life in Slovenia" the following results were obtained: most parents in Slovenia (92.4%) with children up to the age of 15 are employed (Rus et al., 1984). Most young and middle-aged people live in dual-earner families. One-earner families are mainly one parent families and two parent families in which one of the parents is already retired. Among all parents under the age of 55 with children at home, there are only few (approximately 6%) who are not economically active. Formal monetary resources of young and middle-aged families are related to the number of regularly employed members.

Most families (more than three quarters) in which one or two parents are not regularly employed live below the officially declared social security level (indicated by average income per capita in the household). The worst positions in the households are those of women under the age of 55 who are not regularly employed. Although two-earner families have better economic conditions than one-earner families, not all of the former are above the declared social security level.

The economic crisis accompanied by the rapid monetary inflation in the last five years does not allow parents to make a choice concerning their employment status. They have little or no chance to

---

1. The results from the following surveys are mainly used: "The Problems of Development in Slovenia — 1975," "Quality of Life in Slovenia — 1984" and "Changes in the Life Patterns of Families in Europe — 1982," data from Slovenia. The first two surveys mentioned are done on representative sample for Slovenia, while the last is on a quota sample.

express their capabilities and their own ideas regarding their work (Rus and Arzenšek, 1984; Toš et al., 1986). Also, they are not satisfied with their incomes and about a quarter of parents report their income is not sufficient to cover the expenses of everyday living (Černigoj-Sadar, 1986).

It is generally accepted that participation in social production and public life is the basic condition for human emancipation. If paid work gives no possibilities of earning one's living then such work does not lead to emancipation. In fact, some groups of parents with young children are very limited in their personal and social growth. Young parents have very few opportunities of obtaining autonomy and self-actualization for various reasons, such as unresponsiveness of their work environment, pressing demands of young children and unresolved material problems. Conflicts created by the contradictions of the global societal relations are transferred to the family level. Parents often feel guilty because of their inability to create mutually rewarding relationships. The feeling of powerlessness to change family relations or sometimes also their material conditions creates apathetic behavior with temporary aggressive outbursts.

Basic living amenities for raising a family are not available to most parents until they are well into their thirties. Almost half of the families with preschool children do not have an adequate standard of housing—their flats are overcrowded, have no facilities or are humid (Boh and Černigoj-Sadar, 1986a). The existing housing policy does not provide enough formal opportunities for young parents to obtain an independent home. However, the parents do not stay passive, they invest a lot of their energy in informal work to improve their living conditions.

INFORMAL ECONOMY

In the optimal situation formal and informal resources for satisfying family members' needs should be complementary in their function and content. However, in many cases the expenses for biosocial reproduction are pushed into the sphere of informal work, even when both parents are employed. The equilibrium in combining formal and informal resources for resolving family problems are quite rare. Therefore, the informal resources have a mainly compensatory function and rarely become complementary to the formal

Table 1

Financial resources

Groups of parents who have children at home*	% of respondents who live in households:	
	With two or more employed members	Which have average income per capita 10.000 din and less**
Not employed		
Young and middle-aged:		
Male N – 20	35.0	75.0
Female N – 53	30.8	83.0
Employed		
Young:		
Male N – 94	91.4	53.3
Female N – 143	92.1	63.5

72

Middle-aged with children
up to the age of 15 years:

Male	N – 401	86.7	60.1
Female	N – 314	83.7	53.1

Middle-aged with children
above the age of 15 years:

Male	N – 114	88.5	50.8
Female	N – 130	80.3	49.2

---

* Data for the tables 1 and 2 are taken from the survey "Quality of
  Life in Slovenia 1984".

Legend:

Not employed: housewives, students, unemployed and retired.
Employed: employed and self-employed.
Young: from 15 to 29 years old.
Middle-aged: from 30 to 54 years old.

** 10.042 din represents the social security level. If average income
per capita in the household was 10.042 din or less in 1984, the
members of the household are entitled to different welfare supports.

73

(Boh and Černigoj-Sadar, 1985). In such a situation women carry the main burden.

The regular working time per day is 8 hours. On average, employed mothers spend just as much on the household chores and care for children. The ratio between time spent on housekeeping and regular paid work is 1.2 for young mothers and 0.91 for middle aged mothers with school children. For employed fathers this ratio is from 0.52 to 0.42. Fathers are usually the first to help mothers to solve most family problems but they engage in this for a shorter period, perceive less problems and their supportive social networks are less intensive. In rearing children, fathers take an active part particularly in expressive tasks rather than routine ones. Thus, our data show that all activities connected with family are still highly gender segregated.

Most of women's activities are not time limited, they cannot be postponed and they demand a great deal of personal commitment. Employed mothers almost always live under time pressure and their perception of the household burdens increases with age although time required for household chores remains approximately the same. This indicates an accumulating overload for women.

Household chores and care for children are not the sole commitment when parents have finished their regular paid work. About a quarter of them moonlight, do some additional paid work or work on the farm. Approximately one in three parents has built or is building his/her flat/house. Among all finished new accommodations the proportion of those privately constructed has been steadily rising from 43.6% in 1981 to 58.2% in 1984 (Poročevalec, 1986). To find out the extent of informal work in particular social groups, the following areas of informal work were taken into account for each parent:

— household chores and care for children;
— moonlighting, additional paid work, agricultural work;
— the housing problem solved or is being solved by building or adapting house/flat.

The percentage of parents who are engaged in one, two or three of the above mentioned areas of informal work is shown in Table 2.

Almost all parents are engaged in at least one informal work ac-

Table 2

The extent of informal work

Groups of employed parents with children at home:	Informal work - number of areas %				Number of persons in each group N
	0	1	2	3	
Young:					
Male	0.0	71.3	25.5	3.2	94
Female	0.0	75.4	21.1	3.5	124
Middle-aged with children up to the age of 15 years:					
Male	2.5	49.1	38.9	9.5	401
Female	0.0	60.4	36.1	3.5	313
Middle-aged with children above the age of 15 years:					
Male	28.9	46.5	21.1	3.5	114
Female	0.8	50.8	44.6	3.8	130

tivity. The highest percentage of informal work is done by middle-aged parents with children up to the age of 15. Informal work is a compensation for the inefficient formal economy for middle-aged parents. Young parents exploit a lot of the material and non-material resources of their parents (Boh, K., Černigoj-Sadar, 1985).

Women have been taking part in many activities formally ascribed to men (moonlighting, activities connected with building a flat/house) in addition to their traditional housekeeping and taking care for children. Men, on the other hand, have not taken part much in activities ascribed to women. Concerning the gender differences in informal work the same tendencies are shown as in professional work. Women are those who go out of the spheres traditionally ascribed to them. They provide social and psychological support for others and they also work for others to a greater extent than men.

Gender inequality in the division of labor is common to all European societies (Havio-Mannila, 1986; Michel, 1986; Gershuny, 1984). When the total division of labor in formal and informal work is taken into account, greater inequalities from the leisure perspective can be found in the socialist than in the capitalist countries of Europe. In socialist countries most young and middle-aged women are full time employed. They have less household appliances (which means that they spend more time for routine everyday chores) than women living in capitalist countries where less women are employed and the standard of living is higher, while there is no greater men's involvement in household chores in socialist systems.

LEISURE: FROM SELF-DIRECTED
TO OTHER-DIRECTED ACTIVITIES

There are different patterns in free time activities between men and women in Slovenia.[2] The activities during free time can be divided into two groups: self-directed activities which are mainly intended for the persons who are doing it, such as watching TV, reading, participating in sports or attending a study group are included

---

2. The discussion on leisure is based on two studies done by the author: "Social and psychological factors in transformation of free time" (1984), and "The possibilities in free time" (1986).

in the first group. The second group includes other-directed activities which may have potential material value for other people, not only for the person involved, such as gardening and knitting. The first is more characteristic of men, while the second is more characteristic of women.

The trend from self-directed activities to other-directed activities is characteristic of the transition from young adulthood to the establishment phase. But it is more pronounced for employed men than for employed women. Most women do not change their main directions in leisure. They are mainly directed towards social activities, activities connected with mass-media or towards activities which have some utilitarian value for others, even before they have their own family. But in spite of such reality, more young women than men have aspirations for cultural and sport activities. Such a way of spending leisure is, however, rarely attained even in their mature age. Aspirations for cultural and recreational activities are more often achieved by men. These activities are quite restricted with the arrival of the first child. After the age of thirty, approximately half of the employed fathers drop these kind of leisure activities.

Restriction of cultural, educational and sports activities is common to both sexes in the establishment phase, but for women it comes earlier, even before they have a child, while for men the change comes later when they find out that the family cannot live in inconvenient material conditions. Employed mothers, whatever their age and education, have less choices in their free time than fathers.

Holidays are supposed to be a period of "real choice" and the break with everyday obligations, at least once a year. But only part of our parents approach this "image of leisure." Quite a lot of parents (33%-47%, depending on gender and life stage) spend their holidays at home. And to be at home during holidays means to be involved in all kinds of informal work.

INSTEAD OF CONCLUSION

For most parents there is no choice concerning their employment status and even in free time the possibilities to choose among different kinds of activities are quite limited.

Parents are always at least in a latent if not in a manifest conflict situation, especially those who have high criteria for their quality of life or those for whom paid work and family are shared priorities. This is reflected also in their health condition. Almost all report at least one severe symptom of some disease (Boh and Černigoj-Sadar, 1986b).

On the one hand "to be employed and to have one's family" is a social norm. On the other hand the reality of everyday life rarely allows alternatives. To be without one or the other means very limited access to social resources, an economic and in most cases a psychological one also. So people speak more about the positive influences of paid work and family than about the negative. Dissatisfaction for a long period is unbearable. Therefore, the representations of desired state allow above all positive experience to reach the center of awareness. The awareness of real emancipatory potential (which is de facto very restricted) in different spheres of production and reproduction is pushed out. Such a mechanism is indispensable, not only to make different kinds of alienation bearable but also to satisfy basic personal and social needs. Different kinds of repression help to keep continuity and at least a partial coherence of individual identity. Employed parents are pressed to create "different spaces of individual self-realization," but these are mostly fictitious. These images are revitalized from day to day because people believe in them. They have to believe, otherwise they would have no defense against the pressures of contradictions experienced (Ule, 1986). Our specific social and economic situation forces people to transform unreflectively pragmatic everyday premises of "economy of life" into norms and values. These norms and values are introjected. So the utilitarian ways of life (Cathelat, 1977) in leisure prevail over the expressive. Double or triple burdens are perhaps not chosen, but it seems that they come spontaneously until middle age.

In the context of the recent ideal type (the normative one) of Slovene culture, men and women have equal rights and duties. During the past twenty years women have made great progress in the sphere of public participation (Jogan, 1986). The same can be said for some social policy acts enhancing quality of family life and the provision of public services, but all of this may never suffice some needs of family members. The way of organizing everyday life which would be optimal for all family members is not yet clear.

The patriarchal heritage of men and women intrudes into the representations of optimal relationships among family members which should be realized by a symmetrical division of labor. Until now the symmetrical division of labor looks more like a fiction than a fact (Ule, Mežnarič and Ferligoj, 1978; Černigoj-Sadar, 1984). A "labor of love" is still the domain of women and underevaluated (Piotrkowski, 1979). In fact a process of grafting the new and unclear expectations of old myths is under way. New attributes of men and women are being added to the old. On the other hand, solving problems related to the equality of individual family members are pushed to the margins by other more urgent ones (e.g., ecological, social and economic), which appear both on the individual and macro-level of society. But for the time being, there is still some balance between those people who see equality among family members just as one of the myths which had better fade away and between those for whom equal opportunities of all family members are the basic elements for quality of family life and one of the strategies for future development of society. The supporters of the latter should reconsider the contribution of employed partners to society and the actual possibilities for their personal development. The endeavors for better economic conditions are sometimes counterproductive for the achievement of an equal opportunities goal. Intellectual, emotional, economic and political factors are of equal importance in generating the gender equality. And gender equality is the basic brick in construction of an equalitarian form of life which is only one of the possible forms of life in the future.

REFERENCES

Boh, K. and Černigoj-Sadar, N. Testing New Methods in Extending Social and Rehabilitation Services for Families. Ljubljana: Inštitut za sociologijo, 1985.

Boh, K. and Černigoj-Sadar, N. Otroško varstvo—kazalec kvalitete življenja otrok in družin (Child care—an Indicator of Quality of Life of Children and Families). Ljubljana: Inštitut za sociologijo, 1986a.

Boh, K. and Černigoj-Sadar, N. Zdravstveno stanje prebivalstva v Sloveniji (Health Status of the Population of Slovenia). Ljubljana: Inštitut za sociologijo, 1986b.

Cathelat, B. Les styles de vie des Francais. Alain Stanke, 1977.

Changes in the Life Patterns of Families in Europe. national reports—Vol.I., Vol.II., Vol.III. Vienna: European Centre for Research and Documentation in the Social Sciences, 1984.

Černigoj-Sadar, N. Socialni in psihološki faktorji sprememb v načinu preživljanja prostega časa (Social and Psychological Factors in Transformation of Free Time). Družboslovne razprave 1, Ljubljana: Inštitut za sociologijo, 1984, 126-132.

Černigoj-Sadar, N. Možnosti v izvendelovnem času (The possibilities in Free Time). Družboslovne razprave 4, Ljubljana: Inštitut za sociologijo, 1986, 85-99.

Gershuny, J. Social Innovation and the Division of Labour. New York, Oxford University Press, 1983.

Haavio-Mannila, E. Sex Segregation in Paid and Unpaid Work. Vienna: European Coordination Centre for Research and Documentation in Social Sciences, 1986.

Jogan, M. Ženske na poti od delne družinske do celostne družbene uveljavitve (Women on the Way from Partial Family to Global Social Emancipation). In M. Jogan (Ed.), Ženske in diskriminacija. Ljubljana: Delavska enotnost, 1986.

Michel, A. The Impact of Marriage and Children on the Division of Gender Roles. Vienna: European Coordination Centre for Research and Documentation in Social Sciences, 1986.

Piotrkowski, C.S. *Work and the Family System.* New York: Macmillan, 1979.

Poročilo o stanovanjskem gospodarstvu v SR Sloveniji (ESA-84) (Report about housing economy in Slovenija). Skupščinski Poročevalec, XII, št.21, Ljubljana, 5.8.1986.

Rapoport, R. and Sierakowski, M. Recent Social Trends in Family and Work in Britain. London: Policy Studies Institute, 1982.

Rus, V. and Arzenšek, V. Rad kao sudbina i kao sloboda (Work as a Destiny and as a Freedom). Zagreb: Sveučilišna naklada Liber, 1984.

Rus, V. et al. Kvaliteta življenja v Sloveniji (*Quality of Life in Slovenia*). Ljubljana: Inštitut za sociologijo, 1984.

Toš, N. et al. Slovensko javno mnenje 1986 (Slovene Public Opinion 1986). Ljubljana: Fakulteta za sociologijo, politične vede in novinarstvo, 1986.

Ule, M. Protislovja socialne konstrukcije osebnosti (Contradictions in Social Construction of Personality). Doctoral Dissertation. Ljubljana: Filozofska fakulteta, 1984.

Ule, M., Mežnarič, S. and Ferligoj, A. Raspodjela svakodnevnih uloga u porodici izmedju želja /društva/ i stvarnosti /porodice/ (Division of Everyday Roles in Family among Aspiration /Society/ and Reality /Family/). Paper presented at VIth Congress of Yugoslavian Psychologist, Sarajevo 1978.

"The Double Presence": A Complex Model of Italian Women's Labor

Franca Bimbi

WOMEN'S LABOR IN THE "ITALIAN MODEL"

Since the Second World War Italy has experienced the extension of the industrial-urban model of society (which views the family as a primarily reproductive unit), the development of the Welfare State and the legal, political and economic emancipation of women.

These processes occurred in a context of profound regional differences, so much so that it has not seemed improper to speak of "three Italies" (Bagnasco 1977). The cultural models of development of North Italy have been imposed on the whole country. However, several changes in political structure, administration and the social policy occurred in the regions of Central Italy first. In the South and Islands, development has shown itself to be very complex: marked internally by profound splits between processes of social emancipation and mechanisms of economic dependence.

Each of the Regions of Central and North-East Italy have demonstrated various social formations and politico/cultural identity. Each region is different, and the small and medium-sized factories found in these areas may be instrumental in responding to economic crises. In particular, this is because of the permanence of fairly traditional mechanisms of the social integration, based on the maintenance of supportive links within the community and family

Franca Bimbi is a member of the faculty in the Department of Sociology, University of Padova, Padova, Italy.

81

(Bagnasco, Trigilia, Messori, 1978; Paci 1980; Anastasia, Rullani, 1981; 1982).

All these economic and social changes occurred within a context of deep social conflict; up to the 60s primarily between capital and labor. From the end of the 60s onwards it is marked by the presence of strong collective movements, including Feminism (Bertolo 1976; Calabrò, Grasso 1985; Melucci 1984). For Italy, the transformation of female labor and of the role of women has occurred in a society that is changing rapidly. In part, that society is still traditional (with deep peasant roots), but it is also modern and has seen rapid processes of the social differentiation.

One result of differentiation is the "Double Presence" (Balbo 1978). This expression refers to the recent experience of women as a consequence of combination of family work with work for the market. It is also an indicator of the transformation in the social identity of women, which no longer tends necessarily to underline the family as the locus for self-recognition and the legitimization of social roles.

In this sense "Double Presence" would permit women to locate themselves within a complex society: it can, in fact, function as a symbolic code which permits the passage between two interpretations of the world: traditional female culture, marked by values primarily connected with expressivity; and modern culture and society, marked by primarily instrumental values. Empirical research has widely documented the constant increase of female labor compared to the constriction of demand on the official market (Padoa Schioppa 1977; Accornero, Carmignani, 1986). This as well can constitute an indicator of the "Double Presence." Continuing at the empirical level, the reality of "Double Presence" appears to be established as the normal life model for adult women in the areas of North Italy that have been industrialized the longest (Barile, Zanuso 1980). Here the woman's responsibility for managing individual needs, economic resources and family roles as well as holding down a job makes her, more than others, appear constrained to sustain the ideology of work in a society which in other respects proclaims the importance of work. But the model is also a reference point for other types of women: adolescents (Merelli 1985), unmarried women who live alone and students (Piccone Stella 1979), young girls from the South or the Islands (Pacifico 1982).

In this paper I propose both to outline the implications of the introduction of Double Presence, in the reproduction/production relationship; and to show the transformation due to the double presence in a diffuse economy — that of the Veneto — (in particular the area around Padua and Verona) (Bimbi 1983; Pristinger 1983).

In general the research into female labor in the Central-North-East regions (Saraceno 1980; Balbo, Cacioppo, May, 1985; Bimbi, Pristinger 1985; Merelli, Nava et al., 1985) has highlighted some specific characteristics of diffuse economy areas. From an economic point of view the research into female labor underlines the importance of the informal economy (Mingione 1983; Capecchi, Pesce 1983; Bimbi, Capecchi 1986). This is a submerged economy and the real figures for female labor are higher than the official ones. As a community economy we can see in it the importance of the exchange of reproductive resources between relatives who do not live under the same roof, though the individual household remains nuclear. Another reason for the importance of the informal economy is that this family work remains primarily female, even though it is structured in a way not too dissimilar to that in the areas that have been industrialized the longest.

From the social point of view one can clearly see the specificity of the formations in these areas, in which the processes of the transformation of the conditions of women occurred without upheaval (Bimbi 1985 bis).

THE CONCEPTUAL STRUCTURE
OF DOUBLE PRESENCE

Up to 20 years ago — at least in Italy — the analysis of the relation between "civil society" and market underlined the dependence and unproductiveness of the former, both economically and politically. The productive structure of the market appeared to the fundamental reference point for political change. What emerging phenomena enable us to consider the relative autonomy of the "civil society" and the conditions of reproduction? What has brought about the heterogeneity of the time within and without the market (Sachs 1986; Balbo 1987)?

We can look at three sectors in which relevant transformations have emerged, that have a bearing on the autonomy of the productive process:

— the family, which since the war has seen the social valorization of women's labor expended in reproductive activity;
— the state, which has assumed a part of the work of reproduction, thus transferred from private to public;
— the political representations which have developed in the "civil society" in the form of social movements.

It is in this context that we can define the double presence.

The term Double Presence is adopted more and more to substitute the more frequent "double work" or "dual role" and is in some way a new synthesis of both. The expression refers to a conceptual framework for the analysis of women's labor which takes into account both of the specific areas of female production: the work of reproduction and work for the market. Within the concept there are two related areas of analysis: one is relative to the quantitative aspects of the female work force; time of work, the work load and social working day of women: and the other is relative to the mechanisms of the female mode of production (Prokop 1978; Bianchi 1981; Balbo, Bianchi 1982).

In the first area, focus is on the economic function of the work of reproduction. This consists in the management/combination of the resources to which the family has access, (direct, indirect salaries, other income, services), to maximize the response to the need of individuals. This implies that the labor of women permits access, presence and turnover in the labor market for adult members and others.

The second factor demonstrates a double movement between the compartmentalization of the market and the undoubted subordination of presence in the market to that in the family (where the essential work is that of reproduction).

The double presence hypothesis suggests the existence of a network of selective processes open to women with regard to work, the family and its members, which is based on the view that "taking care of others" is the major model of female action.

This same model could explain in part: the low contractualization of the domestic labor of women, (even in a context where the ideology of a double career is accepted) and the reciprocal attraction between women and the social services sector requiring few qualifications.

Structural transformations and recent political initiatives by women are the conditions for the hypothesis of Double Presence.

For the structural aspect we must emphasize three factors: redefinition of the work of reproduction, increase in formal and general education of women, mass access to paid work.

It is possible to speak of Double presence rather than housewives/working women or simply double jobs, when there is created, within the work of reproduction, objective areas of access.

Such access is more to the application of rules than labor for the market. The relationship between female and maternal role can be examined in relation to two factors: the fall in birthrate and the spread of contraception (De Sandre 1982, Federici 1984); the focusing on the psycho/emotional aspects of domestic/family labor and their connection with sources of socialization such as school and social services. These two factors indicate a drastic re-definition of domestic labor and represent a qualitative jump in family organization and female self-awareness, even though the daily and weekly hour load of domestic labor doesn't diminish at all.

Another factor is the formal and general education of women (Chiaretti, Bimbi, Piazza 1981). This is connected to the definition of Double Presence because of the access of women to institutions of higher education which represent a channel of socialization contradictory to the orientation towards the family, but which has also been a vehicle for the professionalization of domestic and maternal labor. The development of the social services sector and its sizeable employment of women has meant that even poorly qualified female workers can have paid work which involves interpersonal relationships.

The development of mass media, TV, radio and publications results in the permanent education of women, which reinforces the image and the experience of Double Presence. Within the processes of increasing formal education of women one can note channels of socialization towards the public area and the re-definition of the private.

The principle characteristic of this access to paid work, which distinguishes this phase with respect to previous historical periods, is that it appears obligatory, in some way "natural" for all women.

That is not to say the female presence on the labor market is not different, differentiated and discriminated against but perhaps it is in the same way for all women. The figure of the middle class woman compelled to be a housewife forever tends to disappear as does the halo of privilege around some women present in certain male-dominated professions. All women must work, want to to a certain extent, and do so at least in certain periods of their lives. Capitalism has made paid work for women "natural." It is an important historic step, often not shown in the statistics. The development of information technology and the service sector, the compartmentalization and interrelation of markets are phenomena which have made this possible, as has the development of the Welfare State.

The two processes outlined above: the re-definition of the work of reproduction and the formal education of women — are not absolutely unconnected with that more sizeable, diversified and less subordinate presence of women on the labor market. The redefinition of the work of reproduction appears as the antecedent necessary for the development of the hypothesis of Double Presence. In fact, the hypothesis of Double Presence is, for Italy, a hypothesis of the 70s, while the work of reproduction has been substantially altered since the war, and mass education of women begins in the mid-60s.

The reminder that the timetables of the three transformations (i.e., the work of reproduction, female education, and widened access to the job market) do not coincide, highlights both the influence of the first two on the third and their effectiveness over a longer period. It also underlines the notion that the changes date from different periods for different actors.

With the reference to women one must, as an antecedent and basis for the hypothesis of Double Presence, recall some specific events in the course of Italian politics:

1. the struggle of causal workers, the conflicts for equal pay; from the end of the 50s to the beginning of the 60s (Law of Equality 1956),
2. the conflicts for social services (from Maternity Schools 1964 to Family Planning Clinics 1975),
3. the struggle against domestic labor and inequality in the family (New Family Rights Bill 1975, Divorce 1970-74),
4. the conflicts for the re-appropriation of the body (Abortion 1978-1981, Projected laws on Rape from 1979).

Reference to these events clarifies the politico-cultural context in which our hypothesis is located: from the culture of emancipation in the 60s to the culture of liberation in the 70s; from the demand for equality to the assertion of difference; from the demand for access, to the job market to the re-definition of the family.

From this brief outline one can see the complexity of our hypothesis, in its extension of the role of women, and in the multiplicity of the cultural variables. The hypothesis does more than open up one field of enquiry. It is concerned with the division of workloads within the family, and so, ultimately, with the question of female identity. (See Diagram 1.)

From the diagram it is clear that Double Presence has wider significance and implications than those focused on by empirical research into female labor. It covers a wide range of factors relative to the condition of women.

The first thing to disappear in this hypothesis is the dichotomy of housewife/worker, both as mutually exclusive experiences and as opposed ways of life, with contrasting attitudes and behavior.

The Double Presence appears as the form taken today by the female role, in which converge the normative models of family organization and the market, as well as the transformation produced in these areas by the women themselves.

The central part of the diagram (C) outlines the relation and connection between different experiences, above all in the areas of reproduction through such public institutions such as schools and social services. They indicate significant interchanges between work and the work of reproduction, the mode of female production and

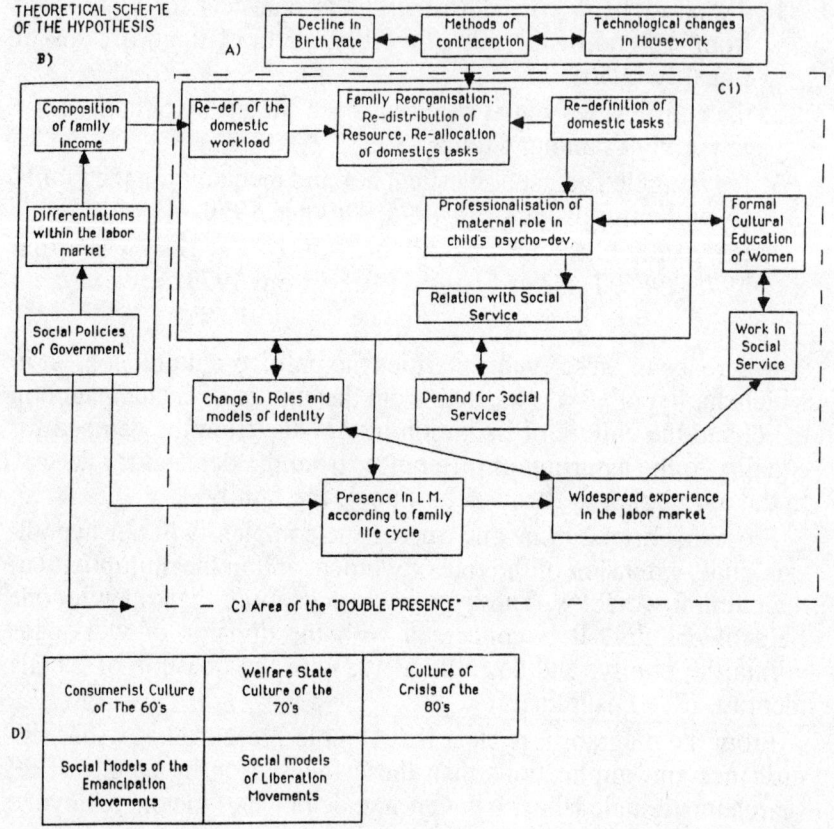

THEORETICAL SCHEME OF THE HYPOTHESIS

DIAGRAM 1

the production of goods and services, the work of communication and work for the market.

These are areas in which Double Presence is the key to labor. Here the models of care of others and the logic according to which work is organized meet, within an institutional framework and this is where the demands made by the family have to be reconciled with the economic limits of the system of social services and the needs of providers of such services, the majority of whom are women.

It is no accident that Double Presence occurs along with the cultural model of reproduction which we have described as the culture of welfare. This was unthinkable before the 70s because it was in that period that Italian women were doubly emancipated: both in reproduction and work. During the 70s women acquired the rights of citizenship; emancipation in the family and work place. This process, linked to the access to social services which substitute domestic labor, and given the demand for female labor in the service sector, corresponds to the highest degree of women's emancipation. Emancipation is not achieved through paid labor as long as the woman is not able to negotiate in the area which is considered her principle form of reproductive activity and her "basic" social role.

THE DOUBLE PRESENCE IN AN AREA OF "DIFFUSE ECONOMY": A "REDEFINED OBLIGATION"?

Relevant phenomena of social transformation emerge as we analyze the expansion of the double presence from the areas of the core to those of peripheral economy; and within this movement from urban centres of a commercial/tertiary type to contexts of greater residential and productive dispersion.[1]

The Veneto region of Northeast Italy appears, from many points of view, the ideal place for tests of this kind.

Research into the peripheral economy in this area (Bagnasco, Trigilia, 1984) underlines the function of the family within the productive network. It functions as a collection of economic resources for micro enterprises and it serves as a powerful instrument for social integration through the transmission of traditional political, moral and religious values.[2]

In this context emerges the importance of the Catholic social identity, as a traditional cultural resource, useful for maintaining the relationship between the political system and processes of modernization of production.

However this traditional sub-cultural identity has undergone deep changes in recent history. Research into the secularization of religion, already underway in the early 70s, has shown for the Veneto a drop in participation in religious practices and in the adhesion to some fundamental creeds of catholicism which is analogous, if not superior, to those in other areas of Italy (Guizzardi 1976). Furthermore the participation in the feminist movement of the 70s (Bertolo 1976) and the vote in the referenda on divorce (1974) and abortion (1981) are further proof of the secularization of family values.

The demographic behavior of the population supplies further indications of the reduction in the Catholic hegemony where family morals are concerned. The Veneto since the war has gradually fallen into line with other areas of North Italy, and now has a rate of population growth which is almost zero; even though maintaining a slightly higher average number of children, greater presence of numerous families and a more limited number of abortions. All these variables have a different importance in areas of greater or lesser urbanization or in social classes of more or less recent peasant origin. The analysis of these phenomena permits the expansion of the double presence hypothesis to peripheral economies. Even though one cannot doubt the influence of work for the market on gender changes within the family, the modernization of family behavior parallels or precedes the substantial presence of women on the labor market. It is a question of two inter-related phenomena rather than a relation of cause and effect, starting from emancipation through work. The women interviewed—a random sample of 400 married women between 20 and 50 years old living with their husbands—represent the social stratum most conditioned by both the mechanism of reproduction and production (Bimbi, Pristinger 1985). From an objective point of view they are deprived of those dynamic possibilities which consist in not yet having a family of one's own.

One specific aim of this investigation was to discover if, in an area of diffuse economy, the family structure, reproduction and the division of domestic labor differed significantly from the models which emerged from research carried out in industrial/urban contexts. The results can be interpreted as revealing both the effect of the process of modernization of family models in the region concerned and maintenance of a broadly traditional gender-based division of duties, based on the structural data and quantitative analysis.

The Family and the Home

Some characteristics of the interviewees relative to their relationship with the market confirm observations on the analysis of the family structure in the sample of 400 women, 48.3% currently are working and 51.5% are housewives. Work experience is the normal course of career of women. Only 44 of the women had never worked (11.1%), while 40.5% had worked in the recent past.

At the same time, giving up jobs was experienced by 44.8% of the interviewees: 75.8% had never returned to the workplace. If we add to these data that the reason for giving up work is predominantly linked to the family cycle (marriage and the birth of children in 42.7% of the cases), and 32% of the interviewees said they had never stopped working, then the image received is contradictory. Work for the market is a general experience. However discontinuity is due to taking on family roles and duties. The result is double presence, not as an addition of two jobs but as a process of transfer and reorientation of female identity between two spheres, according to the demands the family makes on the woman.

There are subjective components in this situation. 41.9% of the women in the sample who are, at present, housewives say that they are ready to work, compared with 25.1% of working women who report they are ready to "only take care of the home." Data indicate the contradiction between the two aspects (work for the market and domestic work) but do not explain this contradiction. The double presence hypothesis is further supported in that 41.6% of working women chose reduced hours and 19.7% do not work outside the home, while 38.8% managed to reconcile full time work with family duties. Taking the 50.1% who work, have worked or are looking for a first job as indicative of a trend then we can see that responsibility for the family does not exempt one from work for the market. But the latter is heavily conditioned by family domestic work. It is interdependence of the market and domestic work which concerns, in different ways, 89% of the women in the sample. The majority of women have or have had paid work during their lives.

The interviewees consisted of two generations: 31.1% were between 20 and 30; 41.5% between 31 and 40, and 27.3% between 41 and 50. The distance between the two generations is shown by the fact that 8.4% are under 25 and 12.2% are over 45.

The distribution of employed women, according to profession, gives the following (Bimbi, Pristinger 1985):

manager	.5%	professional/semi-prof.	2.1%
clerk	24.4%	shopkeeper	12.4%
teacher	15.0%	craft work, work at home	13.0%
manual worker	25.9%	agricultural worker	6.7%

They are distributed over the following areas of economic activity (Table 1).

With regard to size of family, 24.8% had one child, 40.1% of the interviewees had two children, 14.5% had three children, 6.8% had four or more and 13.8% had none.

The distribution of numbers of children by age (Table 2) confirms the tendency to have not more than two children. A smaller number of cases may have decided to postpone the birth of the first child.

This birth rate does not vary significantly with geographical location. There are, however, significant differences in family size between working women and housewives (see Table 3): there are extreme differences regarding women with three or more children and those who are childless.

Education is an important factor in the postponement or reduction of number of children. This immediately introduces the questions of contraception (see Table 4): there are significant differences between the distinction, "working women" and "housewives" in the use of contraception. Women who report that they do not use contraceptives (at present) are approximately 22.2% of the sample. The difference between employed women and housewives is the greater use of the pill among the former and of the fertile period method by the latter. Contraception is generally used by women (77.9%) and this is a check on fertility. These practices work in spite of the strong imbalance in favour of the use of traditional and less certain methods.

Other data relative to the technology of domestic work or to the comforts — services connected to its performance and the well-being

TABLE 1. Employed women by area of economic activity and demographic size of town of residence

TOWN	Agric.	Ind.	Trade, Tur, Bank, Ins. Trans.,Prof.	Teach.Ed. Pub. Adm. Other Serv.	TOTAL
Principle Town (Padova & Verona)	26,7	19,3	38,2	45,3	34,0
> 10.000 inh	-	21,1	14,5	15,6	15,7
5.000-10.000 inh.	20,0	22,8	30,9	21,9	24,6
TOTAL	7,9	29,8	28,8	33,5	100,0

Source: F. Bimbi, F. Pristinger, 1985

93

TABLE 2. Number of children by age group of women

N° of chil. / Age	No chil.	1chil.	2chil.	3chil.	4chil.	5chil. or more	TOT.	N°
20 – 30	26,0	41,5	29,3	3,3	/	/	100	123
31 – 40	7,9	20,1	51,2	14,0	5,5	1,2	100	164
41 – 50	9,3	12,0	37,0	27,8	9,3	4,6	100	108
TOTAL								395

TABLE 3. Concentration of number of children according to professional situation of mothers

N° of chil. Prof.sit.	No chil.	1chil.	2chil.	3chil.	4chil.	5chil. or more	TOT.	N°
employed	20,7	27,5	36,3	9,3	4,7	1,6	100	193
housewife	7,3	22,3	43,7	19,4	5,3	1,9	100	206
TOTAL								399

TABLE 4. Method of contraception according to professional situation of women from 20-45 years

Method Prof. sit.	Coitus inter.	Fertile period	pill	coil	diaphragm	condom	sterili zation	non used	TOT.
Employed	35,5	45,1	21,0	6,5	1,4	10,9	/	19,6	100
housewife	38,1	12,9	8,8	4,1	/	10,9	0,7	24,5	100
total	36,8	9,1	14,7	5,3	0,7	10,9	0,4	22,1	100
cases	105	26	42	15	2	31	1	63	285

of the family, give an even further differentiated picture of the relationship between woman and home. We can thus identify certain general strategies with regard to family resources: the ownership of the home as an objective, some facilities and basic electrical gadgets (fridge, washing machine) as the actual situation and TV and car as more lasting consumer durables.

However there emerges a rather low level of development in the technology of domestic work. Furthermore, 61.9% of women possess a sewing-machine and 41.5% use it to make clothes for the family. The job of family dressmaker introduces the importance of home-consumption in general, as a sign of a combination between saving money and the output of domestic labor. This situation permits a distribution of resources but holds back the organization and technical composition of domestic work. The sewing and making-up of clothes for the family also differs significantly according to geographical location.

Family Domestic Work

The timetable for domestic work described by the interviewees expresses both objective and subjective aspects: the amount of time used for duties, at home and outside the home, and how much time is covered by what the women describe as work and how much time is demanded by their role. In this study there were five women who said they did nothing during the week. Approximately 35.5% reported that they did from 4 to 8 hours of domestic work on a working day.

For example, Saturday is the day one does more domestic work and on Sunday domestic work is almost halved, and this picture is more for working women than housewives. It is a question of two very different rhythms of work. Family work for a working woman is greatly reduced during the week compared to a housewife.[3]

The working women do most of the domestic work on Saturday but tend to free themselves of it (much more than the housewives) on Sunday. If gainful employment is the condition for the reduction of domestic work (which is, however, added to the other job) such a reduction is also linked to age and qualifications. It is not that the youngest work less but the others who work much more.[4] Objective variables therefore, like having young children, are added to other cultural variables, such as the "habits" of domestic work acquired by older women, for whom one might expect the chance to reduce or share the work in a family composed mainly of adults.

Education emerges as a very important factor in differences of domestic timetable. At the two extremes the situations are opposed. The women with least formal education (no qualifications, elementary school certificate) perform in a working day, 12% up to 4 hours of work, from 4 to 8 hours 37.4% and more than 8 hours 50.5%. Of the interviewees with secondary school certificate and degree, 53.3% have a timetable of less than 4 hours; 30% between 4 and 8 hours; and 16.7% more the 8 hours. The latter work significantly less than the others on Saturday and Sunday.[5] Finally that which most determines differences in the timetable of domestic work is having children, in particular children under the age of 15.[6]

This brief summary enables a description of domestic work load dynamics. There is a relative elasticity which is linked to the work situation of the women, age, education and number of children. The concentration of the duties of family work in the hands of the mother-wife is striking. Table 5 is indicative of this.

On domestic family-work (from making the beds to ironing) help for or substitution of the women is very scarce, while it appears much more possible in family bureaucratic work. On the whole the interchangeability is greater for domestic work tasks performed outside the home (shopping and hospital visiting) and for bureaucratic work which involves money (banking, post office, tax and insurance) and/or intellectual content (school and medical visit). But substitution (values for duties performed mainly by others) reaches high levels only for duties involving family finances.

Who helps and who substitutes? And what is the importance of the variables of profession and geography? In all the tasks in which there is little help, taking turns or substitutions, the distinction housewife-working woman is important. In making beds, cooking, washing-up, washing, ironing, visiting doctor and school the housewife is helped less. In shopping and hospital visiting the woman is helped little even if she is working but is helped more than in the duties performed in the home. In baking and post office, paying taxes and insurance, both housewife and working woman is helped substantially. For these last two duties furthermore she is substituted more in communities of less than 5,000 inhabitants than in the larger towns. In general, in the smallest communities there are more people, besides the interviewee, who take part in domestic work, even if not through taking turns and substitution. Furthermore, women working full time are helped — substituted more than those working part-time or those working at home, who in general are more exclusively charged with all household duties.

In general, husbands help and substitute more in bureaucratic duties[7] than other family members. In duties outside the home, such as shopping and hospital visiting, they contribute only slightly more than in other duties performed within the home, from making the beds to ironing, and still much less than other family members.[8] In the group of duties involving family-bureaucratic work it is the husband who helps and substitutes most. In the group of family-domestic work it is mainly the women of the house (mothers, mothers-in-law, daughters).

There is an unequal division of work between husband and wife. If anything, there is an extension of the work of reproduction beyond the family for some of the duties which traditionally are the preserve of men. The husband's timetable of domestic work increases significantly if the woman is working outside the home rather than in the role of housewife. Factors such as the age and education of the husband have a weaker effect, linked more to the choices and opportunities of the woman than of the partner. Domestic work of up to four hours a day is done by 34.5% of ordinary clerks-office workers. For teachers and managers the figure is 23.4%; skilled workers 19.4% and for all others, from higher managers and entrepreneurs to laborers and shopkeepers, it is less than 17.1%. The wife in 82.1% of the cases said that the husband did nothing during the week: 78.1% reported nothing on Saturday and 83.4% nothing on Sunday.

The difference of the "presence" of the husbands in the work of reproduction is evident in couples with children under age 15. Considering such fundamental duties as material care and attention to school work along with some duties which are only improperly described as secondary — playing with children, reading, taking children for walks, the imbalance between the time spent by mother and

TABLE 5. The sharing of domestic work

Who does it tasks	interviewee alone	mainly interviewee with help	in turns	mainly others	TOT.	CASES
making beds	73,4	18,3	4,3	4,0	100	399
cooking	79,2	6,8	8,8	5,3	100	399
washing up	75,7	12,0	7,3	5,0	100	399
shopping	67,8	9,8	16,6	5,8	100	399

washing	87,1	5,6	2,0	5,3	100	395
ironing	79,8	11,8	2,5	5,8	100	397
banking and post	43,6	9,8	23,1	23,6	100	399
tax and insurance	39,1	8,3	22,6	30,1	100	399
medical	65,5	6,2	19,8	8,5	100	388
hospital visits	71,3	6,0	17,1	5,7	100	334
school	79,7	4,0	10,7	5,7	100	300

father is noteworthy. More than 80% of fathers only look after their children for less than a half hour a day.

"Maternal" care is reduced less, even where the woman is working. One can understand how housewives spend only a little more time than working women in looking after children. More often it is the level of education which brings about a change. As it increases there is a significant increase in the time spent playing with children and taking them out. A form of behavior certainly linked to a cultural background but also to certain professions (teachers, manager) with less demanding timetables and a more equally balanced family structure of duties. The husband of the working woman takes slightly more part in the more material duties (dressing children, preparing food): 12.2% of these husbands take part in some such activity for about an hour a day as against 6.2% of the housewives' husbands. In the major towns, compared to the smaller, furthermore, there emerges a greater participation by men in both these duties and in taking the children out. The two factors of being a full time housewife and living outside the cities combine to create the most demanding living condition.

CONCLUSION

The results of the field research outline an example of Double Presence: involving the composition of the family and the definition and division of domestic work in relation to jobs.

The Double Presence blends with a situation of diffuse economy. As in other contexts in North Italy of a more core economy complexion, double labor, for reproduction and for the market, defines the situation of women. In the same way the structure of the family is decidedly nuclear and the demographic tendencies confirm a trend towards more established birth control, while, as elsewhere, the division of domestic labor is reorganized, modernizing but not substantially changing the traditional gender roles.

However, the difference between the cities of Padua and Verona and the smaller towns (< 5000 inh.), typical of a peripheral economy, seems important for several reasons. In the smaller towns, to be working corresponds less to a change in the family structure. One is helped by the husband significantly less, even though demographically the family tends to be bigger. One is less involved in the financial and bureaucratic tasks of the household; one studies less and one has a more discontinuous work history. These and other data, which tend in the opposite direction in the major towns, suggest a difference, in terms of emancipation and the widening of citizenship, between the experience of a double job (associated with more traditional family models) and the double presence, to which corresponds a more marked and equal ability to direct oneself both in the world of the family and of work. To understand the experience of double presence in areas of an ancient peasant culture, one must investigate changes at more specifically cultural levels, relative to different resources for the construction of social identity of women. In research into the conditions of motherhood over the two generations previous to the present (mothers and grandmothers) conducted in two Venetian towns (Conegliano, near Treviso and Limena near Padua) of older and more recent industrialization respectively (Moro, Perin, Zecchinato 1981), one can see the movement of motherhood from being understood as a "biological obligation" to its consideration as the fulfillment of family and marital life. This being faced by peasant mothers nearly a generation later than those women who have experienced factory work or emigration. The daughters who are adult women of today, will have assimilated, during their socialization, the marks of this temporal difference in the changed models of female identity models. At the moment, in the experience of double presence, behind similar behavior patterns or an analogous organization of daily life, there may, therefore, be concealed different motivations and conflicts. These also must be investigated in their various socio-cultural contexts, to place the experience of work within the diverse structures of time and social processes.

NOTES

1. In this case 400 married women aged between 20 and 50 living with their husband were interviewed. The sample was also divided according to size of town and prevalent economic activity. This was to take into account the "spread" of economic activity which is typical of peripheral economy.

2. It is a region in which the Christian Democrats are politically predominant,

thanks to the traditional and integral presence of the Catholic church. Various Authors, 1984, *Il Veneto, Storia delle regioni d'Italia*. Torino, Einaudi.

3. 46.6% of working women had a domestic timetable less than 4 hours as against 4.9% of the housewives; 22.5% of which had a timetable of between 12 and 20 hours as opposed to 3.7% of working women.

4. In the group of women under 30, 38.3% worked during the week between 4 and 8 hours.

5. On Saturday 46.4% of those with a degree worked less than 4 hours; the percentage rises to 63.4% for Sunday. Women with elementary school certificates who on Saturday work less than 4 hours number only 11.4%, for Sunday this figure is 29.1%.

6. In this case for those who have only one child less than 15 years old 37.6% work, during the week, between 4 and 8 hours, whilst 38.3% work more than 8 hours. For those who have 2 children under 15 we find 40.3% work between 4 and 8 hours and 41.1% more than 8 hours. Those with 3 children under 15 work over 8 hours in 6.86% of the cases.

7. In going to the bank or post office, husbands account for 64% of the help and 81.7% of the substitution. For other variables we have the following figures: tax and insurance—67.6% of the help and 83.9% of the substitution; medical visits—70.8% of the help and 79.4% of the substitution; school—75% of the help and 70.6% of the substitution.

8. In shopping, husbands account for 37.5% of the help and 47.6% of the substitution; in hospital visiting for 38.1% of the help and 36.8% of the substitution.

REFERENCES

Accornero A. and Carmignani F. *I paradossi della disoccupazione*, Bologna, Il Mulino, 1986.

Anastasia B., and Rullani E. La nuova periferia industriale, Saggio sul modello veneto, *Materiali veneti*, Venezia, 17/18, 1982.

Bagnasco A. *Tre Italie. La problematica territoriale dello sviluppo italiano*. Bologna, Il Mulino, 1977.

Bagnasco A., Trigilia C., and Messori M. *Le problematiche dello sviluppo italiano*. Milano, Feltrinelli, 1978.

Bagnasco A., Tigilia C. (ed.) *Società e politica nelle aree di piccola impresa, il caso di Bassano*. Venezia, Arsenale, 1984.

Balbo L. La doppia presenza, *Inchiesta*, Bari, 32, 1978.

Balbo L. and BIANCHI M. *Ricomposizioni*. Milano, Angeli, 1982.

Balbo L., Cacioppo M., and May P. *Vincoli e strategie della vita familiare in Emilia*. Rapporto di recerca, Bologna: Regione Emilia-Romagna, 1985.

Balbo L., (ed). *Time to Care*. Milano, Angeli, 1987.

Barile P. and Zanuso L. (eds). *Lavoro femminile e condizione familiare*. Milano, Angeli, 1980.

Bertolo C. *Analisi storica del Movimento Femminista in Italia*, tesi di laurea, Università di Padova, 1976.

Bianchi M. *I servizi sociali*, Bari, De Donato, 1981.

Bimbi F. L'identità possibile: innovazione e ambivalenze della doppia presenza, *Schema*, Padova, 11/12, 1983.

Bimbi F., and Pristinger F. (eds.) *Profili sovrapposti*, Milano, Angeli, 1985.

Bimbi F., and Capecchi V. (eds.). *Strutture e strategie della vita quotidiana*, Milano, Angeli, 1986.

Bimbi F. (bis), Premessa, Merelli M., Nava P. et al., *Giochi di equilibrio*, Milano, Angeli, 1985.

Calabro A., and Grasso L. (eds.). *Dal movimento femminista al femminismo diffuso*, Milano, Angeli, 1985.

Capecchi V., and Pesce A. Itinerario bibliografico sull'economia informale, *Inchiesta*, 59/60, 1983.

Chiaretti G., Bimbi F., and Piazza M. Donne e conoscenza, *Inchiesta*, 49/50, 1981.

De Sandre P., (ed.). *Indagine sulla fecondità in Italia-1979*, Bologna, Tecnoprint, 1982.

Federici N. *Procreazione, famiglia, lavoro della donna*, Torino, Loescher, 1984.

Guizzardi G. Territorio e religione. Ipotesi di lavoro sul "caso veneto," *Città e Regione*, Firenze, 6, 1976.

Melucci A., (ed.) *Altri codici*, Bologna, Il Mulino, 1984.

Merelli M. *Protagoniste di sè stesse*, Milano, Angeli, 1985.

Merelli A., Nava P. et al. *Giochi di equilibrio*, Milano, Angeli, 1985.

Mingione E. *Urbanizzazione, classi sociali e lavoro informale*, Milano, Angeli, 1983.

Moro A., Perin E., and Zecchinato O. *Percorsi della maternità in due generazioni di donne*, Tesi di laurea, Università di Padova, 1981.

Paci M., (ed.). *Famiglia e mercato del lavoro in una economia periferica*, Milano, Angeli, 1980.

Pacifico M. *Casalinghe in fabbrica*. Napoli, Sintesi, 1982.

Padoa-Schioppa F. *La forza lavoro femminile*. Bologna, Il Mulino, 1977.

Piccone S.S. *Ragazze del sud*. Roma, Editori Riuniti, 1979.

Pristinger F. Il lavoro femminile in un'area ad economia periferica, *Schema*, Padova, 11/12, 1983.

Prokop U. *Realtà e desiderio: l'ambivalenza femminile*. Milano, Feltrinelli, 1978.

Sachs I. *I tempi spazi dello sviluppo*, in F. Bimbi, V. Capecchi, *Strutture e strategie della vita quotidiana*. Milano, Angeli, 1986.

Saraceno C., (ed.) *Il lavoro maldiviso*. Bari, De Donato, 1980.

Influence of Work Place Sex Segregation on Family Life

Elina Haavio-Mannila

SUMMARY. The purpose of the article is to examine the influence of the sex structure, i.e., the proportion of men and women doing the same sort of work and having daily contacts, at work on family life. The data consists of mail responses by 692 married or cohabiting men and 667 women in 11 occupational groups in Southern Finland. The data was analyzed by using cross tabulations and path analysis.

The results indicate that integration of men and women in paid work is sometimes problematic for the family. It is connected with work romances, involvement in work at the expense of the family, career competition between the spouses, and unhappiness in marriage. But women also profit from sex integration of work in their family life. As the husbands of women working with men participate in domestic work at home more than other husbands, these women often consider their marriages to be happy.

INTRODUCTION

All over the world, industries, occupations, jobs and work places are segregated by sex. The consequences of this sexual division of labor are in many ways more advantageous for men than for women (e.g., Dex, 1985, Kauppinen-Toropainen et al., 1987, Reskin and Hartman, 1986, 9-17).

In the context of a research project on "Women in Men's and Women's Jobs," Kauppinen-Toropainen, Kandolin and Haavio-Mannila (1987) examined whether women profit (regarding the

---

Elina Haavio-Mannila is Associate Professor, University of Helsinki, Department of Sociology, Franzeninkatu 13, SF-00500 Helsinki, Finland.

107

quality of their work) from performing the same sort of work as men. The qualitative aspects of work studied were the following: autonomy at work, lack of routinization of work, the compulsory rhythm of work, and the demands for social skills. We also analyzed monthly pay and its variation according to functional segregation of work. The empirical data came from the Finnish Study on Working Conditions (1984), which is a representative sample of 4502 persons of the Finnish wage-earning population of whom 48% were women and 52% men. Our results indicate that women often profit from the fact that they perform the same sort of work as men. This benefit was more apparent for white-collar than for blue-collar women. For men the effects of segregation on job characteristics were the opposite. They often profit from sex-segregated work. Social status played a major role regarding the qualitative aspects of work.

In this article, some effects of sex segregation of paid work on family life will be examined. The influence of the employment status and the relative social status of the spouses on the division of labor and power in the family and on marital happiness has been studied earlier (e.g., Berk, 1980, Edgell, 1980, Niemi et al., 1981, Young and Wilmott, 1973). Effects of sex segregation of occupations, jobs and places of employment on family life have not, as far as I know, been systematically studied even though these phenomena are related to each other. This relationship was stated, for example, by the Committee on Women's Employment and Related Social Issues in the United States: "The household division of labor appears to share with job segregation a resistance to change, and the two are likely to be mutually reinforcing. The failure of husband's household time to respond to their wives' paid work may contribute to their wives' choices regarding paid work . . . segregation reduces the resources women bring to the marital unit and thus, potentially, their power in the household" (Reskin and Hartman, 1986, 16-17).

Division of labor and power in the family is not the only family matter, which is likely to be affected by job segregation. *Career competition between the spouses* is probably more common when the husband and the wife do the same kind of work than when their occupational experiences are totally different. As we will see, women working in sex-integrated jobs especially intensifies comparisons about job advancement and earnings between the spouses and creates competition between them.

Work and family are not always easy to combine. According to an earlier Finnish study, wives and husbands who stay at home report slightly more *marital cohesion* and love than working ones (Haavio-Mannila et al., 1984, 162). There are no earlier data on the effect of sex integration of work on marital satisfaction.

Contacts between men and women at work often lead to friendship, romances and sexual harassment (Haavio-Mannila et al., 1987). *Erotic and sexual relationships between men and women at work* may compete with or even substitute for marital relationships at home and strain the marital relationship.

Commitment to or *involvement in paid work* even at the expense of the family is common in modern entrepreneurial organizations (cf. Kanter, 1987). In particular, women's emotional attachment to coworkers of the opposite sex is connected to high work commitment (Haavio-Mannila, 1982).

The purpose of this article is to empirically investigate the influence of the sex structure, i.e., the proportion of women and men doing the same sort of work and having daily contacts, at work on family life. Three aspects of family life will be studied: (1) career competition between the spouses, (2) division of domestic labor and power at home, and (3) marital happiness. The influence of the sex structure of the work place is thought to be mediated by two work-centered factors: (1) the incidence of romances at work, and (2) work commitment at the expense of the family.

THE DATA

The data consist of answers to questionnaires sent by mail to randomly selected male and female trade union members of eleven occupational groups in Southern Finland in 1986 as part of the study "Women in Men's and Women's Jobs" by Elina Haavio-Mannila, Kaisa Kauppinen-Toropainen and Irja Kandolin. The response rates varied between 52 and 75 percent in different occupational groups.

In Finland, 85 percent of the employed people belong to trade unions. Thus the data cover relatively well the members of the occupational groups selected for the study.

The groups were chosen on the basis of their sex ratios and socio-economic status. In our study we included as female-dominated groups (in the order from the highest to the lowest status group) dentists (66% women in 1980), mental health nurses (68% women), nurses for handicapped children (92% women), and waitresses (81% women). The male-dominated groups selected were architects (29% women), police officers (2% women), technicians (9% women), metal workers (8% women), and construction workers (8% women). The sexually mixed groups studied were journalists (42% women) and rubber and plastic workers (42% women).

In each occupational group about a hundred men and the same number of women returned the questionnaire. Only married and cohabiting persons were included in the present analysis, which is based on replies by 692 men and 667 women (72% of the total of 1884 respondents).

The average age of the men was 40 years and of the women, 39 years. Men had been at work for 19 years, women 16 years. About 85 percent of the respondents were married; 15 percent were cohabiting without marriage. Of the men 81% had children, of the women 73%. One third of the respondents had a university education, 40% other vocational education, and the rest had only attended vocational courses or had no vocational education. About 40% of the respondents were upper white collar employees, 40% were lower white collar workers, and the rest, 20%, manual workers. More than half of the work places of the respondents, 58%, were situated in the Helsinki metropolitan area, 25% were in other towns or cities, and 17% in rural communities.

More than forty percent of the respondents worked in the public sector, as state or municipal employees, 40% were employed by private companies or persons, and one tenth were independent entrepreneurs.

Only 52% of the men and 55% of the women had regular daytime work. About one-third performed shift work, and the rest had other kinds of working time arrangements — for example, regular morning, evening or weekend jobs. The average daily hours of work were 8.0 for men and 7.7 for women.

The number of coworkers met daily at work was about ten for both sexes. Men had more subordinates, 4.4, than women, 2.2.

Twenty-two percent of the men and 39% of the women were super-vised at work by a woman.

Our respondents are not statistically representative of the total employed population of Finland. For example, their social status is higher, and they more often work in "opposite sex occupations."

RESULTS

Sex Segregation of Work Tasks and Daily Interaction

In our study, we have made a distinction between functional sex segregation and physical or social separation of men and women at work (cf. Reskin and Hartman, 1986). Functional segregation means that men and women perform different work tasks. Physical or social separation refers to the daily contacts between men and women and means that men and women hardly ever meet each other during their working hours. Even though the functional segregation in the Finnish labor market is intensive, men and women have numerous daily contacts with each other (Haavio-Mannila, 1984, 12-15, Kauppinen-Toropainen et al., 1987).

In order to study the influence of the sex structure of the work place on family life, we divided the respondents into four groups:

1. Persons are defined as *sex-segregated* when they are both functionally and socially segregated from the opposite sex. This means that most of the persons who perform the same sort of work and with whom the respondent has daily contact at the place of work are of his or her own sex.
2. People are defined to occupy *complementary* work roles when their work tasks are shared primarily by persons of their own sex and when they are in daily contact with at least as many persons of the opposite sex as of their own. Existing in this group is functional segregation, but social integration, of men and women.
3. In *integrated or balanced* work role sets approximately equal numbers of men and women do the same sort of work and are

in daily contact with each other. This is a situation of both functional and social integration of the sexes.

4. We defined as *tokens* those persons who share the same work tasks mainly or only with persons of the opposite sex and who have daily contacts with both men and women or only with the opposite sex. Like the balanced group, tokens are both functionally and socially integrated with the opposite sex, but they differ from it by being in a minority position at work.

In order to make the connections between a person's position in the sex structure at the place of employment and his or her family life more comprehensible, some features of the work of the four groups, formed on the basis of their functional and social sex segregation, will now be described.

Due to the strict segregation of the labor market by sex, many characteristics of the tokens closely resemble those of the sex-segregated persons of the other sex. Almost two-thirds of the token men and of the segregated women work in municipal jobs. On the other hand, one-third of the segregated men and token women are state employees. The employers of sex-integrated men and women are almost identical. Men in complementary jobs are more often than women state or private employees, whereas women in this group more often work for a municipality.

Sex-integrated men and women have higher social status than the others: they often are architects and journalists (Table 1). Manual workers, particularly construction and metal workers, are most often represented among segregated men and complementary women. Token men are mainly high-status dentists and middle status nurses; token women are either high-status architects and journalists or middle-status policewomen and technicians.

Tokens of both sexes are about five years younger than the others. They are less often formally married, and they do not have children to the same extent as members of the other groups.

These social and demographic differences between the groups based on sex segregation may interfere with the connections between the sex structure of the work place and the family life. Thus their effect was controlled by calculating partial correlations. The results were unaffected by these controls.

TABLE 1. Social status and occupation according to sex integration of job and sex, %

Social status and occupation	Position in the sex structure of the place of employment				
	Segregated	Complementary	Balanced	Token	Total
Men					
Upper white collar:					
Dentist	–	5	18	33	13
Journalist	3	11	21	3	12
Architect	12	15	18	2	14
Lower white collar:					
Nurse for mentally handicapped children	–	1	11	28	8
Mental health nurse	1	3	16	27	11
Police	23	27	1	–	12
Technician	17	22	1	–	10
Worker:					
Waiter	–	2	9	4	5
Rubber worker	6	7	3	2	5
Metal worker	8	4	2	1	3
Construction worker	30	3	–	–	7
	100	100	100	100	100
(N)	(144)	(174)	(276)	(94)	(688)
p < .001					
Women					
Upper white collar:					
Dentist	27	28	12	1	16
Journalist	2	3	20	10	10
Architect	2	4	23	25	14
Lower white collar:					
Nurse for mentally handicapped children	25	7	6	–	10
Mental health nurse	16	14	15	–	12
Police	–	–	–	28	6
Technician	7	5	5	28	10
Worker:					
Waiter	2	9	10	1	6
Rubber worker	14	6	3	1	6
Metal worker	4	14	2	4	5
Construction worker	1	10	4	4	6
	100	100	100	100	100
(N)	(153)	(139)	(236)	(134)	(662)
p < .001					

There are some consequences of sex integration of work which, as we will see, are relevant from the point of view of the family. In the following, two such aspects are discussed: informal interaction and sentiments of affection between men and women at work and involvement in work even at the expense of the family.

Informal Interaction Between the Sexes at Work

People who share the same work tasks become friends with, get attracted to and fall in love with their coworkers (Haavio-Mannila et al., 1987). This corresponds to the propositions by George C. Homans, who, in "The Human Group" (1951), stated that common activity in the formal work organization leads to informal interaction and sentiments of affection between coworkers. In our present data also, one can observe a close relationship between sex integration of work and friendship and love between coworkers of the opposite sex (Table 2).

Men have more friends of the opposite sex at work than do women in three of the four groups based on the type and degree of sex segregation. Only token women report friends of the opposite sex slightly more often than do token men.

There is no gender gap in the proportions of people having experienced romances at work during their lifetime. In the complementary and balanced groups, men have more commonly than women become attracted to or fallen in love with a coworker while being married to somebody else. Unfaithfulness in marriage — half of the romances have led to sexual intercourse — still seems to be more a male than a female behavior pattern in Finland.

Work Commitment

One-third of our respondents do not "stop thinking about their work when they come home," and one-fifth "sometimes tend to forget their family and devote themselves to their work" (Table 3). There are no sex differences in the work commitment at the expense of the family. Similar results have been reported earlier (Haavio-Mannila et al., 1984). In Finland, professional women in particular are committed to their work, even more than men in equivalent

TABLE 2. Opposite-sex friendships and romances at work according to sex integration of job and sex, %

| | Position in the sex structure of the place of employment | | | | |
	Segregated	Complementary	Balanced	Token	Total
Has opposite-sex friends at work Men	33	48	70	57	56
p < .001					
Women	14	27	51	65	37
p < .001					
Has become attracted or fallen in love at work					
Men					
- during lifetime	26	42	58	63	48
p < .001					
Women	27	36	56	69	47
p < .001					
- while being Men married to somebody else	13	28	38	33	30
p < .001					
Women	11	11	13	30	22
p < .001					

N see Table 1.

social status groups. And correspondingly, professional men report higher family commitment than occupationally comparable women. Professionals seem to consider it to be socially desirable to point out that they are not tied to traditional sex roles: women stress their work commitment and men their family involvement.

Sex segregation of work has more influence on women's than on men's work commitment, as one can see from Table 3. The closer women work with men, the more involved they are in their work, even at the expense of the family. In this way, sex integration of work may be a threat to the family. Men who work in complementary and balanced work role sets are more involved in their work than are sex-segregated and token men.

TABLE 3. Work commitment at the expense of the family according to sex integration of job and sex, %

	Position in the sex structure of the place of employment				
	Segregated	Complementary	Balanced	Token	Total
When I come home, I completely stop thinking about my work, disagrees completely or somewhat %	Men 37 ns. Women 21 p < .05	35 33	40 33	33 40	37 31
I sometimes tend to forget my family and devote myself completely to my work, agrees completely or somewhat %	Men 17 ns Women 14 p < .01	26 14	25 23	16 31	22 21
Work commitment[a], means	Men 5.2 3 > 1,4, p < .05	5.6	5.6	5.1	5.5
	Women 4.8 3,4 > 1, p < .001; 3 > 2, p < .01; 4 > 2, p < .001; 4 > 3, p < .05	5.0	5.5	5.9	5.3

N see Table 1.

[a] Sum scale based on the two indicators above; values range from 2 (least committed) to 10 (most committed). The correlation between the items is .40.

Career Competition

Almost forty years ago, Talcott Parsons argued that the American marriage was too fragile to sustain competition at comparable skill levels between spouses (Parsons, 1949). He thought that it is functional for the marital relationship that only one of the spouses takes care of the instrumental task of providing economic resources for the family. In that way it is possible to avoid career competition between the spouses which can be destructive to the marriage.

In Finland, three-fourths of all married women are gainfully employed. In our research material, 86% of the wives of the male respondents and 91% of the husbands of the female respondents were working for pay. In addition to the situation of having two economic providers in the family, possibilities for career competition between the spouses are increased by the fact that in a large majority of the families husbands and wives have roughly equal social status (Table 4).

The wide categories used in measuring the social status of the spouses were: (1) upper-white-collar, (2) lower-white-collar and (3) manual worker. Spouses who stay at home were considered to have lower status than their gainfully employed partners.

More often than the others, sex-segregated men and women have "matriarchal" families in which the social status of the wife is higher than that of the husband. In many of these cases the wife is a lower-white-collar worker and the husband a manual worker.

Only one-fourth of the male and 12% of the female respondents live in a "patriarchal" family in which the occupational status of the husband is higher than that of the wife. Even though most families in our study do not follow the American typical nuclear family pattern according to which the wife stays at home or at least has a lower status job than the husband, career competition between marital partners is rare. Only 2% of the men and 4% of the women said that they sometimes experience competition over job success and earnings, and 4% of the men and 8% of the women found it difficult to answer the question. An overwhelming majority, four-fifths of both sexes, reported that they do not compete over job success or earnings with their spouse.

There is a statistically significant relationship between sex integration of job and career competition in the family among women. The more sex integrated the job, the more often the wife feels that she is competing over job success and earnings with her husband (Table 5). Sex integration of a job increases men's feelings of career competition with the spouse only very slightly.

Division of Domestic Work and Power in the Family

In three out of four families examined in Table 6, the wife participates more in housework than does the husband. Domestic chores are equally divided between the spouses in slightly more than every

TABLE 4. Relative social status of the spouses according to sex integration of job and sex, %

Relative social status of the spouses	Position in the sex structure of the place of employment				
	Segre-gated	Comple-mentary	Balanced	Token	Total
Men					
Wife has a higher status	25	14	9	7	14
Spouses have the same status	59	60	64	67	62
Husband has a higher status [a]	16	26	27	26	24
	100	100	100	100	100
	p < .001				
Women					
Wife has a higher status [a]	25	16	15	16	18
Spouses have the same status	61	72	77	69	70
Husband has a higher status	14	12	9	15	12
	100	100	100	100	100
	p < .05				

N see Table 1.

[a] Includes families in which the spouse is not gainfully employed. Their proportion is shown in Table 5.

fifth family. Only in one out of twenty families does the husband do more housework than the wife.

There is no discrepancy between the evaluations about the division of housework made by husbands and wives in our material. In earlier studies (e.g., Berk and Shih, 1980, Haavio-Mannila, 1980), both spouses have overestimated their own share of housework. Both sexes have given "socially desirable" answers from their perspective without thinking that their responses can be compared with those given by the opposite sex. This inconsistency of the results has been publicly discussed in Finland. That may be one reason for the compatibility of the responses given by men and women in our present study.

TABLE 5. Career competition according to sex segregation of job and sex, %

Do you and your spouse sometimes compete over job-success or earnings?	Position in the sex structure of the place of employmnet				
	Segre-gated	Comple-mentary	Balanced	Token	Total
Men					
We compete	1	1	2	2	2
Hard to say	5	4	7	8	4
We do not compete	80	83	80	77	80
Wife is not gainfully employed	15	13	13	15	14
	100 ns.	100	100	100	100
Women					
We compete	3	2	3	8	4
Hard to say	8	8	12	23	8
We do not compete	83	82	79	71	79
Husband is not gainfully employed	9	10	9	6	9
	100	100	100	100	100
	p < .05				

N see Table 1.

Position in the work place sex structure of the male respondents is connected to division of housework at home in a statistically significant way. Men working in sexually balanced jobs and in token positions participate more in domestic work than men having sex-segregated and complementary jobs. There are two kinds of spill-overs from paid to unpaid work here: (1) men in traditional female jobs share domestic work with their wives; and (2) men in traditional male jobs keep their hands off "female" household tasks. There is no connection between sex segregation of paid and unpaid work among women.

Men's and women's answers differ in their perceptions about the division of power in the family, i.e., which of the spouses has more influence on important decisions concerning the family. Thirty percent of the men but only 18% of the women reported that the husband has more power than the wife. Only 11% of the men but 18% of the women saw the decisions in their family as female dominated. Both sexes overestimate their own power in the family in the same way as spouses earlier overestimated their share of housework

TABLE 6. Family life: Division of domestic work and marital happiness according to sex segregation of job and sex, % and scale means

| Family life | Position in the sex structure of the place of employment | | | | |
	Segre-gated	Comple-mentary	Balanced	Token	Total
<u>Division of domestic work:</u>	Men				
Husband does more housework	4	5	6	10	6
Spouses do equally as much housework	17	17	24	28	21
Wife does more housework	79	78	70	62	73
	100	100	100	100	100
	p < .05				
	Women				
Husband does more housework	5	4	2	8	4
Spouses do equally as much housework	23	19	26	23	23
Wife does more housework	72	78	72	69	73
	100	100	100	100	100
	ns				
<u>Marital happiness:</u> <u>Scale means</u>[a]	Men				
	13.9	13.4	13.0	13.5	13.3
	1 > 3, p < .01				
	Women				
	13.3	13.8	13.2	12.9	13.3
	2 > 4, p < .05				

N see Table 1.

[a] Sum scale based on the following four variables:
Do you regard your marriage or cohabition as very unhappy... perfect (7 alternatives)

Are you satisfied with your sex life with your spouse? Very satisfied ... very unsatisfied (5 alternatives)

How would you describe your marriage or cohabition? Is it
- sharing of entire life experience (wanting to be together as much as possible)? Yes - no
- vital love relationship? Yes - no

The reliability of the scale was .73. The answers to the four items were reclassified so that each of them has the same weight on the total scale (see discussion above). Women experienced a little more often than men (66% versus 58%) the existence of a total equality between the sexes in the family decision making in their home.

Men's conceptions about their own superior power in family decisions decline linearly, when one moves from the sex-segregated groups to the token group: the correlation coefficient between husband's family power and the degree of sex segregation in his job is .11**. Among women no connection between power in family decisions and sex segregation of work was found.

To conclude: when men share paid work with women, they also share domestic work and power at home with the wife. There is, in this respect, a clear spillover of behavior patterns from work to the family among men, but not among women.

Marital Happiness

Marital happiness was measured by a sum scale based on four indicators: (1) own evaluation of marital happiness; (2) satisfaction with sex life with spouse; and, referring to Cuber and Harroff (1965), living in (3) a vital or (4) a total marriage (see footnote a in Table 6).

Men's and women's marriages are, on the average, equally happy. Men in sex-segregated and women in complementary jobs report the highest marital happiness. Men in the balanced group and women in the token group are least happily married. Even though differences between the four sex segregation groups are small, they indicate that traditional division of labor between men and women (i.e., sex segregation of jobs) is more compatible with a happy marriage than a non-traditional division (i.e., sex integration of jobs).

Paths Between Work and Family Life

Connections between sex segregation of work and the indicators of family life studied here are not very strong. Nevertheless, there are connections between the dependent variables which strengthen the effects of sex segregation on family life. For example, work commitment correlates with work place romances, career competition between the spouses, and marital unhappiness. The unhappiness of marriage is, in addition, connected to career competition between the spouses and, among women, to lack of husband's participation in housework.

These relationships between work and family variables were examined by using path analysis (see, for example, Macdonald, 1977) as a research technique. The results are shown in Table 7 and as a graph in Figure 1. Even though statistically significant, the standardized regression coefficients are low, and the percent of variance explained (R^2) is small. The results thus tell only a minuscule part of the whole story of all the relationships between work and family life.

In path analysis, one assumes a certain causal order between the variables. On the basis of our cross-sectional survey data, it is impossible to definitely say which factors are causes and which are effects. Nevertheless, I will use causal terminology to simplify the presentation. But one should not take this causality as more than a hypothetical chain of events. The connections or correlations are, however, real.

The paths from sex integration of paid work to the quality of marriage are different for men and women. For men, the following paths are detected (Table 7):

TABLE 7. Path analyses of relationships between some work and family variables. Standardized regression coefficients and proportions of variance explained (R^2)

Dependent variables	Independent variables					R^2
	Sex integration of work	Work romance	Work commitment	Career competition	Husband's house work	
Men						
Work romance	.25***	-	-	-	-	.06
Work commitment	-.01	.11**	-	-	-	.01
Career competition	.04	-.01	.12***	-	.14***	.04
Husband's house-work	.16***	-	-	-	-	.02
Marital happiness	-.02	-.14***	-.11**	-.07*	-.04	.05
Women						
Work romance	.28***	-	-	-	-	.08
Work commitment	.15**	.15**	-	-	-	.06
Career competition	.11**	-	.12**	-	-	.02
Husband's house-work	.02	-	.13**	-	-	.02
Marital happiness	-.06	-.03	-.07*	-.15***	.17***	.06

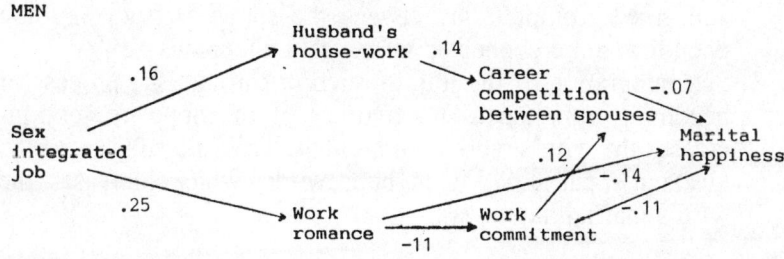

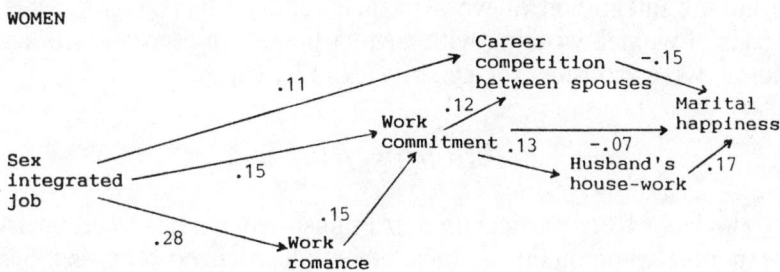

FIGURE 1. Paths from work to family life (based on Table 7)

1. Sex integration of the job increases the participation of men in domestic work. It is connected to career competition with the wife, which leads to unhappy marriage.
2. Sex integration of the job is followed by work place romances, which correlate with marital disharmony.
3. Sex integration of the job leads to romances at work. They are connected to high work commitment, which creates career competition between the spouses, which in turn decreases marital happiness.

For women the following three paths were detected:

1. Sex integration of the job leads to work commitment of the wife and career competition between the spouses. Both of these phenomena cause marital unhappiness.
2. Sex integration of the job leads to romances at work. These are followed by work commitment at the expense of the family

and career competition between the spouses. Both of these phenomena are connected to marital unhappiness.

3. Sex integration of the job, as such or through the process of becoming attracted to a coworker of the opposite sex, increases the wife's work commitment. This in turn leads to the husband's participation in housework, which increases the wife's marital happiness.

The consequences of sex integration of jobs are somewhat problematic from the point of view of the family. But women also profit from sex integration of work in their family life. When the husbands of women working with men participate in domestic work at home, wives consider their marriages to be happy.

DISCUSSION

The labor force participation of Finnish women has traditionally been more common than in most other industrialized countries. Sex segregation of work is nevertheless as prevalent as anywhere in the world. The results reported here indicate that integration of men and women in paid work is problematic for the family. It is connected with work place romances, involvement in work at the expense of the family, career competition between the spouses, and unhappiness in marriage.

According to Alice Rossi (1970, 283), career competition in the family "does not necessarily mean conflict. It can be a social spice and a source of pride and stimulation in a marriage of equals." Among our respondents, competition over job success and earnings often leads to marital disharmony, however.

But our results also reveal that only in a tiny proportion of all families is there any career competition between the spouses. Thus, even though correlations between variables indicate that sex integration of jobs is connected to marital problems, there are only a few families in which these problems arise. In the same way, it is worth noticing that only 37% of the men and 31% of the women think about their work at home and that even fewer, 22% of the men and 21% of the women sometimes forget their family because of their involvement in paid work.

Influence of the degree of sex integration of a job on the quality of marriage is not only negative. Women in sex-integrated jobs who have work place romances and are committed to their work are happily married when their husbands participate in domestic work. This result implics that for a woman it is possible to combine work in a mixed sex group with happy marital life. But that happens only when her husband assumes an active role in running the household.

"A change toward sex equality may cause some temporary marital dislocations, but this is not sufficient reason to expect all women to remain enclosed in the past," Alice Rossi (1970) wrote in her "immodest proposal" for equality between the sexes. In Finland sex integration at work is still connected to some marital disturbances. But our results also show that problems can be avoided or solved when both spouses in practice follow the ideology of true sex equality for example, when the husband participates in domestic work as much as does the wife.

REFERENCES

Berk, S.F. (ed.). *Women and Household Labor*. Beverly Hills/London: Sage, 1980.

Berk, S.F. and A. Shih. Contributions to household labor: Comparing wives' and husbands' reports. Pp. 191-227 in Sarah F. Berk (ed.), *Women and Household Labor* (Vol.5). London: Sage, 1980.

Cuber, J.F. and P.B. Harroff. *The Significant Americans: A Study of Sexual Behavior among the Affluent*. New York: Appleton-Century, 1965.

Dex, S. *The Sexual Division of Work*. New York: St. Martin's Press, 1985.

Edgell, S. *Middle Class Couples*. London: George Allen & Unwin, 1980.

Haavio-Mannila, E. Kodinhoitotehtävien jakautuminen perheessä (Division of household tasks in the family). *Sosiologia* 17: 185-194, 1980.

Haavio-Mannila, E. Työn laatu ja työpaikkarakkaudet (Quality of work and workplace romances). *Sosiologia* 19: 225-236, 1982.

Havvio-Mannila, E., R. Jallinoja, and Harriet Strandell. Perhe, työ ja tunteet (Family, Work, and Emotions). Juva: WSOY, 1984.

Haavio-Mannila, E., K. Kauppinen-Toropainen, and I. Kandolin. The effect of sex composition of the workplace on friendship, romance, and sex at work. Pp. 123-137 in Barbara A. Gutek, Ann H. Stromberg and Laurie Larwood (eds.) *Women and Work Volume 3*. Newbury Park: Sage, 1987.

Homans, G.C. *The Human Group*. New York: Routledge & Kegan Paul, 1951.

Kanter, R.M. Toward the entrepreneurial society? Dilemmas and contradictions of work and organizational innovations. Public lecture at Harvard University, Department of Sociology, April 16, 1987.

Kauppinen-Toropainen, K., I. Kandolin, and E. Haavio-Mannila. Sex segregation of work in Finland and the quality of women's work. *Journal of Organizational Behavior* 9:15-27, 1988.

Macdonald, K.J. Path analysis. Pp. 81-104 in Colm A. O'Muircheartaigh and Clive Payne (eds.), *The Analysis of Survey Data Vol. 2: Model Fitting*. London-New York-Sydney-Toronto: John Wiley & Sons, 1977.

Niemi, I., S. Kiiski, and M. Liikkanen. Suomalaisten ajankäyttö (Use of Time in Finland). Helsinki: Central Statistical Office of Finland. Studies No. 65, 1981.

Parsons, T. 1949. *Essays in Sociological Theory Pure and Applied*. Glencoe, Illinois: Free Press, 1949.

Reskin, B.F. and Heidi I. Hartman. *Women's Work, Men's Work: Sex Segregation on the Job*. Washington, D.C.: National Academy Press, 1986.

Rossi, A.S. 1970. Equality between the sexes. Pp. 262-309 in Meyer Barash and Alice Scourby (eds.), *Marriage and the Family: A Comparative Analysis of Contemporary Problems*. New York: Random House.

Young, M. and P. Wilmott. *The Symmetrical Family*. London: Routledge & Kegan Paul, 1973.

Care Giving and Socialization in the View of Declining Fertility and Increasing Female Employment

An-Magritt Jensen

While the population explosion, presently as well as in the long run, seems to be one of the more fundamental global problems, the industrialized countries will in the near future be faced with reduced population figures. Some countries like Denmark and West Germany have already experienced decreasing population for several years. The total fertility rate is presently far below replacement level in several West European countries. In this paper the demographic situation in Norway will serve as an illustration of this new development. Corresponding tendencies will be found in most western countries, but Norway is one of the few countries which has appointed a population commission to investigate this development.

Since the Second World War, fertility level and labour force participation especially among married women and mothers in Norway have shown a wide range of variations. The changes may be interpreted as a transition in the lives of women from a situation characterized by the prevalence of "internal roles" such as the parental, the conjugal and the domestic roles to a situation where "external roles" like the occupational and the community roles are more outstanding.

This might be supplemented by a strengthening of "mixed roles"

An-Magritt Jensen is at the Norwegian Institute for Urban and Regional Research, Oslo, Norway.

The author wishes to thank Bjørg Moen, Central Bureau of Statistics for valuable comments.

like the kin and the individual roles (Oppong 1980, Federici 1981). One consequence of this shift is an "externalization" of some of the functions formerly being a part of housewives' work. The topic of the paper is the adjustment on the part of society to the shift of women's roles from internal to external. My intentions are to devote some reflections to the effects of this externalization for care giving. I also will raise the question whether there might be other, more indirect effects for the socialization process of children, which also should be taken into consideration for social policy.

DECLINING FERTILITY RATES

The "baby-boom" period in Norway lasted until 1964 when the total fertility rate culminated at 2.98. From this year we had a sharp downward trend until 1975 when it levelled off, however, the fertility was still declining as shown in Figure 1. The fertility decline from the end of the 1960s amounts to 40 percent. The total fertility rate in 1985, at 1.68 is quite below the level of replacement. To find a corresponding low numerical level of births as today's level we must go one hundred and fifty years back in history. The fertility development implicates a reduction of the Norwegian population from the end of the century (NOU 1984:26).

The fertility decline may be traced to a reduction of the size of the family. Fewer children are born, but so far the data sources do not indicate rising percentages of childless women. According to the Norwegian Fertility Survey in 1977, more than 90 percent of the women have born children, and the normative family size is two or three children (Noack and Østby, 1984). Several families do not, however, fulfill this norm. One reason for this may be the substantial changes in the family pattern itself. The number and percentage of couples living in unwed cohabitation have increased. In 1980 about 10 percent of the age group 20 to 25 was living in cohabitation without marriage (Ostby and Strom Bull 1986) compared to 25 percent in marriage at the same age group (Statistical Yearbook 1982). There has also been an increase in the number of female-headed families, in accordance with the development in divorces and in number of births to unmarried women. In 1984 half of the families in Norway were either people living alone (that is without a

Figure 1. Total fertility rate for 1960 - 1985.

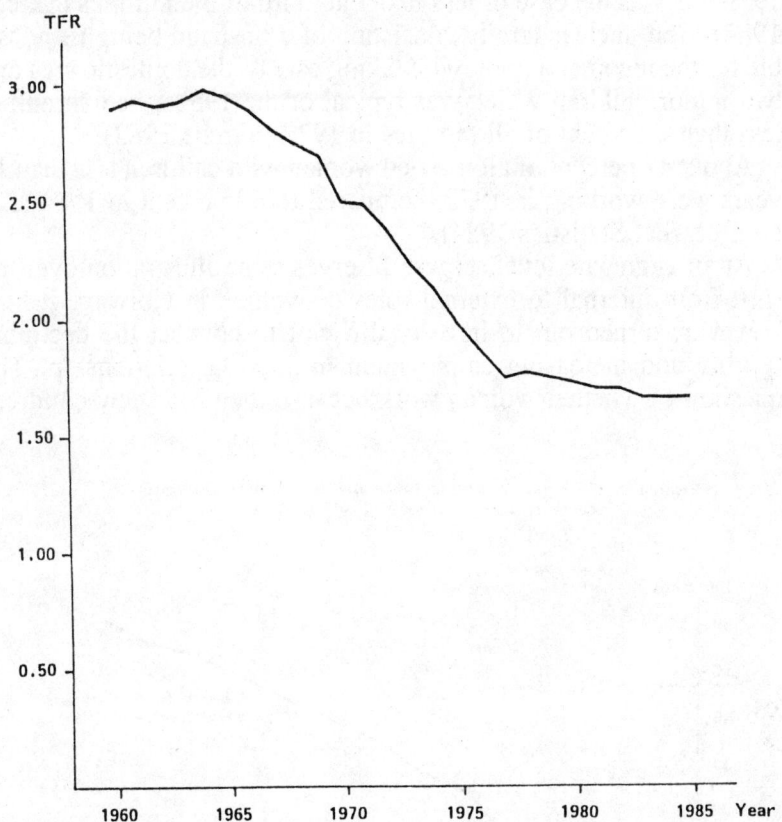

partner) or single parents. The number of children to parents living in unwed cohabitation or in disrupted families is clearly lower than in nuclear families.

INCREASING FEMALE EMPLOYMENT RATES

The fertility decline coincided with increasing labour force participation among married women. During the last 15 years Norway has changed from a society with one breadwinner, to a society with two breadwinners in the family. As late as 1972 the majority of all families (55 percent) were based on the husband's income alone. In 1979 this was the case of less than one third of the families (Skrede 1982). The nuclear family consisting of a husband being responsible for the income, a housewife taking care of the domestic area and two minor children which was typical of the 1950s, had shrunk to less than 4 percent of all families in 1979 (Skrede 1982).

About 42 percent of all married women with children less than 16 years were working in 1972, compared to 69 percent in 1984 (Labour Market Statistics 1984).

At an aggregate level, Figure 2 serves as an illustration over the shift from internal to external roles of women in Norway. It has, however, turned out to be very difficult to connect the declining fertility and increasing employment in a causal relationship. The question of whether women work because they have few children,

Figure 2. Changes in labour force participation[1] and total fertility rate.

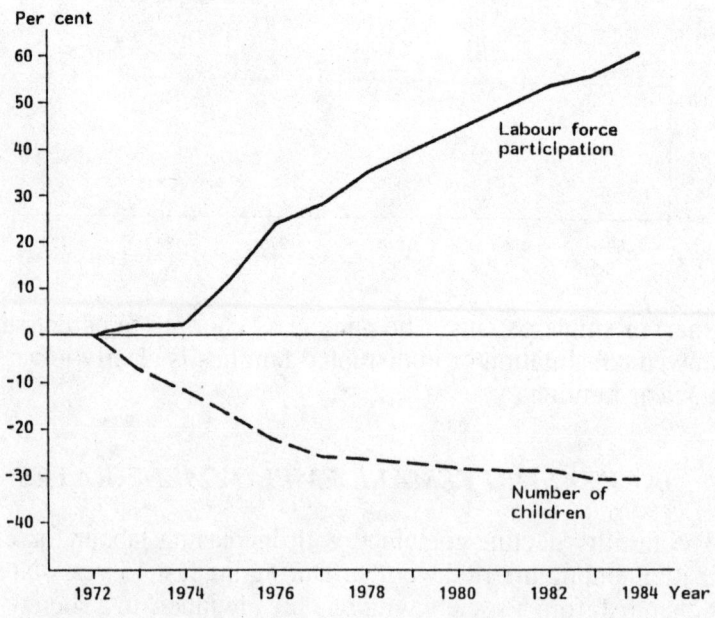

1) Married women with children below 16 years.

or the other way around remains unanswered. The usual solution to employment and childbearing seems to be a limitation of both activities. Part time work accounts for 54 percent of the female labour force (Skrede 1986), and is especially common through the childbearing years.

There seem to be no important differences in the fertility pattern between housewives and women who work part time or for shorter periods, regardless of how we measure the labour force participation (at a certain point of time or accumulated work experience during time in marriage) (Jensen 1983). If we concentrate on women with an extensive employment pattern, however, we do find a clear impact on fertility. Table 1 shows the probability of a second child among all women who have been economically active at all after the first child, compared to women who have been economically active without interruption in the same period. The probability of giving birth to a second child was reduced with 40 percent in the last group mentioned. It is interesting to note that women at the highest level of education do not have any reduction in the second child fertility, while lower educated women clearly have. On the other hand, it is still not usual to work without interruption after the first child, only 14 percent had this employment pattern in 1980 (Jensen and Schweder 1986).

THE WELFARE STATE AND FEMALE EMPLOYMENT

The years of the seventies has been called a decade of transformation. These are the important years of the development of the Norwegian Welfare State. The public share of employed persons increased both for men and women through the seventies, but the increase was far stronger for the women. By 1983 the public sector was dominated by female employees by 58 percent, compared to 48 percent ten years earlier. Almost half of all the employed women were working within the public sector in 1980. This was the case of 25 percent of the employed men. As many as three quarters of the public employed women were working within the educational, health and social services, compared to only one third of the men (Skrede 1986).

A substantial part of the increasing female employment was absorbed into the public sector. The state obtained increases in the tax income from the employed women, but it also was confronted with extended demands for social policy. These demands might be divided in two groups. The first group relates to the welfare entitlements given through employment. The other group relates to the needs created through the decreased access to informal care giving.

The most important social political entitlements to employed mothers are paid maternity leave (18 weeks), 10 days to stay home with a sick child (this is an entitlement to both parents; fathers, however, seldom use it), and one hour a day for breast-feeding. These reforms directed towards the mothers as employees let Norway fall far behind other parts of Scandinavia. To use Sweden as an example, the paid maternity leave is 36 weeks, and the parents have 60 days to stay home with a sick child.

The employment gave the women entitlements which formerly were directed towards private solutions. Between 15 and 20 percent of women between the ages of 20 and 67 are now supported primarily by national insurance. The corresponding figures for men are between 5 and 10 percent. For many women the seventies meant a transition from private (that is familial) to public dependency (Hernes 1982, Skrede 1986).

The external role of women represents a challenge for social policy, as social policy in many ways seems to have been a "push" factor of the development in female labour force participation. The expansion of the public social services created new opportunities for female labour force participation, but the demands for social policy which is a result of females leaving some of their traditional care functions, far exceeds the supply. The dilemma of the welfare state is that in order to take care of some social services, other needs are created. What are the social political consequences of externalization of the female role for the elderly and the children, two groups formerly dependent of the housewives?

CARE GIVING FOR ELDERLY PERSONS

One effect of the transition of the female role, from internal to external, could be a decrease in the potential of informal care. We might concentrate on elderly persons first.

An analysis of the informal care giving in 1980 shows that as many as 60 percent of women between 55 and 64 years in 1980 have supplied informal care to adults in the course of their life, compared to less than 40 percent of the men, as Figure 3 indicates (Lingsom 1986). The average number of years with care experience of women in age group 45 to 66 was 4.2 years and the care recipient was most frequently parents or parents in law. Changes in the pattern of informal care giving from 1950 to 1981 showed no decline in the propensity of female care for parents and parents in law. The typical care giver is employed and the large majority say that care giving have has no effect on their employment (Lingsom 1986).

One question is in what way the future system of informal care giving is affected by the transition of the female role. Until now the women in the actual life phases of care giving to the older generation have been less frequently employed and more often work part time, compared to the younger women who will constitute the potential of care givers of the future. By calculating the number of middle aged females in relation to the number of elderly people we get an expression of the "potential of care giving" in the society.

Figure 3. Percentage of men and women who have given care to adults in the course of their life, in groups for age at the time of interview.

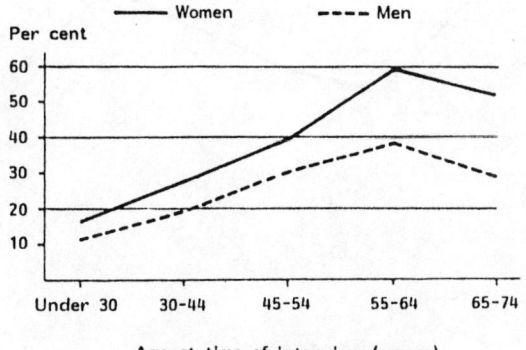

Age at time of interview (years)

Source: Lingsom, 1986

Figure 4 gives a projection of this potential until the year 2040. It shows that we are in the process of a dramatic decrease in the ratio of middle aged women and elderly persons over 80 years, which will last until 1990. By then, the post-war "baby-boom" generations give an upward trend. But to which degree will these women be available for informal care? By the year 2000 when the economically active mothers of today are about 50 to 60 years old they will have been established in the labour force through a long life. These women will be confronted with a demand for care from their parents and parents in law, which far exceeds the demands towards the middle aged women of today. This is due to the demographic

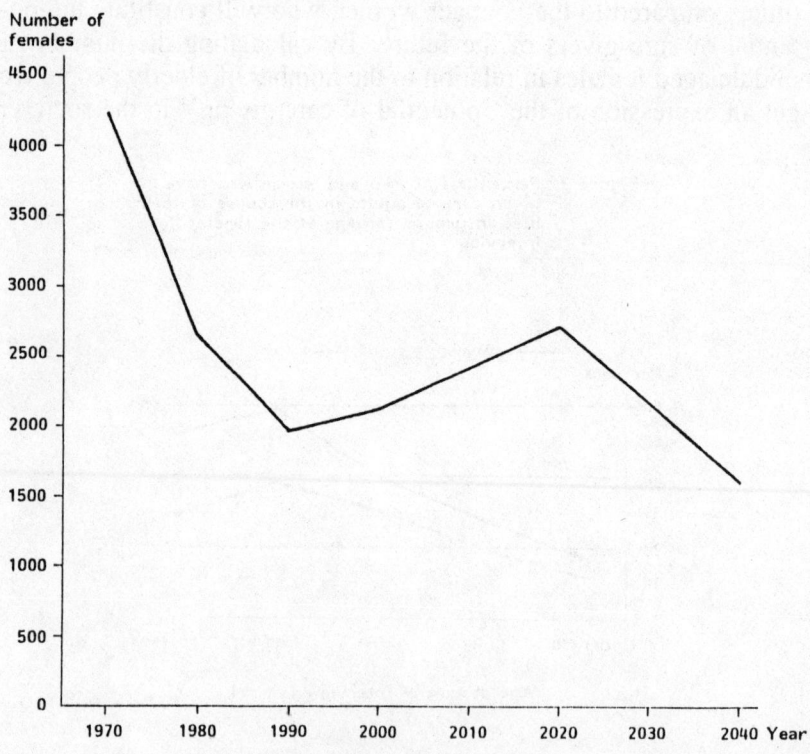

Figure 4. Future potencial of care giving among women 45-59 years per 1000 elderly people.

Source: Population Committee 1984, table 11.34

changes in Norway with a clear increase in the number of elderly persons. To keep pace with today's supply of institutional care an extension of 40 percent is needed. Even today, however, we have a serious undercovering of institutional care.

The aging of the population together with the considerable under supply of formal care for elderly people represents one of the great challenges of an adjustment of the social policy to the external role of women. This challenge will reach us in its full amplitude within the next 20 years. Other effects already have reached us and I will concentrate on these effects in the continuation.

CHILD CARE

The decrease in the number of children clearly results in public savings on expenses to children. In a country like Norway, where health care as well as education are common entitlements free to everybody, these savings are considerable. At the same time the employed mothers increase the public income through their payment of taxes. But the employment also involves expenses.

The most obvious consequence of employed mothers is increasing demands for organized child care. About one half of the mothers with pre-school children, 7 is the age of school start in Norway, are employed. The need for child care institutions during working hours is clear and is also a part of the formal family policy. The Child Care Law of 1975 accepted in principle that child care is among the common services of the welfare state. The actual situation is, however, that more than 70 percent of the pre-school children lack any kind of public child care (Leira 1986). Also, the scanty benefit of public child care covers a wide variety of daily opening hours. A substantial part of the kindergartens is open for less than 6 hours while a full time working day lasts for 8 hours. Only 10 percent of the full time employed mothers can leave the pre-school child at a public full time child care institution. Even at the full time centres mothers have problems with the opening hours. A mother working in the industry, for example, starts her working day at 7 o'clock. The day care centres open at 8 o'clock and sometimes a quarter to 8.

Some kind of child care is a prerequisite of the two wage families with minor children. Analyses have revealed a considerable puzzle of solutions in the daily life of the families regarding the child care arrangements (Wadel 1983). Still, according to recent surveys 45 percent of the two wage families where both husband and wife work full time and with a child less than 10 years, say they have had no child care arrangement outside the family (Opdahl 1984).

By the Child Care Law of 1975, the state admitted its responsibility for child care. Still the supply of day care centres is so far behind the demand that it is appropriate to ask whether social policy is directed towards children at all. Through the uneven development of the employment policy and social policy, children seem to be the ones left outside the welfare system.

A BLACK MARKET FOR CARE GIVING

What happens to the children who have working mothers and who do not have any public child care? The deficit of child care institutions has created a demand for various kinds of private arrangements. The most common arrangement is to hire a housewife as child minder either in her or in your own house. The child minders often have small children themselves. Calculations of the differences between the demand and the supply in public child care, indicates in fact that child minding has been the most expansive single female profession during the years of increasing female employment. This profession is, however, not contributing to the official figures of female employment. The great bulk of the child minders are not working at the official labour market. They do not pay taxes off their income and they do not have any rights regarding social security as ordinary employees.

One consequence of the uneven development of employment policy and social policy, is in fact criminalization of a great part of those women who are not registered as employed, for taking part in the black market of economy. The housewives are in this sense criminalized, but at the same time they are the victims being actually employed without having any of the welfare entitlements canalized through employment. One example is the entitlement of paid sick leave. Another example is the old age pensions, which are earnings-related. About 75 percent of those receiving minimum pensions today are women (Hernes 1986). Today's child minders are de facto employed, but since they do not pay taxes they do not either add any extra to their future pensions. These consequences of the transition to the welfare state are not obviously admitted.

Another consequence is the arbitrariness and lack of public control regarding the atmosphere and pedagogic principles of up-bringing. The fact is that the employed mothers are completely dependent on the child minders. There is a clear, but tacit, acceptance of this situation from the authorities. Alternatively the state would have to finance a public child care which at the moment far exceeds the limits of the social policy directed towards children.

The private market of child care is a necessary adjustment to the failure of social policy to take responsibility for care functions of working mothers. Today the lack of responsibility for the children has found its solution in the black market economy. What then, seems to be a probable solution of a future imbalance between demand and supply in the care of elderly persons? So far Norway does not have a black market for care of elderly persons, this is, however, known from other parts of the industrialized world. The increasing demand for care for elderly persons, combined with a shrinking potential of informal care represents a challenge of great importance for social policy.

The development of fertility and employment creates new demands for a social policy directed towards the caring functions formerly performed by the housewives. It also creates a new situation of growing up. This situation is an indirect consequence of several societal changes. I will illustrate some changes in childhood which might be connected to the decreasing fertility and increasing employment. My point of departure is that not only the direct effects of the externalization of the female role, but also other, more indirect effects ought to be met at a social political level.

FEMINIZATION OF CHILDHOOD

It is reasonable to believe that the transformation of the female role from internal to external will affect the socialization of children. At first sight it seems obvious that one consequence of the increased female employment is a more equal share between men and women in the upbringing of the next generation. I will discuss this in view of changes in family patterns as well as employment patterns. As a first point of view I will argue that the shrinking family size has strengthened the adult dominance over childhood. My next question is whether the adult contact has been more dominated by females over time. The question is based on the observation of increased feminization of the public sector and a possible increased structural distance between men and children.

If we look at the changes of the family pattern first, two important changes have taken place influencing the daily life of children.

1. A greater share of the women have children and
2. they have fewer children each.

The pattern of large families with visiting childless aunts and uncles has almost disappeared. The children are now a blessing available to almost everybody, with the exception of single men. On the other hand, children themselves are in many ways robbed of one important factor in their lives, a rich access to playmates. Most children have only one brother or sister who are not necessarily a suitable age as a playmate. This might also be the case of the families in the neighbourhood. Children who are not in a day care arrangement of some sort or other, may be left alone with their mothers for considerable parts of the day. Because of the more even distribution of the children and the lower number of siblings in general, the relationship between the adult and child is a more dominant feature of the socialization process on behalf of children's relations to each other.

The indirect effect of the development of divorces, must also be taken into account. Regardless of the causal relationship of employment and marital disruption (these are all tendencies difficult to isolate) the effect is a strengthening of the female dominance over children. More than 90 percent of the single parent families (which is at the moment the fastest growing family type in Norway) are female-headed.

In addition to the family pattern, the employment pattern as well means a strengthening of the female dominance over children. Mothers have left their internal roles and have handed over children to paid child minders. But women still carry out the same kind of task as they have done. Women take charge of the caring system. There has been an increase in the proportion who get paid for these functions, but they still are the care givers.

Children will almost without exception be taken care of by a woman, either their own mother or a woman who gets paid for this work. Due to the female dominance of the public sector children also will meet a woman more often when services are needed outside the home. In contrast to some decades ago they will now meet females as dentists, doctors at the health station and as social workers. Even the schoolteachers have increasingly become a female profession. (obs. sjekk dette)

At the same time it is reasonable to ask whether a development of increasing distance of relations between men and children have taken place. This is not an obvious assumption and the tendencies are not as clear as the development of strengthened relations between children and women. The assumption of increased distance between men and children is based on the economic situation of the families with small children and the structural changes of the labour market. On the other hand some cultural changes may have worked in the opposite direction.

Let's first have a look at the economic situation of families with small children.

The entrance of married women into the labour market has had several economic consequences for families with small children. One consequence has been the immediate improvement of the economy of the two-earners' families compared to families with one income. In a competition of scarce goods, like housing, the two-earner families have got an advantage as they in general would be able to pay a higher price than the one-earner family. With a substantial growth in the proportion of two-earner families, however, a general increase in housing costs took place (Berge 1982). The one-earner families had to find some solutions and the relative advantage of the two-earner families diminished.

An analysis comparing the living conditions of families without children to families with small children has revealed a lower level of family income in the last mentioned family-type. As many as one third of fathers with small children have longer working days than the ordinary 8 hours. A substantial part of the fathers hardly reach home before the child goes to bed. Studies of time use have shown that fathers with pre-school children on average spend considerable less time together with children, compared to the mothers. Even full time employed mothers spend an average of 2 hours more than fathers together with children (Lingsom and Ellingsæter 1983).

The families are squeezed during childbearing years and this squeeze consists of an economic as well as a time dimension. Fathers spending less time with the family is one result of this situation.

A second factor that might implicate an increased distance between men and children is the structural change of the labour market. The primary industry some decades ago, with a partial integration of children in the daily work, has diminished considerably on behalf of the secondary and tertiary industries and has changed into a modern, technical industry. Children are effectively cut off from these parts of the labour market and thereby from a natural contact with men through labour situations.

Maybe it is right to say that children somehow are let out of the male world, but at the same time men may have increased their engagement in the female world; like in housework or caregiving. We do not know very much about this. If we look at housework first, there are few indications that men have increased their engagement in this field. Results from a study of children's work show that while there are variations in children's use of time to housework dependent on the mothers employment, the same is not the case for men. Preliminary conclusions from this study are that children, not men, are the counterparts in housework of employed women (Solberg and Vestby 1986). But they have increased their engagement in child care. According to the study of changes in time use, married men with children under 7 years of age spent on the average one half hour per day on child care by the beginning of the 70s. Ten years later this had increased to one hour per day. More optimistic on behalf of men's relations to children are the figures showing that the percentage of fathers participating in care activities during a day rose from 51 to 70 percent through the 70s. So, there are some indications of men taking a more active, and maybe a more positive role in child care. An increase of half an hour daily in child care over the last ten years, however, is hardly impressive.

I will not follow this line of argument any longer. My point is that during the period of externalization of the female role, we also have had a strengthening of the relations between adults and children. I have suggested that this strengthening is especially valid for the relation between women and children.

I will argue that a public responsibility of the child care system is important for children not only in order to have available play-mates, but also in order to escape the feminine dominance in their lives. Not only does the mother have claims regarding a proper child care system. The child has as well. Kindergartens will strengthen children's possibilities to play with each other. The female dominance will to a certain degree be weakened by a guaranteed access to playmates. In order to promote the father's role in child rearing, however, social policy is hardly enough. This seems to challenge the employment policy as well as the established sex segregation in society.

WELFARE IMPLICATIONS
OF POPULATION DEVELOPMENT

The result of the squeeze of families with small children may be found in the fertility development. Today's fertility rate will result in a population decline by the end of the century. By the year 2100 the population will have shrunk from 4 million people to 3 million with today's fertility trends. On this background Norway appointed a Population Committee in 1981; reproduction and population structure was the focus of the Committee. The Committee should give a description of the population development, propose measures to meet the problems of this development and consider whether an active policy to influence birth rates is desirable and within the range of political possibility. The Population Committee concluded its work by fall 1984 (NOU 1984:26).

According to the conclusions of the Population Committee, the Norwegian society should have a policy of stabilizing the fertility close to the replacement level in order to avoid sharp variations in the population structure. The main proposals of the Committee were social political. The Committee stressed the necessity of a radical improvement of the living conditions of families with children. Among the measures proposed were:

1. extended salaried maternity leave (from 18 weeks to one year)
2. sufficient supply of kindergartens
3. public arrangements during the first years of school, when the child spends only a few hours at school
4. an improvement of the economic situation of families with small children through public transfers.

According to the Population Committee, a population policy must have as a point of departure the general living conditions of families with small children. An improvement of these conditions is regarded as necessary to raise the number of children. It is, however, argued that such an improvement in the living conditions is a social political aim which does not necessarily influence the birthrates.

By the presentation of the report of the Population Committee some attention was drawn to the increase in the number of elderly people. The commentators concentrated on the reproduction aspects, the desirability and possibility of increasing fertility, and on problems connected with the long-term development of the "dependency ratio." But altogether little attention was given by the mass media to the conclusions of the Population Committee.

Also at the political level the conclusions of the Population Committee was given little attention. A next governmental committee, "On Family Policy," did not take up the proposals of the "Population Committee" in the direction of a significant improvement of family welfare (Foss, Moen and Mønnesland 1985).

There are few signs of radical improvements as a result of the proposals of the Population Committee. So far, and despite Norway being one of very few western countries with a governmental report on the fertility decline, we cannot say that Norway has a policy in order to prevent a long term decreasing population.

CONCLUDING REMARKS

The lack of public child care may have hampered the rate of employment among women with small children. Compared to another Scandinavian country, Sweden, which has far better public child care as well as welfare entitlements of working mothers, Norway has a low level of employment in this life phase. About one half of women with children below 7 years are employed. These mothers have joined the labour market in spite of difficulties with their child care arrangements. This has put considerable strain on the living conditions of families with small children as the private arrangements are more costly and more unreliable compared to public child care. Two-earner families seldom have more than two children and it is reasonable that the policy of public child care is one among several factors that disfavours another child.

During the development of decreasing fertility and increasing female employment rates, the children seem to be squeezed between the family need of an extra income and the shortage of political responsibility for the next generations. Families still have the main responsibility of the children, but structural changes in society leave families incapable of a fulfillment of the responsibility. As a result families may reduce their number of children to a degree which questions the future population.

The number of children born is of vital importance for the future of any society. The difference between the two child family and the three child family is exactly the long term difference between extinction and population explosion. Over time a society continuing to exist must manage to persuade a certain proportion of the families to have three children (Berge 1982). This draws attention to the fact that social policy is not only a question of moral principles of living standards in a prosperous society like Norway. Social policy is one of several prerequisites of interest to society itself, in the long term order of existence.

REFERENCES

Berge, E. Fertility and the First Child. INAS, January, 1982.
Central Bureau of Statistics. Statistical Yearbook, NOS B 298, 1982.
Central Bureau of Statistics. Labour Market Statistics, NOS B 545, 1984.
Federici, N. Effects of Social Policies on Women's Roles and the Demographic Consequences in Developed Countries. International Population Conference, Vol.3, Manila, 1981.
Foss, O., B. Moen and J. Mønnesland. Regional Imbalances and Public Policy in a Zero Growth Population. Contributed paper, IUSSP General Conference, Firenze, 1985.

Hernes, H.M. The Public Transition of the Family, In Womens Research: Contributions to Social Theory (red. Haukaa, Hoel and Haavind), Norwegian University Press (in Norwegian), 1982.

Hernes, H.M. The Impact of Public Policy in Individual Lives; a Life Course Approach, Institute for Social Research, Oslo, February, 1986.

Jensen, A.M. Working Mothers — Fewer Children? Changes in Number of Children, Education and Employment. Article 147, Central Bureau of Statistics, Norway (in Norwegian), 1983.

Jensen, A.M. and T. Schweder. The Engine of Fertility — Influenced by Interbirth Employment? Discussion Paper no. 15, Central Bureau of Statistics, 1986.

Leira, A. Children, Family and the Welfare State. News of Women's Research, no. 2 (in Norwegian), 1986.

Lingsom, S. Care Giving Over the Life Course. Institute for Social Research, Oslo, February, 1986.

Lingsom, S. and A.L. Ellingsæter. Work, Leisure and Time Spent with Others. Changes in time use in the 70s. Statistical Analysis No.49, Central Bureau of Statistics, 1983.

Norwegian Public Reports. Population Development. No. 26 (In Norwegian), 1984.

Noack, T. and L. Østby. Childless or Childfree? A descriptive study of sterilization, infecundity and intentional childlessness. Scandinavian Population Studies, 6:2, Stockholm, 1984.

Opdahl, S. Single Parents Living Conditions and Time Use. Report No. 16, Central Bureau of Statistics, Norway (in Norwegian), 1984.

Oppong, C. A Synopsis of Seven Roles and Status of Women. An outline of a conceptual and methodological approach. ILO World Employment Programme, research working paper, 1980.

Skrede, K. Provider Income and Family Economy. Institute of Applied Social Research (INAS), Report no. 16 (in Norwegian), 1982.

Skrede, K. Shaping Women's Lives — The Impact of Recent Social Change in Norway. Paper for the conference "Life Course, Family and Work: Research and Policy." INAS, Oslo, 1986.

Wadel, C. (red). Organizing Dailylife. Norwegian University Press, Oslo (in Norwegian), 1983.

Solberg, A. and G.M. Vestby. Children's Working Life. Report, forthcoming, Norwegian Urban and Regional Institute (in Norwegian), 1986.

Østby, L. and K. Strom Bull. Extent and Distribution of Cohabitation without Marriage. Journal of Jurisprudence, offprint (in Norwegian), 1986.

Social and Economic Aspects
of the Family
in an Italian Peripheral Area

Patrizia David
Giovanna Vicarelli

SUMMARY. From analyses carried out in the 70s, the family emerges as a system of economic management and a complement to Market and State. Besides having been of undeniable importance in terms of a more detailed perception of the family as a whole in Italian society, this result has also attributed greater possibilities of interpretation to the models of analysis of social reality itself. The choice of a specific territorial research dimension proved in addition to be a particularly determining factor for major accuracy in this analysis. This paper presents the principle results emerging from studies carried out on the family unit by the group of sociologists of the University of Ancona, whose research activities related to the social economic context of the region clearly underline the full ability of the family to play an active economic role in society.

It seems possible to affirm that the 70s represent a turning point for sociological studies on the family. A substantially new approach of considering the family emerged from the research carried out in this period, one which undermined the principle models of interpretation. This new way of regarding the domestic community consists fundamentally of no longer considering it as being in a residual and marginal position with respect to the process of economic regulation of modern society; a view affirmed by traditional sociology,

Patrizia David and Giovanna Vicarelli are researchers in Sociology at the University of Ancona (Italy). This article results from common work of research and discussion. Nevertheless, P. David wrote the first part and G. Vicarelli the second one.

which relegated the family to an exclusively superstructural framework or to the sub-system of human relationships. It denied the family any form of economic functionality.

We do not intend to dwell on an analysis of the cultural processes which have led to a different approach in the interpretation of the domestic community. This has by now been fully examined and clarified. Our attention mainly concerns the results attained and the different methods of research adopted.

From analyses carried out in the 70s the family emerges with its own system of economic regulation aside from those of the Market and the State. This activity of economic regulation assumed by the family passes through three substantial types of functions. The first is related to the production and transformation of goods and services with which the family proves to be involved. This includes the consumer process, a complex one involving decisions and transformation of raw materials purchased on the market and also in the direct production of goods and services for self-consumption. This function, considered internally, aims at satisfying the needs of the single members of the family while externally, with respect to the productive system, there results in restraining reproduction costs of the labor force. In addition the family constitutes a central element in the distribution process of resources. This function makes it possible to attain an important achievement in terms of social integration through the "private" management of the inequalities produced by the market.

The second function, identified by a series of territorial researches, is exercised by the family in relation to that particular form of production development, for small companies, which are very widespread over a territory which is still substantially tied to agriculture and which characterizes the central north-east areas of Italy. In these areas the family does not limit itself to producing for self-consumption but operates as a real and proper company for the market, inserting itself directly into the local processes of production. A third type of economic function carried out by the family related to the management of its own members with respect to their working capacity is where the family assumes a double characteristic: it represents the place of distribution of different types of work, e.g., domestic, for the informal economy or the market, between the different components on a sexual and generational basis. It constitutes a key element for the differentiation of the labor force in the market.

The briefly summarized results on the new interpretation of the role of the family in society have contributed greater interpretation capacity to the models of analysis of social reality. Also this new way of regarding the family was not attained by following an unequivocal course in the methods adopted and disciplinary approach used. It is the result of various research paradigms originating from the diffusion of different interests around the family theme. We retain it to be particularly stimulating to underline several of these paradigms: the first made it possible to reconduct studies on the contemporary family over a long term period; this was possible with the acquisition and re-elaboration of the results of historical research within other than family frameworks of analysis, e.g., the labor market, the industrialization process and the formation of the modern State.

Secondly, the choice of a territorial area of research, intended as an "organization principle of social phenomena" (Bagnasco, Messori 1978, p. 220) proved to be particularly determining for a more complete analysis where the family is considered in its particular interrelations with specific forms of State and Market. The object of analysis, according to this approach, is the "territorial formation" as the delimited territorial meaning of the concept of social-economic formation in the hypothesis that a "compatible system" subsists between the structural and the superstructural elements which characterize it.

Finally, a third paradigm is represented by considering the family as a dynamic organization of needs and resources, not as a static entity, which changes as life cycles vary. The validity of results from sociological studies on the family appear to be highly correlated to the fact that their models of interpretation have taken into account dimensions of analyses particular to other disciplinary approaches, such as, historical, economical, anthropological and demographic analyses.[1]

We would now like to present the research studies on the family carried out over the last ten years by a group of sociologists at

Ancona, Italy,[2] as concrete examples of the complex method of analysis already mentioned.

In their initial phase, research activities carried out in the Marches are part of studies on productive decentralization which at the beginning of the 70s identified the importance of capitalistic accumulation of the small industrial and artisan companies in Italy largely located in various well defined areas. The Marches Region represents an area in which productive decentralization is particularly widespread. The initial survey[3] was formulated on the hypothesis that its persistence and vitality was explained not only in terms of demand, involving the production structure characteristics and national capitalistic accumulation, but also in terms of the available labor force and its reproduction processes. The objective of the research was to determine the role the family would play in this type of production context. The hypothesis is that the different types of work which feed the dispersed production system would find their origin in a social context where the extended family and the farming domestic community still played an important role.

The economic-territorial paradigm on which research activities were initially based made it possible to identify the existence of a particular type of family with specific prerogatives in the economic and productive fields. This has been identified as the "family company." This description is aimed to draw attention to a specific and complex method of organization and operation of the domestic community in the Marches Region.

The typical family in the survey proved to have certain peculiarities with respect to the model relevant to industrial society. With respect to its structure, it was "extended" or "multiple" in well over a third of the cases considered, with a net prevalence of the paternal line. Second, the different types of working activities interwoven within the same family framework became immediately evident, ranging from those for the market, and which were placed according to a "regular-irregular" scale in terms of both the working relationship and hours of work or the periodicity of the work itself, to informal types of activities, such as the care of a vegetable garden, breeding farm animals and the activities of the domestic artisan, to actual domestic work itself. These activities proved to be subdivided between the different members of the family, no member excluded, according to a rigid model of the division of roles and functions based on the sex and age of the family members, but which were in part subject to change proportionally to the life cycles of the family.

It proved, in fact, to have a great ability to manage the labor force of its members, to which it met the requirements of the production system perfectly, in terms of a flexible labor force at a low cost, and at the same time guaranteeing a subsistence basis for itself through the use of resources from different sectors and activities.

In the same way, it became evident how the family was following wider strategies through this working logic, thereby involving more generations, all of which aimed fundamentally at preventing the "proletarization" of the family labor force. The accentuated ability of the family-company to centralize and control resources permitted the formulation of investment strategies to the extent that true "family-firms" were formed. This type of domestic community proved therefore to be a determining factor for the very development of the particular local production structure. Analyses of the phenomenon moved, therefore, to examine a longer period of time, in order to identify the historical factors at the basis of this specific family model.

Historical research carried out in the Region, studies regarding its agriculture,[4] supplied bases for verification of the hypothesis of the existence of continuity both culturally and economically between the farming family which in the past characterized the local community and the typical family model of small company industrialization. The Marches Region, together with other regions in central and north-east Italy which experienced a similar type of industrialization, represent an area where historically, share-cropping management has always been very widespread, thus delaying the introduction of more modern farming management methods. The historical share-cropping crisis of the '50s was responsible for a limited formation of large farming companies and of wage-earning farm workers. More frequently it gave way to the constitution of small family units.

The necessity of integrating the family income in those cases where the size and productivity of the land did not make it possible to reach adequate resources, produced a large labor force which moved towards the industrial and artisan sector, which at the time where emerging. The passage of various members of the farming family to activities in the industrial sector, did not modify its organization and cultural characteristics. The out-of-company activities of some of its members, more than an alternative to the family farming company and therefore the start of its progressive abandon, proved to be the result of a more rational division of work within the domestic community (Pieroni 1983). This continued to be the framework within which the minor industrial energies (of sharecropping derivation) of the head-of-the-family were being expended.

Through its experience of part-time farming it made possible for families to accumulate capital and to acquire extra-farming abilities. The potential of these energies together with the large labor force available allowed the farming family to become the central element of the gradual passage of the local community from a farming production structure to an industrial structure without involving radical changes of its traditional values.

Subsequent surveys, which were based essentially on a territorial-economic approach and on the concept of the family-company, validated the results obtained during the course of this initial survey.

In research based on social and health services for the population of an area of the region with typically peripheral development,[5] reference to the family and territory was recognized as crucial for an analysis of factors which prevent or deviate awareness of the risks existing for health and the participation of the population in social service and health activities. Regarding the request for social health services of a sample of families residing in one of the communities in the area[6] demonstrated that "farming and industrial work in the footwear sector, in small companies and at home" required "long working hours, short holidays, high health risks and accidents" just as "the daily toil in the fields and factories." Workers in both settings experienced "living conditions which very often did not offer the minimum indispensable health facilities" (Mori, Paci 1979, p. 49).

The population did not seem to have acquired any type of awareness of the causes of existing health risks related to their particular living and working conditions. It was as though the awareness of social and environmental risks were compressed "within a private outlook of the health problem" (Mori, Paci, 1979, p. 22) in which the family, in its configuration typical of the peripheral economy areas, played a determining role, and proved to function essentially as a "filter or defence screen for personal privacy" (Mori, Paci 1979, p. 23) rather than as access to the different forms of social participation and health prevention.

If, on the one hand, the characterization of the local community in a traditional cultural sense was at the basis of the same economic development which had invested large areas of the region, on the other hand seemed to prevent the growth of health and social awareness.

The survival of traditional cultural practices was found to be widespread within the dominating social structures in peripheral economies. The role of the "extended" family and the local community proved to be central in the analysis of child labor in a survey carried out in 1980 in several footwear-farming municipalities in the region.[7] The hypothesis on which this research was based was that the phenomenon of child labor in the small-industry areas was directly related to the particular co-relation existing in those same areas between the production and the family system. The vitality of the family model of farming origin is the determining cause of the phenomenon rather than due to the economic necessity of the families of the children.

Even though the existence of different methods of using children according to different family strategies was in fact identified, the early working experience appeared clearly as an integral element of the local cultural heritage. It proved to be the cause and effect of that "market mobilization" which had introduced the diffusion of acquisitive economic strategies and cultural orientation. It implied the acceptance of the market as a system of social regulation, into areas characterized by a growth model based on the small industry (Bagnasco 1985).

Behind this apparent uniformity, regarding the duties and sectors of occupation, the phenomenon of child labor proved to have some rather significant differences within the context analyzed. The principle reason was found "in the different position of the family

within the local system of production and distribution of resources"
(David 1986, p. 43). These children were, in fact, acquiring different behavior patterns through their working experiences, not only
because of the sex but because of their social class. The family, in
particular, proved to be the principle environment in which behavior patterns conforming to the formation of managerial and wage-
earning labor force mentalities, were developed. The analysis revealed how

> different the prospects could be, at a class articulation level
> within the local environment, for those children whose work-
> ing activities lay within valid family acquisitive strategies with
> respect to those who, on the other hand, belonged to not very
> dynamic families from an economic and social point of view.
> (David 1986, p. 43)

The concept of the "family-company" as has already been
stated, had been coined to identify the economic and productive
characteristics of those domestic groups which had proved to be
typical of peripheral economic activities. Subsequent surveys demonstrated, however, that it was possible to use this concept in non-
peripheral economic areas, which in some ways were opposite and
complementary to those already considered.

The family, in a survey carried out between 1978 and 1979 in the
city of Ancona, appeared equally able to carry out an active economic role, both in production for the market and, above all, in
making the best possible use of the resources necessary for the welfare of its components.[8]

The family's managerial ability proved to be crucial. For example, in approximately one-third of the cases examined the male
heads of the family have a secondary autonomous and free professional activity, besides a dependent primary one in the public sector. Even though the work involved was carried out for different
economic reasons and, in part, to achieve a professional fulfillment,
something which was not possible in the primary working activity,
they were nonetheless all sustained by family motivation and organization whose premises were related to those traditional domestic

groups, such as farmers or artisans from which the majority of the people interviewed had originated.

At the same time the family demonstrated that it knew how to activate working strategies and acquire monetary resources to increase the level of its income and the quality of its life style over and above the economic level and social conditions determined by the social class to which the head of the family belonged. The family proved, for example, to be able to organize itself so as to make use of the advantages deriving from female labor in the public services sector, which because of its particular working hours and flexibility generally makes it possible for women to maintain their domestic role unaltered. It was able to draw advantage from the irregular work of children introduced prematurely into the labor market and from state benefits through cohabitation with elderly or disabled relations which in many cases increased family resources considerably.

The most relevant factor, however, was the different configuration of family strategies with respect to their economic-social position, life-cycle and generation differences. Among young families, those without children or with preschool age children, there were relatively few cases where there was a single source of income. There was a very high integration of income, especially among the families of office clerks and teachers, which was attained both by the remunerated work of women or by a second job of the men, or both. Families which more often than others had a single working income, were those with school-age children, particularly among specialized workers and administrative staff, because of the drastic reduction of female labor. An increasing number of children worked and this was sometimes added to a second job held by the father. In families with children over the school-age, the presence of different working activities was very high and the pattern of employment very similar to those in the first few years of matrimony. It should, however, be noted that the integration of the family income in the families of teachers and office clerks came almost exclusively from the work of women or from the second job by the head of the family while the integration of income in families of laborers came essentially from the work of their children.

There were different methods of organization for the various individuals involved in work for the market or for the different levels of labor effort and resources obtained. Most important, however was the different choices made by the families according to the reproduction processes and conservation of the labor force. Concern was for the growth and education of the children and to satisfy the daily requirements of all the members of the family. If in the more wealthy families, the majority of resources accumulated made it possible to consider both these processes, the less wealthy families managed to obtain adequate resources to meet the family's daily needs only to the obvious disadvantage of a higher level of reproduction of the working ability of their children who were taken from school at a relatively early age and introduced into the labor market. In those cases where, despite a low income, an attempt was being made to "invest" on the children, the living standard was decidedly low and precarious (Vicarelli, 1982).

The functions of the economic regulation of the family which were in this way confirmed in an urban and economically different setting from the situation to be found in rural and widely-spread industrialized districts, also emerged in terms of the utilization of the social and health services offered by the public sector. A further survey on the basic social-health services offered in the city of Ancona and in five boundary municipalities, confirmed that families directly involved in production activities for the market were not fully aware of the working risks and dangers for health, especially artisan families. It also became apparent that public services were not only unable to substitute the tasks of the family but neither were they able to integrate those provided by the family. The survey proved that a large part of the care and assistance afforded to non-autonomous elderly, chronically ill and disabled persons came from the family, just as did a large part of the basic health assistance.

The extension of our research in time and space led us, at the beginning of the 80s to identify the importance of two additional factors in the analysis of the economic role of the family. First, it became apparent that the strategies in the domestic organization in relation to the family life-cycle with respect to the number of children and their birth were a determining factor. Moreover, demographic statistics indicated a considerable change in this period, even in an area as traditional as the Marches Region. The birth rate dropped from 15.8% in 1961 to 9.8% in 1983 and the average number of children per woman born from 2.04 in 1961 to 1.36 in 1983.

Second it became evident that it was necessary to consider the impact between the social policies implemented in the country in the 70s and the economic role of the family, in the specific territorial configuration, experienced in the Marches Region. The social and health services offered could modify the behavior of the families in terms of assistance and care of dependent members, which had traditionally been performed by the family, or, on the contrary, could reconfirm the complementary and integrative role of domestic groups.

It was on this basis with the territorial paradigm extended in consideration of the role of the welfare state and a new paradigm emerging in relation to family demographic dynamics, that a further survey was carried out in collaboration with the Institute of Mathematics and Statistics of the University of Ancona. The research, "Fertility, Family and Social Services" which is currently underway, aims to construct a model of analysis and micro-simulation on the basis of data on domestic groups which have been collected over the years by the Institute of Sociology; demographic data obtained from the population census; and results obtained from the National Survey on families, the first of its kind in Italy carried out by the Central Statistical Office (ISTAT). While the intention is to arrive at the construction of a micro-simulated model of fertility in the Marches Region, based on family groups instead of individuals, another objective is to test the possibility of verifying the potential demand of social services for children by families in the Marches Region in future years. If the survey will enhance the eventual choices of socio-economic policies, it will also be possible to extend analysis on the family and, therefore, consider the complexity of the social factors which seem to effect its behavior.

The necessity of studying family patterns in relation to the changes that involve the Market, the State and the informal network of relations, friendships and volunteers in subsequent historical events and in a specific territorial formation seem, more than ever, the objective with which to make comparisons in future research work on the family.[9]

NOTES

1. Cf as essential references for this paragraph: Balbo, 1976, Chisté, Del Re, Forti 1979; Ingrosso 1979; Del Boca, Turvani 1980; Paci 1980; IRER, 1980; Cutrufeli 1980; Saraceno 1981; David, Vicarelli 1983.

2. Research was carried out at the Institute of History and Sociology of the Faculty of Economics of Ancona; much of this research was supervised by Prof. M. Paci.

3. The research, carried out in 1976 in six municipalities of the Region, involved a total of 650 families. The hypotheses and the results were presented in the collective volume edited by M. Paci, "Family and the labor market in a peripheral economy" Angeli 1980. Other papers regarding research: the monographic edition of Inchiesta, No. 20, 1976; Ascoli 1977, David, 1978; Vinay, 1978.

4. See, particularly, Coletti, 1925; Anselmi 1978a, Anselmi 1978b.

5. The research was carried out on behalf of the Health and Social Security Board of the Marches Region, in 1977, amongst the population of the Media Valle del Tenna. For hypotheses and results see, Mori, Paci 1979; Bellabarba 1979; Vinay 1979.

6. The survey was carried out on 30 families at Monte S. Pietrangeli cf Vinay 1979.

7. The research was carried out in Junior Schools (3rd, 4th and 5th Classes) and secondary schools in seven municipalities between the province of Macerata and that of Ascoli Piceno; a total of 2850 children were interviewed, of which 60% proved to be working or to have worked. Cf. Vinay, 1984; David 1986.

8. The research "The Policy of Occupation and Secondary Working Activities" supervised by Prof. M. Paci and coordinated at a national level by six universities, was carried out on a sample of working males in Secondary Schools, Hospital Staff, Municipality Staff, the State Railways and the National Electricity Company and in a large chemical industry in the city of Ancona. For results see the collective volume edited by M. Paci, "State, Market and Occupation", Il Mulino, 1985.

9. The results of the research carried out in 1980-81 were published in Vinay, 1981; Vicarelli, 1982; Paci, Pettenati, 1985.

REFERENCES

Anselmi S. (a cura di). *Economia e società: Le Marche tra XV e XX secolo*, Bologna, 1978a.

Anselmi S. *Mezzadri e terre nelle Marche*, Bologna, 1978b.

Ascoli U. Rigidità dei ruoli familiari e offerta di lavoro femminile, in *Inchiesta*, n. 30, 1977.

Balbo L. *Stato di famiglia*, Milano: Estas, 1976.

Bagnasco A., M. Messori, C. Trigilia *Le problematiche dello sviluppo italiano*, Milano: Feltrinelli, 1978.

Bagnasco A. Dal mondo contadino alla mobilitazione di mercato, in Bagnasco e Trigilia (a cura di), *Società e politica nelle aree di piccola impresa. Il caso della Valdelsa*, Milano: F. Angeli, 1985.

Bellabara G. *Indagine sul fabbisogno dei servizi sociali e sanitari presso la popolazione della media valle del Tenna. Vol. II Strutture e caratteristiche dei servizi sociali e sanitari esistenti*, Ancona, 1979.

Chisté L., A. Del Re, E. Forti. *Oltre il lavoro domestico*, Milano: Feltrinelli, 1979.

Cutrufelli M.E. *Economia e politica dei sentimenti*, Roma: Editori Riuniti, 1980.

David P. Il ruolo della donna nell'economia periferica, in *Inchiesta* n. 34, 1978.

David P. Il lavoro minorile in un sistema ad economia diffusa, in *Economia Marche*, n. 1, 1986.

David P., G. Vicarelli (a cura di) *L'azienda famiglia*, Bari: Laterza, 1983.

Ingrosso M. *Produzione sociale e lavoro domestico*, Milano: F. Angeli, 1979.

IRER. *Lavoro femminile e condizione familiare*, Milano F. Angeli, 1980.

Mori, M., M. Paci *Indagine sul fabbisogno di servizi sociali e sanitari presso la popolazione della media valle del Tenna. Vol. I Rapporto di sintesi*, Ancona, 1979.

Paci M. (a cura di), *Famiglia e mercato del lavoro in una economia periferica*, Milano: F. Angeli, 1980.

Paci M. (a cura di) *Stato, mercato, occupazione. Il doppio lavoro nell'area anconetana*, Bologna: Il Mulino, 19

Paci M., P. Pettenati. *I servizi socio-sanitari di base*, Ancona, Università degli Studi di Ancona, 1985.

Pieroni O. *Agricolture a tempo parziale*, Bologna Il Mulino, 1983.

Saraceno C. *Il lavoro mal diviso*, Bari: De Donato, 1980.

Vicarelli G. L'azienda famiglia: una ipotesi interpretativa, in David e Vicarelli, *La famiglia nello sviluppo capitalistico italiano*, Ancona, 1981.

Vicarelli G. Strategie familiari nel sistema delle garanzie, in *Inchiesta* n. 56, 1982.

Vinay P. *Indagine sul fabbisogno di servizi sociali e sanitari presso la popolazione della media valle del Tenna. Vol. III Coscienza del rischio e atteggiamento della popolazione verso i servizi socio-sanitari*, Ancona, 1979.

Vinay P. *La domanda di servizi socio-sanitari: il comportamento della famiglia*, Ancona, 1981.

Vinay P., *La realtà del lavoro minorile nella economia periferica*, Ancona, Università degli Studi di Ancona, 1984.

Tradition and Modernity
in the Family Farm:
A Case Study

Bruno Hildenbrand

TRENDS IN THE DEVELOPMENT
OF THE RURAL FAMILY:
LINEAR MODERNIZATION?

For years there have been two diametrically opposed points of view among West German researchers on the consequences of modernization processes in agriculture. One group maintains that agriculture is increasingly losing its traditional characteristics and is being completely absorbed into the industrial capitalistic sector (Lutz 1986). The other group contends that on account of its particular structure agricultural production cannot do without traditional elements. This is already evident in spite of all trends towards industrialization and concentration on a historical and transcultural basis, the agricultural family farm has proved itself to be the most satisfying form of rural economy. Support for this theory is that there is a marked tendency in West Germany towards the single-owner farm. At the same time, the number of jobs for farm workers in agriculture who are not owners has decreased from 18% in 1945 to 5% in 1983. Attention has also been called to the significantly lower rate of agricultural production achieved by the large agricultural co-operatives in the socialist countries (Haushofer 1958, Planck 1985, Mendras 1967).

The limits to which agriculture can be industrialized are that in

Dr. Bruno Hildenbrand is Hochschulassistent, Johann Wolfgang Goethe-Universitat, Fachbereich Gesellschaftswissenschaften, West Germany.

159

industrial production the machines are stationary and the material to be manufactured mobile while in agricultural production the situation is exactly the opposite: the manufacturing basis, the earth, is stationary and the machines mobile. This is a prohibiting factor in the use of machinery on a large scale. Moreover, there are traditional factors such as the time which limits production because animals and plants are all bound together in unalterable growth and maturing processes.

If these factors are not taken into consideration, then society will have to be prepared to accept enormous dangers to the preservation of the natural basis of life itself. Soil erosion, high nitrate levels in drinking water and the buildup of chemicals in plant and animal tissue are the now familiar catch phrases.

Just as a total industrialization of agricultural production is not a viable system, the often quoted view that the rural family has been totally absorbed by the social organization of the urban family is simply not tenable. It is true that in its outward form the rural family is increasingly similar to that of the urban family (Egner 1980, Schelsky 1967), but there are four characteristics which ensure that there is always a structural difference between urban and rural families.

1. The rural family is not only just a unit of consumption, but also a production unit.
2. The choice of marriage partner is being increasingly influenced by emotional considerations, but factors such as dowry and capacity to work are still of central importance when selecting a partner.
3. Just as the land is stationary, so also is the rural family, and thus one of its most important characteristics is its permanent residence in a fixed place.
4. Several generations continue to live on the farm with each other and to organize the work jointly.

Tradition and modernity on the family farm exist side by side in a remarkable relationship to each other which I intend to examine in detail. This is followed by the case reconstruction of the situation of an average farming family which demonstrates the relationship between traditional and modern aspects of family. While this is structurally essential for farming families, it need not necessarily be disadvantageous, but carries within it considerable potential for innovation.

THE RELATIONSHIP BETWEEN TRADITIONAL AND MODERN ASPECTS OF THE SOCIAL ORGANIZATION OF FAMILY FARMS

In the traditional model of the farm the family is organized around the principle of the division of labor. The rules of marriage are designed to protect the continuity of the farm, and the succession to ownership of the farm is also geared towards continuity whereby the inheritor enjoys a privileged position. This form of organization, which is specifically concerned with the continuity and permanence of the family farm, corresponds to a view of life which places the farm at the centre of all decisions and subordinates the individual aspirations of family members to the security and permanence of the farm (Weber-Kellermann 1969, 1977).

Although the traditional orientation which places the farm at the centre of the decision-making process continues to be upheld, the reality of the situation on the farm with regard to work organization as well as financial and commercial considerations has distanced itself from traditional ideas. Since the fifties, over half the farmers have abandoned farming as their sole means of livelihood. They have continued to farm as a supplement to their income, but their main employment is in industry. The remaining farms were only able to survive as viable production units capable of supporting a family by adopting measures leading to radical specialization and rationalization. The industrialization of the farms that this process entailed led to capital becoming an extremely important factor while the advantages of the family-run farm with its teams of flexible workers willing to labor without regard for their own health and safety decreased. In the last thirty years the use of borrowed capital for the operation of farms has increased five-fold in West Germany, and the average debt per hectare is almost 4,000 DM. Changing market structures have enforced a standardization and mass production of products so that the traditional individual self-sufficiency of the farm has been undermined and has become directly dependent on market forces. The farm owner and his wife now find that they have need of know-how not only in the traditional skills of planting, harvesting and husbandry, but also in management, marketing and technology.

Along with this specific multiplicity of the skills required by farmers, each decision affecting the management of the farm also affects the family so that particularistic and universalistic aspects of social organization on the farm are superimposed on each other (Bergmann 1969, van Deenen 1971). Mendras (1967: 322) gives an instructive example of this process: The purchase of a tractor not only represents an investment for the farm, it also simplifies work on the farm. It is a status symbol for the whole family and a concession on the part of the father to the son in order to encourage him to stay on the farm.

With regard to family organization, far-reaching changes have taken place which question the model of the family farm. In particular, the increase in individualized behavior patterns is one area in which the rural family is becoming more and more assimilated with the urban family. An example of this is the earlier age of marriage which is no longer compatible with the traditional succession of the generations on the farm and which coupled with the generally longer life-expectancy gives rise to the situation whereby four generations live on the farm at the same time, two of which fall in the age group needing to earn a living. With the present tendency towards single-owner units, this must inevitably lead to conflicts. Another characteristic of increasingly individualized behavior patterns is that the succession to and management of the farm is no longer the sole imaginable alternative for the son. As a result, the idea of continuity, which is of central importance to the family farm, is being steadily undermined. For the farming couple this means that on account of the uncertain future of the farm, their mentality, which has always placed the requirements of the farm first and which continues to find expression as a traditional set of values, must adapt to the perspective of the possible futility of future efforts to modernize. On the one hand, the traditional model of the dominance of the farm to which individual interests are subordinated can only be maintained by increased efforts to modernize which allow for an intensified individual and flexible reaction to economic and social trends. On the other hand, this reaction threatens to become meaningless on a permanent basis should the son of the farming couple decide to leave the farm in order to follow an alternative biographical development for the same individual reasons and motivations previously adopted by the managing farmer in order to keep his farm going.

METHODS

The following case study of the Hahn family illustrates the problem posed by tradition and modernity in the rural farm. This case study is not to illustrate an already formulated theory, but is along with other case studies intended to generate a theory (Glaser & Strauss 1973, Strauss 1987). Our understanding of the individual case is one of individual generality in the sense that we are concerned with elaborating the relationship between general structures in which the individual is located as well as the emerging individual actions and meaning structures being active in the context of these general structures.

Individual case reconstructions are not an isolated phenomenon but have their place within a collective system. The formulation of a theory is the result of an accumulation of individual case reconstructions. The theoretical assertions which have already been elaborated with regard to the Hahn family and the connections between them are based on minimal contrasting (comparison with similarly situated cases) and maximal contrasting (comparison with opposite cases) (Glaser & Strauss 1973, Hildenbrand 1988). Individual case analyses interpreted in this manner are capable of separating the factors which determine the specific nature of a case from those which typify the historical situation and the positioning of a case in the framework of a social structure. In this sense, general statements are possible in the area of sociological research which deals with case reconstruction.

Some remarks on the method used: The data presented are based on a conversation held with the family in which we asked those present to narrate the history of their family (Hildenbrand and Jahn 1988).

After each conversation a written record of our observations was made, noting where the conversation had taken place and describing the house and its furnishings.

The conversation about the history of the family was transferred to paper, taking into account pauses, interruptions and intonations. In our evaluation we first dealt with the events and their sequence as they appeared in the biography of the family. Examined was the extent of knowledge and interpretation put on past events and their relevance to family members when they recollected or thematized them. Finally, these interpretations were analyzed under the aspect of their interactive production. In evaluating the observations and notes we made, the spatial organization of the family (seating positions, plan of the house, etc.) as it reflects life patterns and structures was reconstructed in view of the theme under discussion here.

In the course of each family analysis these evaluations led to the formulation of a concept with the status of a case structure hypothesis which expresses the family structure in question. The comparisons between the families are based on these premises.

THE HAHN FAMILY

In 1934 Otto Hahn, the present farm owner and eldest of two children (a sister followed in 1941), was born into a farming family who had lived on this farm for several generations. In 1957 he married Gerda, a girl from the same village who comes from a background of farmers and small craftsmen. In 1967 he took over the management of the family farm which at that time comprised 10 hectares. Today he farms 70 hectares, two thirds of which is leased.[1]

The farm is situated in the uplands on the edge of the Rhein-Main area, the second most heavily populated region of Germany. Dairy farming, meat production, and feedstuffs are the three main areas of production on the farm. The size of the farm is sufficient to provide a living for three generations with extra income provided by work done outside the farm.

The considerable expansion in terms of land and the accompanying mechanization for its management was financed by the earnings of Otto Hahn who worked as a woodcutter, cabinet maker, carpenter, mason, bricklayer and lorry driver, as well as by the good income of his father who was also a meat inspector.

At the time of this inquiry, the family living on the farm consisted of eight people from four generations: the proprietors Otto and Gerda Hahn; Paul and Barbara Hahn, Otto's parents; Uwe, son and designated successor of Otto Hahn; Uwe's wife, Sonja; and their two children, a boy and a girl. Uwe's sister Iris, is studying to be an interpreter for Chinese and comes home regularly for the weekend.

After finishing school at the age of sixteen with the German Intermediate Certificate, Uwe Hahn did an agricultural apprenticeship. He then worked for a year in an agricultural research station owned by a major company. In the meantime, he also passed his exams in agricultural training. Sonja is a housewife with no other occupation apart from the household and rearing the children.

At a relatively early stage, the Hahn family took the necessary decisions for continuing to run the farm on a full-time basis. After the early purchase of a tractor in 1953, they extended the farm buildings, then situated in the village, by constructing a large barn in 1954/55. However, as conditions in the village did not allow for further development of the farm buildings, and as after Otto and Gerda Hahn's marriage with the subsequent birth of their two children accommodation problems arose, the family decided to build a new farm complex outside the village.

This plan was financed partly by a special credit at a minimal rate of interest and partly by Otto Hahn's own contributions. He worked as a mason for the firm that built the new farm unit during the period it was under construction. Due to the concentrated efforts of all the family, it was possible to complete the phase of restructuring the farm in just under two years. The difficult financial situation was eased when the old farm buildings were sold for a good price and also by the steady income provided by Otto Hahn's work outside the farm, although he never tried to develop this earning potential into an alternative to a full-time living from agriculture. His extra work, which allowed him to acquire skills that were of great use in running his own farm, was always undertaken with the goal of securing the farm and ensuring its continuing expansion and modernization.

As is clear from all they narrated about the construction of a new farm unit that the Hahn family displays a very positive orientation towards agriculture, which finds expression in their energetic striving towards integration and continuity, as well as in a willingness to take risks in order to achieve what they want, and to invest all their labor potential in it. The succession to the farm is characterized by offering the future owners (Otto and Uwe) the opportunity to take part in the production and decision-making processes on a gradual basis so that they can continuously prepare for their full function as manager later on. When he was 58, Paul Hahn handed over legal control of the farm to Otto, who at that time had managed the farm as a tenant for the previous three years. In practice, however, Paul Hahn withdrew from the key position of farm manager at the age of 44, parallel with the upsurge in the trend towards increased mechanization, and so made it possible for his son to take over progressively the central role on the farm.

This correspondence between the withdrawal of the old farmer and the integration of the young one is influenced and supported by Paul Hahn's financial independence due to his income as a meat inspector, and also by the beginning of qualitative changes in agricultural production. Paul more or less dissociates himself from the new developments of the technical age and leaves the stage to the younger generation.

Paul Hahn continued to orient himself towards the farm, even during the period when his main income came from his occupation as a meat inspector. This is evident in his willingness to work on the farm in his free time and in his continuing to finance the next generation in their efforts to modernize the farm.

As well as Otto Hahn, Gerda, his wife, has a central position on the farm. She comes from a part-time farming family and had no difficulty integrating into the Hahn household. Above all, she was not in competition nor subject to the control of the woman in charge of the household (at the time of the marriage, this was her husband's grandmother). On account of her positive personal relationship with this woman, which was mainly based on her qualities as an excellent worker, she was soon recognized as having an important role to play, especially in the difficult time of building the new farm complex. This important role comes into focus during the modernization phase when her second child is born and Barbara Hahn becomes so ill that she has to be nursed. Gerda Hahn takes on all these duties and thus documents her participation in the common interest and so attains after a short period a central position in the area of farm production allotted to the female members.

Gerda Hahn's efforts in connection with the new farm unit must also be seen against the background of her own interests which were directed towards improving the cramped living accommodation available to the family at that time.

Uwe Hahn is also called upon early to take over a position of responsibility on the farm. This is mainly caused by his father beginning to suffer from the effects of long years of hard labor in and off the farm, and he, therefore, leaves most of the work outside in the fields to his son. Like his father, Uwe Hahn is integrated without question into the traditional succession to the management of the farm.

Before the construction of the new farm buildings, nine people lived in cramped living conditions. Gerda and Otto Hahn, for example, had to share a bedroom with their two children. The household was managed by Otto Hahn's grandmother. His own mother, Barbara Hahn, who was in poor health, had only a minor role. Gerda Hahn worked with her husband in the fields.

When the grandmother died, Gerda Hahn took over the position of woman in charge of the household, which she further secured by passing her examinations in agriculture.

As already indicated, from the beginning Gerda Hahn was interested in separating the core family from the rest of the farm household. After moving to the new farm complex outside the village, the situation regarding living accommodations improved greatly. The common household was kept for the present. After his marriage, Uwe Hahn with his wife and new-born daughter moved into the second house which had been built on the farm in the meantime, and which was intended as living quarters for the older couple in their retirement. His parents and grandparents remain in the two-story house and share a common household. It is here that the combined living-room kitchen is situated, which is the centre of family

life. Uwe and his family eat their midday meal here. This arrangement of the communal midday meal is Gerda Hahn's idea, who
considers it a necessary counterbalance to the separation of the core
family from the rest of the family household. As far as the organizational aspect of the family farm is concerned, the family midday
meal offers its members an opportunity to discuss and coordinate
work needing to be done and prospective plans. From the emotional
perspective it represents for Otto Hahn in particular a memory of
the traditional lifestyle before the construction of the new farm
complex. He appears to miss the warmth of this lifestyle while on
the other hand, for Gerda Hahn and her daughter this particular
quality of family farm life increasingly appears to be rather artificial
in character.

THE HAHN FAMILY IN RELATION TO TRADITION AND MODERNITY

In the introduction to this article the theory was advanced that on
the one hand the traditional model of orientation towards the farm
and its continuity can only be sustained by increased efforts to modernize and by an increasingly individual and flexible reaction to
social and economic trends, while on the other hand this reinforced
individualization undermines the attitudes which accept the interests of the farm as paramount, and thus endangers the unity of the
family-run farm.

The future of the Hahn family's farm appears to be secure in spite
of this because the individual parties succeed in maintaining simultaneously two opposing orientations:

On the one hand, the Hahn family has decided on a process of
strict modernization. Very early on, they decided to build a modern
farm complex, they mechanized, and in the course of outside work
they learned many extra skills which were of great benefit in the
effective management of the farm. By taking on this extra work
outside the farm they provided themselves with the means of fi-
nancing its further expansion. This process of differentiation in the
field of specialized knowledge for running the farm was paralleled
by an analogous development in the family sphere. The core family
emerged more strongly and there was a trend away from patriar-

chal-authoritarian forms of interaction to ones based on the principle of sharing between partners.

On the other hand, the traditional orientation towards the farm is
retained. The income gained from non-agricultural activities is
added to the farm capital and is not used for private consumption.
The work outside the farm does not give rise to the situation
whereby it develops into a work orientation so strong as to be in
direct competition with the interests of the farm. As a result, the
readiness on the part of its members to work without regard to personal health and safety and to refrain from personal consumption
ensures the future stability of the farm as a whole. The conditions of
interaction based on the principle of sharing between partners exist
not only between the married couples, but also between the older
and younger generations. This ensures that the next successor to the
farm undergoes from an early age the process of socialization which
teaches him to put the interests of the farm before all others. Even
though the core family gains a measure of independence, the common family interests are maintained and emphasized by such central
rituals as the common midday meal.

Thus the Hahn family manages to steer a course between two
orientations which necessarily conflict each other yet interact together. The fact that the continuity of the farm is not permanently
secure is not only due to any structural changes in agriculture on a
large scale, but also to specific family circumstances. Uwe has not
succeeded in integrating his wife as part of the labor force capable
of working the farm. As long as Gerda is able to work, this deficit
can be compensated. When Gerda can no longer cope with the work
burden, then one of the four elements mentioned at the beginning of
this article as constituting the essential structural differences between the urban and the rural family is no longer functional,
namely, that the farmer's choice of wife must be made not only
from the emotional aspect, but from the standpoint of the future
wife's ability to form part of the labor force necessary for running
the farm. On the other hand, since four generations live on the farm
due to early marriages, it is possible that when Gerda retires from
work, the loss of Sonja as part of the farm labor force can be compensated by skipping over a generation. For this to happen, it is
essential that Sonja's and Uwe's son is not only prepared to take

over management of the farm, but also to make an early marriage according to traditional patterns.

THE POSITION OF THE HAHN FAMILY
IN THE MODERNIZATION PROCESS:
A COMPARISON WITH OTHER FARMS

In our research project we compared different types of farms with each other. In addition to the Hahn family which runs a specialized farm considered average size in the Federal Republic, we also studied family farms carrying on the traditional mixed farming, a farm operating on organic-biodynamic principles, and a large tenant farm with an industrial pig production unit.

The comparative analysis of these family farms revealed several areas in which the conflict inherent in the modernization of production units, which are capable of modernization only to a limited degree, became particularly obvious. For example the families we studied differed from each other in the manner in which they had mastered the increased demands made by the need to modernize. The tenant family farm as well as the family that had decided to switch to organic-biodynamic farming organize their farms along commercial principles and act like innovative managers. This means that they orient their production to meet market requirements and are continually on the lookout for new markets. The other families, including the Hahns, yield to pressure to modernize only to the degree that this is necessary to secure the continuation of the farm. The orientation of these families is directed towards traditional patterns and roles.

Being a farmer in today's world means being obliged to coordinate two spheres which can only be combined with difficulty: on the one hand, there is the compulsion to modernize continually; and on the other hand, there is the recognition that there is a limit to the degree to which natural methods of agricultural production can be modernized.

The simple solution to this dilemma lies in dissolving the conflict by giving up farming altogether, or by deciding on radical industrialization of agricultural production. This step, however, is not in accord with society's interest in the preservation of the natural basis of life. Our research shows that the complex solution can be more easily put into effect on small and average-sized family farms such as that of the Hahn family. Due to their type of farm and family structure they are able to produce food on a natural basis and at the same time modernize their farms. The decisive factor in the continued existence of these farms will be whether government agricultural policy will be able to create the necessary framework to ensure this development.

CONCLUSION

This article deals with the position of the rural family in the process of rationalization taking place in society. It has been the contention of some researchers that agriculture is becoming increasingly absorbed into the industrial sector, and, parallel to this development, the rural family has progressively adjusted its lifestyle to match that of the urban family. Others have maintained, on the other hand, that the structural requirements of agriculture make the traditional elements essential.

With the aid of a case study of a family farm situated at the edge of a heavily populated industrialized region of West Germany, this article seeks to demonstrate that the farm is able to survive because its members succeed in continually modernizing it, on the one hand, and on the other because they succeed in maintaining traditional patterns of orientation, whereby the interests of the farm are paramount, in the face of general tendencies towards individualized behavior.

NOTE

1. This study of the Hahn family was made in the course of the project "Processes of reality construction in collective family history narrations" (Directors Dr. B. Hildenbrand and Prof. Dr. U. Oevermann) which was financed by the Deutsche Forschungsgemeinschaft (German Research Council). The data collection was undertaken by B. Hildenbrand and D. Thoma-Radler, and the data analysis carried out by H. Müller and R. Schmitt.

REFERENCES

Bergmann, T. Der bäuerliche Familienbetrieb—Problematik und Entwicklungstendenzen. In: Zeitschrift für Agrargeschichte und Agrarsoziologie 17, 215-230, 1969.

van Deene, B., Neuere Entwicklungen bäuerlichen Familienlebens. In: Sociologia Ruralis 11, 401-415, 1971.

Egner, E., Epochen im Wandel des Familienhaushalts. In: Seminar: Familie und Gesellschaftsstruktur. Heidi Rosenbaum (Hrsg.). Frankfurt am Main. Suhrkamp, 92-127, 1980.

Glaser, B. & Strauss, A. The Discovery of Grounded Theory—Strategies for Qualitative Research. Chicago Aldine, 1973.

Haushofer, H., Typen agrarischer Lebensformen. Studium Generale 11, 473-480, 1958.

Hildenbrand, B. Modernisierungsprozesse in der Landwirtschaft und ihre Bewältigung—Vergleich einer "normalen" mit einer "schizophrenen" Familie. In: Lüscher, K. et al. (Hrsg.) Die "postmoderne" Familie. Konstanz. Universitäts-Verlag, 297-311, 1988.

Hildenbrand, B. & Jahn, W. "Gemeinsames Erzhählen" und Prozesse der Wirklichkeitskonstruktion im familiengeschichtlichen Gespräch. In: Zeitschrift für Soziologie 17, 203-217, 1988.

Linde, H. Persönlichkeitsbildung in der Landfamilie. In: Soziale Welt 10, 297-309, 1959.

Lutz, B. Die Bauern und die Industrialisierung—Ein Beitrag zur Erklärung von Diskontinuitäten der Entwicklung industrieller Gesellschaften. In: Soziale Welt. Sonderband 4, 119-140, 1986.

Mendras, H. Sociologie du milieu rural. In: Gurvitch, G. (Hrsg.) Traité de Sociologie. Paris, PUF, 315-331, 1967.

Planck, U., Die Landwirtschaft in der Industriegesellschaft und die Industrialisierung der Landwirtschaft. In: Zeitschrift für Agrargeschichte und Agrarsoziologie 33, 56-77, 1985.

Strauss, A. Qualitative Analysis for Social Scientists. Cambridge. Cambridge University Press, 1987.

Schelsky, H. Wandlungen der deutschen Familie in der Gegenwart. Stuttgart. Enke, 1967.

Weber-Kellermann, I. Kontinuität der Familienstruktur? Zum Problem von Geschichtlichkeit und Dauer bei Primärgruppen. In: Kontinuitä t, Geschichtlichkeit und Dauer. Bausinger, H. & Brückner, W. (Hrgs.) Berlin. 143-153, 1969.

Weber-Kellermann, I. Die deutsche Familie—Versuch einer Sozialgeschichte. Frankfurt am Main. Suhrkamp, 1977.

Family and Home Ownership in Australia — The Nexus of Ideologies

Lyn Richards

INTRODUCTION

This paper is based on three contentions. Firstly, to understand family change, we must understand stability, the resilience of old structures and old ideas and their power to shape new families. Secondly, to understand the power of those ideas, we need research on the reshaping of traditional family ideology, not merely assumptions that it is fading or assertions that it remains dominant. And thirdly, to understand ideology, we need both quantitative and qualitative analysis.

Family sociology, committed to monitoring the ways ideas change, oddly has shown little curiosity in the ways ideas hang around, and less in how they hang together. It coexists awkwardly with a critical literature committed to exposing dominant family ideology, so showing little curiosity in empirical evidence about what people actually believe. Too often the stand-off has meant both sides are deprived of insights into processes of family change and non-change. The two approaches have in common only a tendency to assume that there is a traditional family ideology, and that we all know it when we meet it, and a tendency to avoid even defining the concept, let alone specifying the content of the ideology discussed.

Lyn Richards is Senior Lecturer in Sociology at La Trobe University, Melbourne. The project that this paper reports was funded by La Trobe University and the Australian Research Grants Committee.

The approaches are divided not only by theoretical assumptions, but also by methodology. Studies of family values rely normally on survey evidence. If it draws at all on evidence, critical writing on ideology tends to rely on unstructured data. Few studies combine methods, though the study of ideology, however it is defined, surely requires both quantitative data and the acceptance of ideas and qualitative analysis of their meanings and connections (Richards, 1987).

My own working definition, discussed elsewhere, is simple: ideologies are sets of ideas that hang together and hang around, influencing behavior (Richards, 1985a). The present paper reports some results of a five-year study of a new Australian suburb.[1] Quantitative data derived from several surveys and one reinterview of a sample of 160 of the first residents. Qualitative data included five years' participant observation records, unstructured interviews and transcripts of responses in surveys. Analysis was conducted with NUDIST, a concept-based computer package for rigorous exploration of unstructured data.[2]

THE SETTING

My context is the core of "normal" family life, in a heavily promoted, privately developed outer-suburb of Melbourne which I have called Green Views. Almost all of the smart new houses contain intact nuclear families, almost all owning or purchasing their homes. From the start of the project, their accounts made it clear that to study family life in that context required a study of home ownership. Examination of the meanings of home ownership in this setting will demonstrate that they are part of the package of dominating ideas identified in the critical literature as traditional family ideology. But the package is in constant flux, as individuals negotiate with those ideological demands.

Home ownership, like motherhood, had until recently an almost unspotted record as a Good Thing. Like motherhood, it has therefore been taken for granted and little researched, though both impose formidable requirements that impact at some stage on most of the population. They are, I will argue, strongly connected. Australia demonstrates the connection. Possessing one of the highest rates of home ownership of western countries, it has also proved one of the slowest to shift traditional family structures. It remains overwhelmingly a marrying society, and one in which family means nuclear family, childlessness is deviant and gender determines people's social places (Bryson, 1984; Richards, 1985). The increase in married women's workforce participation all but ceased in the mid-seventies; indeed it would have fallen had wives' part-time workforce participation not continued to increase (Richards, 1986). While the average age at marriage and duration of marriage prior to first birth have continued to rise in recent years, singlehood and childlessness have become options for only a small and probably economically favored segment of the society (McDonald, 1988).

So despite the messages of the women's movement, the "ideal nuclear family" seems amazingly resilient (Burns, 1988). In the critical literature, that resilience is explained by the dominance of powerful "ideology," and both motherhood and home ownership are described in those terms. But changes in these ideas and the links between them are little explored. Partly this is because the ideas in "ideologies" of both family and home are rarely specified, so ways in which the two sets support each other are little understood. Mainly it is because the idea of "ideology" is less often a research tool than a label for a critical approach, a sort of theoretical bumper sticker, establishing commitment to certain values, but not affecting the research vehicle, its performance or its destination.

PROPER PATHS TO PRIVATE PLACES: AN IDEOLOGY OF THE FAMILY?

Writings from the women's movement since the 60s have used the concept of ideology as it was designed by Marx to be wielded, a weapon for social struggle and an explanation of stuck societies (Barrett, 1980; Gittins, 1985; Burton, 1985). "Systematically ignored by a majority of 'family' scholars," family ideology has been "taken for granted by a minority" (Bernades, 1985, p. 275). But that minority succeeded in changing the sociological image of family from boring functional necessity to a "focal point of a set of ideologies that resonate throughout society" (Barrett & McIntosh, 1982, p. 29).

And lately the effects of ideology have been less taken for

granted, as research studies tackled the ways in which ideas hang together, masking the realities of social change. Australian studies have led in this area, drawing on interview data, documentary sources, policy statements and historical records. Recent work explores "ideologies" of motherhood (Wearing, 1988), of home and work (Game & Pringle, 1988), of domestic roles and workforce patterns (Bryson, 1984) and of family lives in different settings (Williams, 1983), the effects of such ideologies on those apparently outside them (Marshall, 1987) and on politics and policy (Baldock & Cass, 1984) and the processes by which dominant ideas emerged and were changed (Reiger, 1985).

The evidence is far from conclusive, and the argument uneven. Ignoring sticky questions of how ideology can be shown to exist, many assert that it does and illustrate it with data. Few ask what is to be done with survey evidence that indicates change and widespread rejection of just those ideas claimed to be dominant (Richards, 1984; Glezer, 1984). Almost all offer more understanding of women's than men's experience. The "thereness" of women in past sociology (Lofland, 1975) has been repaid by exclusion of men from much of this recent research (Lewis, 1984; Russell, 1988). But two themes strongly recur, echoing those in overseas literature. The first is that family life is dominated by thinking in terms of two "spheres"—the private world of home and the public world of work. The second is that there is a recognized proper path through adult life.

Private/public, family/work, hers/his: Dichotomous thinking dominates both popular and research pictures of family life. Sociology of the family started in a dualism, celebrating the stabilizing function of women's place in the private family home, and its necessary separation from the world of work and men (Parsons, 1942). Understanding of the origins of modern families was lit by work on the fusing of rural and domestic idylls in which women, home and community stood against the uncaring worlds of industrial work (Davidoff, 1976). The dichotomy of private and public has been used by feminist scholars as a lever for analysis of women's and men's different access to power, status and authority (Rosaldo, 1974; Gamarnikow, 1983). But it has also been attacked, as a myth obscuring the state's invasion of the home (Baldock and Cass,

1983), the interpenetration of family and work in women's lives (Rapp, 1982; Game & Pringle, 1988) and women's vulnerability in private "havens" (Scutt, 1983). Recent commentaries have suggested that complex changes in family lives and built environment are caricatured by equating private/family/hers with suburbia (Saegert, 1980; Harman, 1983).

Whether the world is in fact so divided, and whether the researcher is helped by looking at it that way, research studies show Australians do so. Ideas about women's and men's places, duties, opportunities and options are backed by the assumption that the private world of family is and should be segregated from that other hard world of work. However inappropriate to the patterns of social change, such two-worlds thinking is the background to family life, the way we interpret its demands. But always a changing background (Richards, 1986). The studies show sets of ideas that sound the same hanging together, ideas about gender, family roles, children's needs, but they are accepted unquestioningly by decreasing minorities (Glezer, 1984). They distinguish women's place from the man's world it is in, home from the outside world, unpaid from paid work, love from money. People call them "old" ideas, indicating debate with them. (Richards, 1986a) but their continued power is shown in evidence of guilt and stress for women who work "outside" (Wearing, 1983; Harper & Richards, 1986).

The Proper Paths to those private worlds are also challenged by increasing numbers, but for most Australians there is still a right order for going through family life stages. As most people still see it, marriage is natural and married people have children: marriage indeed *means* children (Richards, 1985; Wearing, 1983). The last decades have seen changes in timing of the steps into family life, for at least some Australians. But there has been little challenge to the *order* of taking those steps and a resurgence of the idea of "proper time" for family stages (MacDonald, 1983). Workforce participation for women is shaped by that proper path, statistically related to age of dependent offspring, across two decades of change in overall participation rates. People's accounts make it clear that good mothers stay home (Harper & Richards 1986). But patterns of both paid work and childbearing are also related to the major financial commitment of most couples buying the home.

THE GREAT AUSTRALIAN IDEOLOGY? —
HOME OWNERSHIP

"The Great Australian Dream" is to own your own home. The observation is commonplace, but few studies have asked why, and fewer have examined just how widespread or uniform is that dream. For most the only evidence is the indisputable fact that an until recently ever-increasing majority of Australian adults were attempting home ownership. Owner occupancy (owner or purchaser) rose to over 70% in the mid-sixties, and still accounted for 68% of households at the 1981 census.

This then is the obvious ideology and critics have drawn the obvious conclusion. "The Great Australian Dream is almost universally held" (Kemeny, 1983, p. 1). But is it? And what is it? Most discussions concentrate on its advantages for capitalism, and its political support (Bell, 1977). Critics have explored the effects of the Dream on the increasing numbers for whom it is out of reach (Cass & Radi, 1983; Burke et al., 1984) and have argued that for Australian housewives it offered a nightmare (Game & Pringle, 1984).

But regularities of behaviour are not evidence of the dominance of ideology however that highly elusive concept is used. We need to know a lot more about why the home is so important, before we can assume home ownership rates indicate ideology rather than merely the absence of alternatives. Few studies have pursued the dream into people's accounts. Yet it is clearly related to the two clusters of family ideas summarized above. The home epitomizes the private world. Australian family reformers emphasized home as "a place of rest and refreshment from the cares of the world" (Reiger, 1985, p. 37). Is that still the dream? And home ownership places people on the proper "ladder of life" (Perin, 1977). In the postwar years the home became symbol of normal family life. "Australia is the small house. Ownership of one in a fenced allotment is as inevitable and unquestionable a goal of the average Australian as marriage" (Boyd, 1968, preface). While family researchers have rarely noticed this theme, people they quote do. "We were both ready to have a child by then. We had the house." (Harper & Richards, 1986, p. 71).

At first glance, surveys of meanings of home offer little evidence of dominant ideology. Rosow (1949), tidied answers into precoded categories, and found his sample of upper-income Americans averaged 4.5 reasons for ownership each. And there are differences within societies by class (Ineichen, 1972). But the very few studies examining people's words show individuals' values are complex, impossible to summarize in lists of categories, and much less practical than they at first look. Rosow found financial reasons "less significant than commonly supposed." Almost half of the reasons were "emotional" (including family).

Decades later, Rakoff reported that while the "obvious" meaning in unstructured interviews was investment, behind this came a tangle of other answers. He concluded that the "multivocality of the house as a symbol reflects the ambiguous meanings Americans attach to the private sphere" (1977, p. 86). A decade, an ocean and a class world away, Holme (1985, p. 69) found two-thirds of her young, British, workingclass respondents gave "financial reasons," but these included "we wanted to get on the house-purchase ladder" (1985, p. 70). And answers were dominated by a sense of the "naturalness" of homeownership (p. 145).

Another ocean away, many of these themes, even the words, recur in Green Views. Reasons for owning look practical. But explored as ideology, all prove to be linked with ideas of family life.

WHY DO YOU WANT TO OWN YOUR OWN HOME?

The purchase of the home was both the overwhelming reason for coming to Green Views and the common link felt with other residents (cf. Gans, 1967). Almost everyone took for granted the necessity for home ownership. Only a fifth of those interviewed had ever even considered not owning, and in most cases it had been considered only as a temporary expedient. Very commonly, they "explained" wanting to own by the fact that they had always wanted to own. "It's our life. It's something that we've always wanted." "It means everything really." They assumed it was a goal for everyone.

> *M*. I think, when we were buying our house, Australians, per head of population, were the greatest homeowners in the world. I think they still could be. So, it's sort of a thing that's born into you . . . I've never come across anybody yet, whether they own a house or don't, that don't want one.

Perhaps the clearest indication of the dominance of background ideas is their being taken for granted (Richards, 1987). "Why do you want to own your own home?" proved an awkward question. It was often answered, like "Why did you get married?" (Richards, 1985a) with, "Everyone does." The words indicated that the need to own a home was taken for granted, all-important and tied to the needs of family.

> *M*. I think it's the biggest step to marriage. That's the biggest step, and your second biggest is usually buying a home. It means everything.

But that nexus of ideas of family and home is not simple. Statistically, our responses say little about family. Green Views residents, like those in other countries, give "hard," practical reasons for owning their homes. Coding up to three responses for each of 160 women and men, we collected 305 answers, of which a third were coded "financial investment/security." Another 18% were in terms of "security of tenure." The other down-to-earth replies, "can do what you want with it," and "owning something/possession" accounted for 24%. So replies explicitly and only about social life and identity were a tiny proportion. "Achievement" and "status" together rated a mere 7%, and the "soft" answers of "privacy" and "stability" only 17%.

Analysis of what people said, however, gives a different picture. Here I will look at three of the keywords: security, control and privacy.

"Security"

This is the off-the-hook answer to "Why own your own home?" The only one-word answer commonly given, it was used in a majority of responses, but rarely explained. Interviewers often had to probe for followup comments to establish even whether this was financial security or security of tenure. A lot of answers were about both, some about neither; "security" has many meanings, so frequently combined it is very hard to extract patterns. But most were about proper paths.

Most obvious is financial security. It has at least three faces in these accounts. Each has its keywords — rent as "wasted money," "security for the future" and "building up." The most common is the first, but it is usually combined with the other two. And those two often turn out to be as much about family and a *family* future, further down the path, as about money. It is a straight path, to "permanence" and stability. "Security. It's sort of our aim from marriage to get a house and then have our family." A retired man recalled his setting out on the proper path to adult life.

> *M*. Owning your own home, in my opinion, was a fundamental thing when I was 16 years of age. And my parents taught that to me. My first thing in life was to buy a home, and then everything came after that.

There was obvious excitement for many in "starting from the beginning with nothing, and moving up to what we've got now." There was also massive confidence, a conviction that once you have the deposit, you are sure of becoming "established."

> *W*. We wanted something that would be our own eventually. And I think the only way we felt we could achieve that was to buy a home and to actually get in and get started on owning something.

> *M*. Security. If I own my own home, if there's payments hanging over my head, I know if anything happened, no one could take the house off me. And therefore my family will always have somewhere to live.

No one could take it? The confidence is amazing, in a setting where mortgagee auctions are quite commonplace. But no one mentioned in this context the insecurity in having "payments hanging over" their heads, though almost all had mortgages.

There was also no comment on the vulnerability of family goals to mortgages. A picture of the homeowner's progress comes firmly through—there is a normal path, from "nothing," through sheets on the window, (when drapes cannot be afforded), to becoming "established." It is ridden, naturally, on two incomes. Those who get the timing wrong pay for their error: these accounts celebrate the contribution of home ownership to the delaying of first birth.

> *W.* If you get married and start to have a family immediately it is virtually impossible to save the deposit for a house. So these families that actually have got the deposit on their house, even if the repayments are pretty steep and they're having a terrible struggle, they've still got their foot in the door of their own block of land and their own house.

It is important not to underestimate the "hard" money reasons for owning. Finance almost always came first, as though it was more acceptable (or more easily explicable?). For some it was the only real reason available. Like Australians generally (Burke et al., 1984, p. 58), these people believed the best thing to do with your money was save towards a home. But when people said their reasons were "purely financial," other factors always slipped in at the end. A childless teacher responded quickly:

> *W.* We wanted something that would be our own eventually. And I think the only way we felt we could achieve that was to buy a home and to actually get in and get started on owning something . . . we wanted financial security.

But even as she thought about it, her answer became blurred:

> *W.* We had never earned a wage before, we hadn't had much money, yes, so it was definitely a financial security thing. Plus we felt that if we were going to have children ever . . . you definitely could never have children in a flat.

Later, she added other reasons, "In my friendship group and my family group, the pressures that I'm getting from other people are, yes, it is good to own your own home and there is something unstable, perhaps, about renting."

Control

Control had at least two meanings, each with its keywords. The most common is negative: no one can "put you out." The second is more positive: you can "do what you want" to your own house. Both, in turn, are obviously about independence from a landlord. But both drew in other themes about the private world, but a particular sort of privacy.

Being "put out" of a rented house (like a dog!) was widely dreaded, and the risks exaggerated. The certainty of "they can't take it away" if you own it is matched by the conviction that "they" can throw you out if you don't. But then these statements, too, are linked with other meanings.

> *M.* A rental agent can put you out of the house when the owners say you've got to get out. If you're in your own home, it depends on you keeping up the payments on whether you stay. I think when you own your own home it's just a basic security. You got your garden—it's just your own piece of Australia, your own piece of the land . . . I feel as if this is my base to go from.

Some shifted from security to "being able to do what you want with it." Keywords again—several phrases stand for freedom from interference. One woman remarked, "Put a nail in the wall, people always say." Not always: we had only four other comments about nails in walls, but forty about other ways of "doing what you want with it." They include having wild parties (2 comments) and being able to repulse neighbours (one comment only in this context, but a recurring theme in others). Most had rented, and had felt niggling constraint.

> *W.* It's not permanent when you're renting . . . You can get kicked out the next week if they feel like it. And you can't do anything. You put a bit of paint on the wall and they'll have a fit.

Control was about adulthood, the home seen as the only place you can express yourself, by "getting it the way you want it" and "making it yours."

> *W.* You can build your own identity, and not have the feeling that you actually belong to somebody else. You start from new and it's your own and nobody has ever lived in it before.

"You" or "we" in these statements always refers to the couple. That children are not mentioned is partly of course because they are seen as neither participating in nor having preferences about "doing it up." But they do not even feature as occupants in these discussions. The house is never portrayed as part of their identity, but literally, it is part of the adults'. "If you are renting," a woman said, "it's not part of you." Children were a strong theme though in the need for stability. One man explained, "I like to have the feeling that I know that something's mine. Especially with a family too, I think."

This is more than just security of tenure. Ten people compared owning with a married life begun in parents' homes (in two cases a caravan at parents'). Others linked it with responsibility and self-sufficiency, all requirements for married life. The significance of the home is infused in many accounts with the significance of transition to adult status. Buying it, for one woman at marriage, was "the start of my own life . . . It's my house. I don't have to answer to anybody." There is a strong message in many of these statements that the home is a necessary part of becoming an independent marital couple, and a necessary condition for having children. No other pathway into family had been considered.

> *M.* Buying me first home, basically it was sort of a new start to life . . . It's mine — no one can take it away . . . security for the future. It's just yours, and you can do whatever you want, without anyone always bugging you.

Like having families, it was "natural," a term that recurs, and families, like the house, are built up from foundations.

M. This is our first home. Our first sort of building up of something together in our marriage. We came in here with four bare walls and not much money and all the rest, like most people, and slowly built it up. It means a lot to us. It's not a house, it's a home. I feel proud, I suppose.

The home for many was a necessary condition for even thinking about family futures — like throwing a six to start the game (Richards, 1980). A young man explained that, "We're self-sufficient." Before they had lived in a caravan at his parents'. "It's helped us PLAN. We tend to plan things now." He summarized, "Security in one respect. To know you've got a proper place to come home to." And owning the home commanded respect. Those failing to follow the proper path were condemned.

W. Couples that get married and just never sort of knuckle down or bother to think, well, we'll buy our own home, well I haven't got much time for them . . . I just think you've got your head screwed on if you get your own home for your children and for yourself . . . I think if you say to someone, we've been able to save . . . I think people do respect you more.

Ownership was not only a metaphor for safety and citizenship, as for Perin's respondents, but also a metaphor for proper family life.

W. Oh yeah, there's a big stigma about renting. Especially around here, where people do OWN them . . . You never come across anybody who actually admits to just renting as a permanent structure. It's always, "Just for the moment, until we can get enough money," or whatever. But people tend to look down on the ones who haven't been able to save up enough for their deposit. And "Fancy getting married and having kids if you don't have your own house!"

Thus this version of the private world links privacy to independence, control, security, "being settled down," "permanence." Not one statement contained regret for the settling, though most had enjoyed the experience of married life in a flat without children. It was, as one woman said, "a natural progression from one thing to another.'' And not one suggested privacy had problems. The child-less teacher again:

> *W.* You live a kind of transient life, I think, when you're a renter. It's definitely an in-out job. You're never home . . . Whereas this is a more, I suppose, settled way of life and more solid way of life because it's your home and it's a different way of looking at things altogether . . . We tend to stay in the home more than we would have in our flat. We're quite happy to stay home in the afternoon, and just enjoy being here . . . It was something we really looked forward to, to having our home and sort of building a future . . . something that we can really work on, something that we can put a lot of ourselves into and get some return out of . . . You know, this is going to be yours, this is going to be ours.

What did she see as the difference between a renter and a home-owner? "Stay-at-homeness, I think . . ." Stay-at-homeness in these accounts was linked to family unity. "We want to be a family, and a good foundation is owning your own home," a young father said. An older man had missed the proper path in early life stages. "Sta-bility, it just basically comes down to stability. It's something that everybody shares in the whole family, sharing."

This is a very specific private world, certainly a container for family, but hardly an idyll of community life. To explore the impli-cations of home ownership in the growth of what Marx and Engels called "the personal life" (Agnew, 1981) is beyond my present scope. But it is important to stress that while many of these com-ments sound casual, they clearly establish the enormous signifi-cance of owning a home.

> *W.* It was when I got married, so it was the start of my own life.
>
> *I.* What does this house mean to you?
>
> *W.* Everything. If I didn't have it, I think I'd just give up really . . . It's my house. I don't have to answer to anybody.

Home and Haven

> *W*. We always wanted a home of our own . . . I wouldn't like to live in a flat. We lived with my husband's parents for two and a half years. I don't know — I want to do things my way in my house. The privacy, the responsibility — setting out there and doing things for ourselves.

In much of the material above has appeared the theme of family isolation that has dominated feminist criticism of suburbia (Allport, 1984). The strongest theme here is "together" — couples "building it up" together, families living in it in togetherness.

> *I*. How do you feel when you walk in the door?

> *M*. It's good to be home. It's ours. It's our home. I've put a lot of work into it — a lot of work we've put in together. And it means a lot to us.

Privacy here is highly complicated, but much more often about achievement of independence than peaceful haven. The private home is seen as unifying couples, marking the start of life together.

> *W*. We're doing things together now. It's ours, so we can do things . . . Freedom, I think, more than anything. If you had to rent a house, it wasn't ours. And here we can come and go as we please and I don't have to worry about committing myself to anyone. It's ours. It's our home. You don't have to worry about anything.

You also don't have to go out of it. What the teacher called "stay-at-homeness" occurred in several eulogies of suburban life. A recent immigrant compared life (with children) before owning.

> *M*. Because you've got a bit of land, a house built on top and you want to do something, you want to do the garden, the back garden, add this one, put this, put that, so you're more interested in what you've got. Before, you rent, you're only interested in getting home, having dinner, watch T.V. Saturday and Sunday, get the car out. You don't have that interest in

getting home, "I have to do this and I have to plant that tree"; not that we have to, we like, we like to do things in the house.

The home in this sense for some literally means a family life; without it, there is no place of peace to hold family together. Privacy is necessary for togetherness, and it is privacy *from* the hard world of work, at least for men, but that's another story. Work, in turn, is *for* the home, *for* the family. When people describe the home in terms of family haven, it always is juxtaposed to the work world, and justifies the work it requires. A Greek-born mother of school-age children thought it "important for everybody to be able to buy their home." I asked why.

W. It means so much, I think. It means a family life. You get so much. I mean, whatever we do, it's for our children as well. It's not just for me and Ron. I mean, we're a family. So everything we do, our home is important.

I. And you'd feel you couldn't do that if you were renting?

W. Oh yes. It's not the same. Although you'd be clean in a rented home and dry, it's not the same. You don't take the same pride that you do in your own, because it's yours . . . You take pleasure in knowing your garden's nice, and in the summer you can sit out and enjoy your home. And you don't really have to go away from home because you have that many things here now.

IT MEANS WHICH FAMILY LIFE?
THE NEXUS OF IDEOLOGIES

The present discussion has only touched on many crucial complexities. In particular, there are no meanings of the home that are the same for women and men; analysis of those gender patterns, and the implications for the debate on women in suburbia, are tackled elsewhere (Richards, forthcoming). But for women and men the threads of ideologies of family and home are tangled. The few accounts of the home that did not use language of family never excluded it. Several people said flatly "It's not an investment to me" — but nobody said "It's not necessary for family."

Very many people volunteered, on the other hand, that the home was necessary, both for getting on the ladder of family life, and also for having children. "For them to grow up in" was a reason for owning, as was simply "it's good for the kids." One father commented that if you didn't own your home, "obviously they wouldn't have a backyard to play in and something they could call their own." The obvious was explored with prompting: were these prerequisites for having the children?

> *M*. I wouldn't call them prerequisites. I think they're an important part of family life. An important part of family life, I believe, IS owning your own home, having somewhere to bring your kids up, some place that's safe for them. It gives them a good family environment.

Family life does not seem to be defined in terms of the home; rather, the link is taken for granted. When asked, later in the interview, to tell us their idea of "a good family life," only five even mentioned the home, and only one ownership.

"Just to have some kids in your house and settle down," he said. Yes, that meant owning it. "I think you've got to have your own house. It's something that's yours and something for your kids." The other definitions of good family life that mentioned home made it just part of the furniture of family. "As long as you're happy and content within your home," one man said. For another, a good family life was "the one I've got. Job, house, home, financial security" as though the package deal was obvious. An older man specified, "Comfortable home, healthy kids, relax and forget work." You couldn't have that, he added, in a flat. Only one woman included "home" in her definition of a good family life, "Same as anyone else's, I suppose. Just to be happy in the home." Some people recited the steps as though no alternative path was possible.

> *M*. Sort of filling the goal that we had when we first got married, waiting five years, saving for a home and achieving that goal, and starting a family.

The proper path is to provide the private place prior to "starting" a family. To fail to provide it was for most people undesirable, for many unthinkable. So an apparent contradiction is built into the nexus of the ideologies. The woman will quite normally be in the workforce in order to achieve the home. The home will quite normally be empty of the family it is necessary for.

It is beyond the scope of the present paper to explore how people negotiate ways out of that contradiction, but important to stress that many do. For some, that contradiction is real and painful: when the "old" ideas of family are firmly held. Like all of the families selling up because the mortgages had proved too much, this couple will buy again as soon as they can afford it. For now her constant worry is childcare.

> *W.* When they were young and that, though, I used to pay for them, but then it got up to $20, each, I worked for them to be looked after . . . Now they just have to stay home, and boy it's awful, I'm just a nervous wreck while it is happening, I hate them being at home. I don't like them having no one to look after them, it really worries me the whole time. But . . . we couldn't live if I gave up the job, you know. And I've always been one that's never permitted the kids to go home from school on their own or anything. . . . I do it now and I don't believe that children should be allowed to do that sort of thing . . . It's really bad for the children, I think, really bad but I just can't do anything about it now, this house is too heavy, this load is too much.

In Green Views, family values retain major elements of traditional family ideology. Women's place is in the home, the family is her priority and her time theirs (Richards, 1987). But its goals are time together, and working together to attain the home. There is little said about the attainment of the peaceful idyll of family and community which the suburban dream encapsulated. Family ideology is reworked in the processes of disentangling its demands, a process in which changing networks is both a strategy and a result. The ideology of home ownership is part of those demands. Listen to people's accounts, and it is obvious that the two sets of ideas interlock, reinforce and support each other — the self-evident truth of one making the truth of the other self-evident. Together they offer a massive and seemingly impenetrable version of the pathways into family life and the private world it promises. Together they ensure that in an estate sold as a "family community" one of the most common phrases is "nobody's home."

To understand the family lives that result is essential to understand their ideological context. This paper has argued for a theory of ideology that stresses the active ways individuals negotiate with dominant ideas, and a methodological approach that combines study of how widely they are accepted with exploration of what they mean to people.

NOTES

1. The avoidance of the stronger concept of "dominant" ideology is deliberate: the importance of studying the active relation of individuals to ideology is central in the forthcoming report of this project, Lyn Richards, *Nobody's Home*, Oxford University Press.

2. Qualitative data analysis used NUDIST, a computer system designed for non-numerical unstructured data indexing, searching and theorizing. See Richards and Richards, 1987.

3. All respondents quoted were married residents of Green Views. Quotations are identified by M.(man) and W.(woman). The interview sections reported here were precoded and taped.

REFERENCES

Allport, C. The Princess in the Castle: Women in the New Social Order Housing. In Women and Labour Publications Collective, *All Her Labours: Embroidering the Framework*. Sydney: Hale and Iremonger, 1984.

Ardener, S. Ground Rules and Social Maps for Women. In S. Ardener ed., *Women and Space*, London: Croom Helm, 1981.

Baldock, C. & Cass, B. (Eds.) *Women, Social Welfare and the State*. Sydney: Allen & Unwin, 1983.

Barrett, M. *Women's Oppression Today*. London: Verso, 1980.

Barrett, M. & McIntosh, M. *The Anti-Social Family*. London: Verso, 1982.

Bernades, J. "Family Ideology": Identification and Exploration. *Sociological Review, 33*, 275-294, 1985.

Boyd, R. *The Australian Ugliness*. Melbourne: Penguin, 1968.

Burton, C. *Subordination*. Sydney: Allen & Unwin, 1985.

Bryson, L. The Australian Patriarchal Family. In L. Bryson & S. Encel (Eds.) *Australian Society* (4th ed.) Melbourne: Cheshire, 1984.

Burke, T., Hancock, L. & Newton, P. *A Roof Over Their Heads: Housing Issues and Families in Australia*. Melbourne: Institute of Family Studies, 1984.

Burns, A. Why Do Women Continue to Marry? In Grieve, N. and Burns, A. (Eds.) *Australian Women: New Feminist Perspectives*. Melbourne: Oxford University Press, 1986.

Cass, B., & Radi, H. Family, Fertility and the Labour Market. In Grieve, N. & Grimshaw, P. (Eds.) *Australian Women: Feminist Perspectives*. Melbourne: O.U.P. Duncan, J. (Ed.) *Housing and Identity*. London: Croom Helm, 1981.

Davidoff, L., Esperence, J. and Newby, H. Landscape with Figures: Home and Community in English Society. In J. Mitchell and A. Oakley (Eds.) *The Rights and Wrongs of Women*, Harmondsworth: Penguin, 139-75, 1976.

Gamarnikow, E. et al. (Eds.) *The Public and the Private*. London: Heinemann, 1983.

Game, A., & Pringle, R. The Making of the Australian Family. In Burns, A. et al. (Eds.) *The Family in the Modern World*. Sydney: Allen & Unwin, 1984.

Gans, H. *The Levittowners*. N.Y.: Vintage Books, 1967.

Glezer, H. Antecedents and Correlates of Marriage and Family Attitudes in Young Australian Men and Women. *XXth International CFR Seminar on Social Change and Family Policies*. Melbourne: Institute of Family Studies, 1984.

Harman, E.J. 'Capitalism, Patriarchy and the City,' Ch 5 in C.V. Baldock and B. Cass (Eds.) *Women, Social Welfare and the State*, Sydney: Allen & Unwin, 1983.

Harper, J. & Richards, L. (revised ed.) *Mothers and Working Mothers*. Melbourne: Penguin, 1986.

Holmes, A. *Housing and Young Families in East London*. London: Routledge & Kegan Paul, 1985.

Ineichen, B. Home Ownership and Manual Workers' Lifestyles. *Sociological Review*, 20, 391-412, 1972.

Kemeny, J. *The Great Australian Nightmare*. Melbourne: Georgian House, 1983.

Lewis, R. Some Changes in Men's Values, Meanings, Roles and Attitudes toward Marriage and the Family in the USA. In *XXth International CFR Seminar on Social Change and Family Policies*, 1984.

Lofland, L. The "Thereness" a of Women: A Selective Review of Urban Sociology. In Millman, M. & Kanter, R.M. (Eds.) *Another Voice*. N.Y.: Anchor Books, 1975.

MacDonald, P. The Baby Boom Generation as Reproducers. *Australian Family Research Conference*. Melbourne: Institute of Family Studies, 1983.

Marshall, H. Not Having Families: A Study of Some Voluntarily Childless Couples. Unpubl. PhD. thesis, La Trobe University, 1986.

McDonald, P. Families in the Future. *Family Matters*, 22, 40-45, 1988.

Parsons, T. Age and Sex in the Social Structure of the United States. *American Sociological Review*, 7, 604-16, 1942.

Perin, C. *Everything in Its Place: Social Order and Land Use in America*. N.J.: Princeton, 1977.

Rakoff, R.M. Ideology in Everyday Life: The Meaning of the House. *Politics and Society*, 7, 85-104, 1977.

Rapp, R. Family and Class in Contemporary America: Notes towards an Understanding of Ideology. *Science and Society*, *42*, 1980.

Reiger, K. *The Disenchantment of the Home*. Melbourne: O.U.P. 1985.

Richards, L. The impossible dream. In D. Davis (Ed.) *Living Together*. Canberra: Centre for Continuing Education, 1980.

Richards, L. Mothers. *Australian Society*, *3*, 40-41, 1984.

Richards, L. *Having Families*. (revised ed.) Melbourne: Penguin, 1985a.

Richards, L. Australian Family Studies. *Contemporary Sociology*, *14*, 1985b.

Richards, L. No Man's Land: Introduction to the revised edition, J. Harper and L. Richards, *Mothers and Working Mothers*, Melbourne: Penguin, 1986.

Richards, L. Ideology at Home? Family and Home Ownership in the Australian Context. Paper to the National Council on Family Relations, Atlanta, 1987.

Richards, L. (forthcoming) *Nobody's Home*. Melbourne: O.U.P.

Richards, L. & Richards, T. Qualitative Data Analysis: Can Computers Do It? *Australian and New Zealand Journal of Sociology*, *23*, 23-25, 1987.

Rosaldo, M. & Lamphere, L. (Eds.) *Women, Culture and Society*. Stanford: Stanford University Press.

Rosow, I. Home Ownership Motives. *American Sociological Review*, *13*, 751-6, 1949.

Russell, G. *The Changing Role of Fathers?* St. Lucia: Univ. of Qld. Press, 1983.

Saegert, S. Masculine Cities and Feminine Suburbs. *Signs*, *5*, s96-s111, 1980.

Scutt, J. *Even in the Best of Homes: Violence in the Family*. Melbourne: Allen & Unwin, 1983.

Seeley, J. R. et al. *Crestwood Heights*. Toronto: University of Toronto Press, 1956.

Wearing, B. *The Ideology of Motherhood*. Sydney: Allen & Unwin, 1983.

Williams, C. *Open Cut*. Sydney: Allen & Unwin, 1983.

Young, M. and Wilmott, P. *Family and Kinship in East London*, London: Penguin, 1962.

Strain and Enrichment in the Role of Employed Mothers in Israel

Ruth Katz

SUMMARY. This paper analyzed some central elements in the dual role behavior of Israeli employed mothers. Two approaches can be distinguished in the study of working mothers specifically, and multiple role sets in general. The role-strain approach maintains that the two sub-roles compete for scarce resources, thus impairing their performance and adversely affecting the role occupant and her contribution to society. The enrichment approach emphasizes the reciprocal complementarity of the sub-roles and, as a result, the advantages which may compensate for the strain. Some of the skills and assets acquired in one aspect of a dual role are likely to help the role occupant improve their performance and ward off burnout.

The balance between strain and enrichment characterizing the Israeli working mother was examined, and the conditions under which strain diminishes while enrichment increases were identified. A representative sample of 1,500 married couples were interviewed by means of a structured questionnaire. The main findings are:

— The average burden, measured in hours, carried by the working mother is larger than the comparable burden on married fathers or on homemakers.
— Decreasing the number of children reduces the gap between self image at work and the one at home, whereas a decrease in the hours of paid employment reduces the sense of burnout.
— Mothers who are rich in resources, schooling, income, and occupational prestige, tend to moderate the role-strain by reducing their tasks: the number of children and the amount of work hours.
— Mothers who are rich in resources are able to recruit hired help

---

Ruth Katz is Professor in the Department of Sociology and Anthropology, and School of Social Work, The Center for Research and Study of the Family, University of Haifa, Mt. Carmel, Haifa, Israel.

195

to ease the burden involved in the dual role, but they do not manage to enlist greater help from their husbands.
— Mothers who are rich in resources succeed in maintaining work continuity more than do mothers having limited resources.
— Mothers who are rich in resources tend to perceive their work as contributing to their children's education.

The findings indicate that the dual role encompasses elements of strain, internal competition for scarce resources as well as elements of enrichment. The general ramifications of these findings pertaining to the employment of women and to sexual equality are discussed.

This paper analyzes some central elements in the behavior of Israeli employed mothers in the light of role theory. The essence of the growth in maternal employment is the merger of two role-sets, which used to be clearly differentiated; and the corpus of research on this subject appears as a continuing examination of the extent to which the linking of the two role-sets has succeeded. Two general approaches — the "pessimistic" and the "optimistic" — can be distinguished.

The first approach, known as "the scarcity approach," was developed by Goode (1960), Moore (1960), and Slater (1963). The dual role is described as a situation in which several tasks compete for scarce resources. As a result strain is generated, which expresses itself in a reduction, both quantitative and qualitative, of the role's outputs, in the depletion of resources-reserves, and the attendant attrition of the role occupant. Roles may differ in regard to the resources required for their performance. However, two basic resources, time and energy, are required in one degree or another for the performance of any role; and these two resources are rigidly limited for all role performers alike. One role performer might be more liberally supplied than another, with requisite instruments, accessories or knowledge. Nonetheless, he or she has no more than the daily round of hours and a bounded quota of energy. The "scarcity approach" predicts negative consequences that express themselves in a decline in the quality of the marriage of the employed mother, in the maladjustment of her children, in physical and emotional fatigue, and finally, in the likelihood of withdrawing from the dual role by quitting work, transferring to part-time work, or even by dissolving the marriage.

The "optimistic" approach does not deny the existence of tensions resulting from the dual role, but rather emphasizes the advantages that are likely to compensate for these tensions: the dual role enriches the individual with additional resources, and some of the skills, connections, and material possessions acquired in one role sustain the other role: i.e., they help the dual role occupant to improve his or her performance and/or to maintain a given level of achievements with less effort and strain. This process of reciprocal enhancement between the different roles of a single person which was designated as "role accumulation" by Sieber (1974), and as "role expansion" by Marks (1977) is applicable to the analysis of various situations in the life of a working mother. For example, the mother-teacher is likely to draw on her professional skill when educating her children, and on her experience as a mother when teaching. Also, the employed wife is able to make use of her income to acquire household implements or to hire help in order to save time and conserve energy that would otherwise be invested in her homemaker role. As the woman's possession of education and income resources increases, so does her participation in making the decisions which determine the character of the family (Bahr, 1974; Blood and Wolfe, 1960; Katz and Peres, 1985; Lupri, 1969; McDonald, 1980; Scanzoni, 1979). It is reasonable to assume that the working mother can utilize her acquired intra-family authority to mobilize assistance from other family members, thereby lessening role-strain and attrition.

Both approaches have received some empirical corroboration though the first approach has been the focus of more research effort and consequently more empirical support. There are two conflicts facing employed mothers: (1) Strain resulting from coinciding time demands of work and family. In addition to her occupational tasks the employed mother usually does most of the housework and is thus overburdened (Bryson, Bryson, Licht and Licht, 1976; Epstein, 1971; Fox and Nickols, 1983; Herman and Gyllstrom, 1977; Rapoport and Rapoport, 1971; 1976; Walker and Woods, 1976), and (2) Strain stemming from conflicting norms or values. The occupational and familial spheres reinforce incompatible behavior patterns. Contemporary culture emphasizes individual growth and fulfillment on the one hand, and family values on the other (Heckman, Bryson and Bryson, 1977; Gordon and Hall, 1974; Hunt and Hunt, 1977; Pleck, 1977).

Nevertheless, a significant number of studies report on women who cope successfully with their multiple roles. This success stems, at least in part from strategies adopted by employed mothers (Elman and Gilbert, 1984; Vanek, 1974; Voydanoff and Kelly, 1984). It has been found that being employed contributes to the material (Rainwater, 1979), as well as to the physical health (Verbrugge, 1983) and to the psychological well-being of mothers (Marcus and Doron, 1985). Thoits (1983; 1986) uses a wider range of role-identities (spouse, parent, employee, group member etc.) as explanatory factors instead of comparing employed with unemployed mother. She reports that possession of multiple role-identities does significantly reduce distress. Lieblich (1986) notes that career women aged 35-57 report less "mid-life crisis" symptoms than that generally indicated in the literature for this age group. She suggests that maternal employment makes it possible to integrate both the masculine and feminine modes of the personality, and that this enables women to meet successfully the challenges of their aging (ibid., 265). Orthner and Axelson (1980) report that married women who were employed full-time and enjoyed high professional status achieved closer companionship with their spouses than did those women employed only part-time.

A general conclusion that can be drawn from theoretical considerations and empirical findings is that in most dual roles, elements of competition and strain coexist with aspects of enhancement and enrichment. The balance between these opposing elements needs to be examined empirically in each relevant situation. Assessment of the balance between strain and enrichment in the role of the employed mother in Israel necessitates some remarks on the overall framework in which this role functions. In contrast to the situation in other industrialized countries, marriage and motherhood are still nearly universal roles in Israel today. Among women aged 40-44, only 2% are not married at present or were never married in the past (Statistical Abstract of Israel, 1984, Table 19b); and only 2.5% of women reach this age and remain childless (Population and Housing Census, 1985). Hence, remaining single as an alternative life style is extremely rare in Israel.

Since the 1950s the entry of women into the Israeli work force has increased markedly, from 22% in 1954 to 40% in the 1980s. In recent years more women than men joined the work force: between 1980-84 there was an increase of 14% of women in the work force and only 7% for men (Working Women in Israel, 1981 and 1984, The Central Bureau of Statistics and the Ministry of Labour and Social Affairs). Two factors, which developed simultaneously in Israel, are related to the growth in maternal employment: higher education and a decrease in fertility. Between 1961 and 1981 the percentage of women completing high school increased from 33% to 47% and the percentage of women who studied at institutions of higher learning went up from 8% to 21%. Since the 1950s the fertility rate of women of Afro-Asian origin dropped by 50% from an average of approximately six children to about three children in 1984 (Statistical Abstract of Israel 1984, Table 14c).

In the context of the demographic and social changes that took place, an attempt will be made to assess the particular balance between strain and enrichment in the role-set of the Israeli employed mother. This balance is probably subject to changes not only over time but also across different groups in the populations. The question to be addressed is: Under what circumstances does role-strain increase in the life of a working mother and in what situations are the negative results outweighed by enrichment and complementary role enhancement? Two principal hypotheses are examined:

I. Role-strain increases as the scope of tasks increases. When the burden of tasks is great, there is high role-strain. And, conversely, a decrease in role-strain follows a lessening in the scope of tasks.

II. Resources at the disposal of the role occupant, i.e., schooling, income and occupational prestige, contribute to the ability to cope with the dual role. From this, the following secondary hypotheses are derived.

IIa. Resources at the disposal of the employed mother enable her to reduce her role-obligations;

IIb. Make it possible to mobilize additional laborpower for household tasks and care for the children;

IIc. Enable her to achieve more continuity in the fulfillment of the occupational role;

IId. Lessen burnout as well as other manifestations of strain;

IIe. Enhance enrichment through complementary role performance, i.e., one undertaking contributes to the performance of the other.

METHODS

Subjects

The sample was designed to represent the population of intact urban Jewish families with minor children; it included 1,500 mothers and their husbands. The respondents were selected by stratified area sampling. Townships were classified into three types: large cities, cities established prior to 1948 and cities established after 1948. An additional stratification was carried out according to geographical location (north, center, south). Each community in the sample was subdivided into statistical areas, and the sample population for each area weighted according to its size. In each household the two spouses were interviewed. The average age of the sample was 37 years for women and 42 years for men; the marriage age was early 20s for women and mid-20s for men; the average number of children for working mothers was 2.8: the mean years of schooling of working mothers was 11.8. Number of children, mean years of schooling, and occupational breakdown of the sample were almost identical to that of the Israeli population at large.

Measures

A questionnaire mostly structured, focusing on behavior and attitudes toward work and family, was administered separately to husbands and wives. Data were collected during winter 1982.

Dependent Variables

Various aspects of role-strain:[1] (1) A sense of burnout by the working mother was expressed in a high degree of agreement with the statement. "I am tired and worn out as a result of the double effort of home and work." (2) Marital dissatisfaction was examined in seven spheres of marital interaction: the division of tasks, socialization of the children, leisure time, intimate relations, financial arrangements, standard of living and mutual understanding (see Arnott, 1972). Responses to these spheres were combined into a unidimensional index of "marital quality" (Katz and Briger, 1988). (3) Dissatisfaction at work: A general question regarding satisfaction at work was presented; response categories ranged over a five-level continuum. (4) Gap between the self image at home and the one at work: A measure of discrepancy between self-image at home and at work was included on the assumption that role-strain will increase as the execution of different assignments by the same person demands more widely differentiated personality characteristics. Self-image was examined by means of a semantic differential (Osgood et al., 1957), which included seven characteristics: emotional-rational, yielding-aggressive, self-confident-lacking in self-confidence, tense-relaxed, bored-interested, sad-happy, feels appreciated-feels disparaged. With the data obtained by this procedure, an average differential between the definition of self in two situations, at home and at work, was calculated.

Various aspects of investment in the double role: This variable was measured by examining number of children, use of hired help in the home (average number of hours per day), the allotment of work time (daily average) to the different tasks: employment, travel time, housework, and child care.

Various aspects of enrichment: This variable was measured in terms of the mother's personal assessment that employment improves her educational capacities as well as the relations between her and her children; that her children "profit" through her being employed; and that her husband takes an interest in her work.

INDEPENDENT VARIABLES

The burden of tasks was indicated by number of children and extent of employment (these variables serve as both dependent and independent variables, but in different hypotheses). As independent variables these factors were organized dichotomously: mothers having a small number of children (1 or 2) and mothers having a large number of children (3 and more), or trichotomously, homemakers, mothers employed half-time or less, and mothers employed full-time.

Resources at the mother's disposal were measured by years of schooling,[2] occupational prestige (operationalized according to Kraus, 1977)[3] and personal income.[4] After dichotomizing these variables (see footnotes 2,3,4) two groups were formed. The group characterized by a high level of these three resources is referred to as "high resource women" and the group having a low level of resources as "low resource women."

Control Variables

The purpose of this study was to assess the net effect of burden and resources on role-strain and on enrichment, therefore background variables that might influence the dependent variable should be controlled. Analyses of variance were performed controlled for the following variables: ethnicity, religiosity and duration of marriage.

FINDINGS

The issue of time-allocation among various tasks included in the same role-set has been extensively discussed in previous research (Gronau, 1976; Leibowitz, 1972; Robinson, 1977; Walker and Woods, 1976). Table 1 shows the amount of time invested by husbands and wives in three main tasks: employment, childcare, and housework.[5]

Overall averages of time invested show that the burden of the working mother is greatest (13.5 hours per day), that of the homemaker is least (9.7 hours), and that of husbands of both categories falls between the two (12.7/12.8 hours). Husbands do not share in the additional burden arising from their wives' employment. The number of hours they devote to their homes and to their children is about the same irrespective of whether or not their wives are employed outside the home. In order to inquire into this constancy in

TABLE 1. Allocation of time (average hours per day) for employed mothers, homemakers and their husbands.

Allocation of Time	Women			Men		
	Employed Mothers		Homemakers	Husbands of Employed Mothers		Husbands of Homemakers
	n=1000		n=500	n=800		n=400
Socialization and child care	3.5	1.4 t=9.6**	4.9	2.0	0.1 t=0.5	1.9
Housework	3.2	1.6 t=13.4**	4.8	1.2	0.1 t= 1.1	1.1
Total work at home	6.7	3.0 t=16.6**	9.7	3.2	0.2 t=1.3	3.0
Travel (to and from work)	0.8		-	0.6		0.6
Employment	6.0		-	8.9	0.3 t=1.8	9.2
Total time outside home	6.8		-	9.5	0.3 t=1.8	9.8
Total time expenditure	13.5	3.8 t=15.3**	9.7	12.7	0.1 t=.88	12.8

Difference between employed mothers and their husbands in allocating time for paid work   2.7;   t=25.0**

Difference between employed mothers and their husbands in allocating time for housework   2.0;   t=31.0**

Difference between employed mothers and their husbands in allocating time for child care   1.5;   t=24.0**

** p ≤ .01

the husband's allocation of time, variances in the allocation of time to the various tasks were compared between men and women (see Table 2).

Evidently husbands' allocation of time for domestic tasks is by far more uniform and less flexible than that of wives. This finding is reversed in the allocation of time to work. Here, where men invest most of their time, the variance among them is greater than among the women. Thus, both husbands and wives allocate their work time in accordance with the needs of their principal area of responsibil-

TABLE 2. Variances of time allocated to various tasks for employed mothers and their husbands, and F values.

Variance in Time Invested	Employed Mothers	Husbands of Employed Mothers	F
	n=1000	n=800	
Employment (including travel)	4.14	5.20	1.25**
Child Care	4.68	2.61	1.79**
Houswork	2.98	1.41	2.11**
Child Care and Housework	8.35	5.21	1.60**
Total	10.81	8.17	1.30**

** $p \leq .01$

ity; a greater variance is found for women at home and for men at work.

Let us now turn to test our hypotheses. To test Hypothesis I, role strain increases as the scope of tasks increase, subjects were divided into four groups according to the measures of burden; number of children and amount of work time outside the home (see Table 3).

The inter-group differences in role-strain are significant according to analysis of variance (see Scheffe, 1959). According to Hypothesis I it is expected that groups 1 and 2, mothers of one or two children, will reveal less role strain than groups 3 and 4, mothers of 3 children or more. It is also implied by Hypothesis I that mothers who are fully employed, groups 1 and 3, will show more strain than part time employed mothers, groups 2 and 4. Referring to dissatisfaction at work and to the gap between self image at home and at work, the first prediction is supported by the data: groups 3 and 4 express higher role strain than groups 1, 2. Referring to the sense of burnout the second prediction holds: groups 1, 2 exceed in expressing burnout than groups 2, 4. In sum, Hypothesis I received partial support, only part of its predictions were corroborated.

Hypothesis II states that resources at the disposal of the employed mother contribute to her ability to cope with the dual role. This

TABLE 3. Measures of role-strain by extent of employment and number of children (schooling, ethnicity, and age of women controlled)

Measures of Role-Strain	Sense of burnout	Marital Dissatisfaction	Dissatisfaction at work	Gap between work/home self image
Female Categories Range (high-low):	7 - 1	0 - 4	5 - 1	6 - 0
1.Employed mothers full-time with 1,2 children (283)	3.20	1.41	2.02	1.16
2.Employed mothers part time with 1,2 children (167)	2.50	1.27	2.06	1.27
3.Employed mothers full time with 3+ children (312)	3.40	1.43	2.15	1.30
4.Employed mothers part time with 3+ children (205)	2.84	1.36	2.16	1.30
Significant differences between categories	1,3>2,4	3>2	3,4>1,2	3,4>1,2

(the categories are arranged according to their numbers)

contribution pervades in all the following sub-hypotheses. In order to test Hypothesis IIa, the direct effect of schooling, occupational prestige, and working mothers' income on reducing the scope of her tasks, two, one-way analyses of variance were conducted. The dependent variables were the number of daily working hours, and the number of children. Ethnic origin, duration of marriage, and degree of religiosity controlled. The sample was divided into two categories according to whether the level of resources was high or low.

Table 4 indicates significant differences in the hypothesized direction: more schooling, occupational prestige, and personal income result in a reduction in the mother's tasks: fewer hours of work and a smaller number of children. In contrast to the men, the

TABLE 4. One-way analysis of variance between employed mothers high and low in resources (dependent variables—work hours and number of children; independent variables—income, schooling and occupational prestige; control variables—duration of marriage, ethnicity and religiosity).

Burden of tasks	Daily working hours:		Number of Children	
Resources	High in Resources	Low in Resources	High in Resources	Low in Resources
Income (per hour)	6.53	6.98	2.75	3.01
(N)	(340)	(343)	(354)	(346)
F	7.86**		7.38**	
Schooling (Years)	6.40	7.09	2.67	3.11
(N)	(348)	(329)	(401)	(337)
F	15.36**		19.49**	
Occupational Prestige	6.53	7.09	2.63	2.94
(N)	(443)	(474)	(456)	(484)
F	15.80**		15.34**	
Combined resources	6.35	7.05	2.78	3.43
(N)	(248)	(174)	(259)	(175)
F	10.00**		20.53**	

** $p \leq .01$

women employed in occupations of higher prestige tend to work fewer hours. A woman with high occupational status receives a higher income per work hour. She is able to cut down the number of working hours while still retaining a reasonable salary. A low status employed woman, however, needs to devote many hours to her work, and because this is done alongside domestic chores, attrition results. A seemingly different explanation is based on the fact that a large proportion of educated women having high professional prestige are employed in teaching where the average work day is shorter than in lower prestige occupations (industry, retail sales). A careful examination of this second explanation reveals that it does not differ from the first. Considering the alternatives available to them in the labor-market, many women tend to prefer occupations compatible with the dual role of wife-mother and breadwinner. The concentration of educated women in these occupations creates pressure to maintain and even extend such work arrangements, (Izraeli, 1983:65).

The tendency for educated women in high prestige jobs to have fewer children is well-established but it is interpreted in various ways. Becker assumed that along with education and status there is an increasing tendency to invest in each child and elevate his or her achievements — a goal that is much easier to attain if the number of children is kept small (1981, ch.2). But whatever the conscious rationalization, the decision to have fewer children obviously diminishes the time demands on the working mother. Hypothesis IIa, that mothers with more resources can mitigate the pressures of the dual role by reducing role obligations, is therefore corroborated.

In order to test Hypothesis IIb, that resources at the disposal of the employed mother make it possible to mobilize additional labor-power for household tasks, the tendency of working women with resources to utilize paid help and/or husband's help (help on the part of other family members was not measured), was examined.

The data in Table 5 corroborates Hypothesis IIb as to hiring paid help. The differences between women high in resources and those lacking resources are all significant and in the expected direction. As is reasonable to assume, income has a very strong impact, but education and prestige also have a significant bearing.

As for the second part of Hypothesis IIb, that the employed mother who has a high level of resources is more capable of enlisting the help of her husband, *no* difference in the number of hours devoted to home and children by husbands of either group was found. In both cases the father allots 3 to 3.25 hours in comparison with double that number of hours invested by the mother.

Testing of the hypothesis regarding each of the mother's resources separately, income, schooling and occupational prestige, showed the same results (data not presented). In sum, then, the working mother who is in possession of resources has an advantage in recruiting paid help, but not in enlisting the aid of her husband.

TABLE 5. One-way analysis of variance between employed mothers high and low in resources (dependent variables — paid help, hours per day; independent variables — income, schooling and occupational prestige; control variables — duration of marriage, ethnicity and religiosity).

| | Paid Help (Hours Per Day) | | |
Resources	Employed Mothers High in resources		Employed Mothers Low in resources
Income (per hour)	1.27		0.62
(N)	(382)		(313)
F		21.00**	
Schooling (years)	1.19		0.56
(N)	(294)		(347)
F		13.60**	
Occupational Prestige	1.13		0.77
(N)	(406)		(399)
F		8.7**	
Combined resources	1.34		0.29
(N)	(177)		(216)
F		26.3**	

** $p \leq .01$

One of the difficulties in the life of the working mother is maintaining continuity in work in spite of family events that are liable to induce her to change her place of work, her occupation, or even to stop working altogether. Hypothesis IIc, resources at the disposal of the employed mother contribute to continuity in the fulfillment of the occupational role, requires an examination of work continuity. Forty-four percent of employed mothers had their career interrupted following changes in family status: 24% stopped work several times. At the same time there are also women who are continuously employed in spite of marrying, giving birth, and related events. Employed mothers with high resources manage more than others to maintain continuous employment. A correlational analysis shows a slight though significant ($p \leq .05$) tendency for work interruptions to decrease with increasing level of education ($r = -.15$) ($p \leqslant$ .05). Analysis of the relation between occupational prestige and work interruptions obtained similar results ($r = -.12$) ($p \leqslant .05$). The working mother with high resources possesses several attributes that facilitate continuity in work: she has fewer children (see Table 4) and starts childbearing at a later age than the mother lacking in resources.[6] Analysis of variance revealed significant differences between women having higher and lower levels of resources. The former postponed the age of bearing their first child: 23.8 compared to 21.7; $F = 38.79$ $p \leqslant .01$.

In order to test Hypothesis IId—that resources make it possible for the employed mother to reduce the results of role strain, such as burnout, one-way analyses of variance on the various dimensions of role-strain, were conducted while controlling for relevant background variables (Table 6).

All the differences between the groups were in the predicted direction, and with the exception of one—the difference in the extent of burnout between women having high or low salary—they were all significant. Hypothesis IId is therefore corroborated. The working mother lacking in resources shows more manifestations of strain than the working mother who is high on resources. Education and occupational prestige have a stronger impact on reducing strain than does income.

To test Hypothesis IIe—that resources have a positive influence on the complementary contribution of one task to the other—the relation between resources and enrichment indicators were measured (see Table 7).

A mother high on resources has a greater tendency to see her work as contributing to her children's development, to her relations with them, as well as to her ability to educate them. The more educated, higher occupational prestige mother benefits both from the contribution of her work to her children and from her husband's greater interest in her work.

DISCUSSION

In previous research the dual role has been analyzed from two perspectives: pessimistic—emphasizing the negative results arising

TABLE 6. One-way analysis of variance between employed mother high and low in resources (dependent variables – measures of enrichment; independent variables – income, schooling and occupational prestige; control variables – duration of marriage, ethnicity and religiousity).

Resources	Shooling		Income		Occ. Prestige		Combined Resources	
Measures of Role Strain	High	Low	High	Low	High	Low	High	Low
Sense of burnout	2.68	3.43	2.84	3.23	2.78	3.29	2.70	3.30
(N)	(397)	(331)	(352)	(340)	(450)	(473)	(258)	(173)
F	13.10**		1.97		13.36**		5.97**	
Marital Dissatisfaction	1.31	1.52	1.29	1.48	1.31	1.45	1.27	1.64
(N)	(331)	(257)	(331)	(306)	(370)	(355)	(242)	(150)
F	12.17**		4.36*		8.00*		11.46**	
Dissatisfaction at work	1.96	2.29	1.9	2.32	1.94	2.25	1.87	2.48
(N)	(397)	(327)	(350)	(342)	(451)	(472)	(258)	(172)
F	16.80**		27.14**		23.67**		28.85**	
Gap between work/ home self images	1.15	1.32	1.18	1.32	1.15	1.34	1.12	1.33
(N)	(387)	(309)	(338)	(324)	(434)	(451)	(249)	(163)
F	6.46**		7.09**		11.27**		6.66**	

*   p $\leq$ .05
**   p $\leq$ .01

from competition for scarce resources or contradiction between norms, and optimistic – the possibility of enrichment, whereby one aspect of the dual role supports the other. Each approach is supported by research findings. The seemingly contradictory conclusions lead to the hypothesis that in most dual roles both strain and enrichment are to be found. In the present study we found evidence not only of the existence of both phenomena, but can also indicate the conditions that cause the balance between them to change. The dual role, as it appears from our findings, is not some kind of "pun-

TABLE 7. One-way analysis of variance between employed mothers high and low in resources (dependent variables — measures of enrichment; independent variables — income, schooling and occupational prestige; control variables — duration of marriage, ethnicity and religiousity).

Measures of Enrichment	Employed Mothers	
	High in resources	Low in resources
Mother's assessment that:		
Her employment improves her educational capacities	2.55	1.98
(N)	(224)	(178)
F	22.88**	
Her employment contributes to her children's development	3.65	3.11
(N)	(224)	(170)
F	18.75**	
Her husband takes an interest in her work	2.84	2.56
(N)	(224)	(170)
F	6.84**	

** $p \leq .01$

ishment'' or burden but rather a challenge enabling more or less successful coping, in accordance with the resources mobilized and the strategy pursued.

Two strategies for coping with the pressures of the dual role have been examined: reducing the tasks and enhancing the reciprocal contribution of one role to the other. In a social context there is a decisive difference between these two strategies. The first represents a cost — the complementing roles receive less; the second represents mainly a profit — role performance becomes easier and less pressing for the actor, while the environment wins outputs of better quality. Working mothers in Israel make use of both strategies. Their ability to succeed in either of them is influenced by the extent of resources at their disposal. A working mother with extensive resources, schooling, income and occupational prestige is able to reduce the burden of the obligations necessitated by the dual task: she tends to bear fewer children, to work fewer hours, and to recruit more hired help from outside the family. As a result of lessening the childbearing task, we found a consistent reduction in two indicators of inter-role strain: dissatisfaction at work and a significant gap between home and work, in self image. A reduction in work hours tends to reduce constantly the sense of burnout.

Resources such as education, occupational prestige, and income help the employed mother to organize her dual role in such a way that the processes of enrichment are enhanced. Two concrete mechanisms achieve this end: First, within the limitations of the job market, she tends to choose occupations in education, or other helping professions, which develop skills relevant to the mother-wife role. Second, she is able to invest part of her personal income in improving the functioning of her home. This ability stems not only from the increased size of the family income but also from the increased say of the working mother in determining expenditure priorities and family consumption (Katz and Peres, 1985). One of the most efficient ways for the employed mother to ease her burden is to invest part of her income in hiring help, in this way enabling her to devote less time to housework and concentrate more on alternative concerns such as education, social activity and leisure. The pursuit of these strategies creates a sense of reciprocity between the roles: the perception that the children benefit and their education improves as a result of the mother's employment.

Evidence of enrichment in the dual role should not divert attention from the social cost entailed. The dual role, as it is understood and performed by a large majority of Israeli working mothers, apparently does not lead toward complete equality between the genders. The working mother tends to invest her resources in achieving a *balance* between the role and not in maximizing her professional achievements. In this way she gains the support and interest of her husband, but not actual help from him in her domestic chores. The entrance of wives and mothers into the work force did not eliminate the sexual division of labor. On this point our findings are in line with the conclusions of several studies on allocation of time (Fox &

Nichols, 1983; Robinson, 1977; Sanik, 1981: Walker & Woods, 1976).

According to our data the ability to regulate role-tasks successfully as well as to benefit from role-enrichment is found chiefly among working mothers who are rich in resources. In other words, the ability to avoid attrition and enhance enrichment in a dual role can be viewed as another expression of social stratification. The social cost of coping with the dual role is apparent in the practice of many affluent working mothers employing household help. Role-strain is "rolled over" onto the shoulders of some other women.

A sober view of the employed mothers' dual role reveals limitations (no gender equality) as well as new problems (increasing stress in another woman's role). But these limitations are not enough to advocate a return to traditional gender roles. Limiting mothers to the home might have social costs that are even higher. Role enrichment may not only compensate the employed mother for part of her stress and strain, it may also generate new qualities of role outputs. Thus, for example, it seems to be easier to educate children toward the ideal of gender-equality if their mothers have professional lives of their own.

In the future more women will probably be joining the work force without being able or wanting to forgo the simultaneous fulfillment of the wife-mother role. This expected development increases the importance of enrichment, in which lies the possibility of blending the roles rather than having to choose between them.

NOTES

1. There is no reason to expect that these aspects will aggregate to a unidimensional scale: (a) manifestations of attrition can appear as a result of various tensions of the dual role; (b) each role-occupant reacts to strain with different manifestations of attrition in accordance with his or her specific vulnerabilities.

2. In order to test the impact of schooling on the dependent variables, two categories were set up: women having studied 0-12 years and women having studied 13 or more years.

3. In order to test the influence of occupational prestige on the dependent variables we divided the sample into two categories: those with a rating of 0-49 on the occupational prestige scale, and those with a rating of 50 and over.

4. Income was also divided into two categories, with the median as the dividing line.

5. These three tasks may not cover *all* activities performed by the husband and/or wife (e.g., bureaucratic and financial arrangements, are not included), but they probably cover most of the familial role obligations.

6. This does not imply a causal order: she may have acquired resources because of the reduction or postponement of childbirth.

REFERENCES

Arnott, C.C. Married women and the pursuit of profit: An exchange theory perspective. *Journal of Marriage and the Family* 34(1): 122-131, 1972.

Hahr, J. Effects on power and division of labour in the family. In L.W. Hoffman and F.I. Nye (eds.), *Working Mothers*, San Francisco: Jossey-Bass, 1974.

Becker, G. *A treatise on the family*. Harvard University Press, Cambridge, Mass. 1981.

Blood, R. and Wolfe, D. *Husbands and wives*. New York: Free Press, 1960.

Bryson, R. B., Bryson, J. B., Licht, M. H., and Licht, B. S. The professional pair: Husband and wife psychologists. *American Psychologist*, 31: 10-16, 1976.

Central Bureau of Statistics. Statistical Abstract of Israel, 1984.

Central Bureau of Statistics. Population and housing census, 1984.

Central Bureau of Statistics and Ministry of Labour and Social Affairs, Working women in Israel, 1981 and 1984.

Elman, M.R. and Gilbert, L. A. Coping strategies for role conflict in married professional women with children. *Family Relations*, 33(2): 317-328, 1984.

Epstein, C. F. Law partners and marital partners. *Human Relations* 24: 549-563, 1971.

Fox, K. D. and Nickols, S. Y. The time crunch — Wife's employment and family work. *Journal of Family Issues* 4(1): 61-82, 1983.

Goode, W. J. A theory of role strain. *American Sociological Review* 25: 483-496, 1960.

Gordon, F. E. and Hall, D. T. Self image and stereotypes of femininity: Their relationship to women's role conflicts and coping. *Journal of Applied Psychology* 59:241-243, 1974.

Gronau, A. The allocation of time of Israeli women. *Journal of Political Economy*, August: S 201-212, 1976.

Heckman, N.A., Bryson, R. and Bryson, J.B. Problems of professional couples: A content analysis. *Journal of Marriage and the Family* 39: 323-330, 1977.

Herman, J. B. and Gyllstrom, K. K. Working men and women: Inter and intra role conflict. *Psychology of Women Quarterly* 1: 319-333, 1977.

Hunt, J. G. and Hunt, L. L. Dilemmas and contradictions of status: The case of the dual-career family. *Social Problems* 24(4): 407-416, 1977.

Israeli, D. N. Israeli women in the work force. *The Jerusalem Quarterly* 27: 59-80, 1983.

Katz, R. and Briger, R. Modernity and the quality of marriage in Israel: The impact of socio-cultural factors on marital satisfaction. *Journal of Comparative Family Studies* 19(3): 371-380, 1988.

Katz, R. and Peres, Y. Is resource theory equally applicable to wives and husbands? *Journal of Comparative Family Studies* 16(1): 1-10, 1985.

Kraus, V. Social grading of occupations. Unpublished Ph.D. Dissertation. The Hebrew University, Jerusalem (in Hebrew), 1977.

Leibowitz, A. Education and the allocation of women's time. *National Bureau of Economic Research*: New York, 1972.

Lieblich, A. Successful career women at mid-life: Crisis and transitions. *Megamot* 29(3): 256-268 (in Hebrew), 1986.

Lupri, E. Contemporary authority patterns in the West German family: A study in cross-national validation. *Journal of Marriage and the Family* 31: 34-44, 1969.

Marcus, Y. and Doron, N. How worthwhile is it for women to work? *Society and Welfare* 6(2-3): 222-232. (in Hebrew), 1985.

Marks, S.R. Multiple roles and role strain: Some notes on human energy, time and commitment. *American Sociological Review* 42: 921-936, 1977.

McDonald, G.W. Family power: The assessment of a decade of theory and research, 1970-1979. *Journal of Marriage and the Family* 42(4): 841-854, 1980.

Moore, W. E. A reconsideration of theories of social change. *American Sociological Review* 25: 810-818, 1960.

Orthner, D. K. and Axelson, L. J. The effects of wife employment on marital sociability. *Journal of Comparative Family Studies* 11(4): 531-545, 1980.

Osgood, C.E., Suci, G.J. and Tennenbaum, P.H. *Measurement of meaning*. Urbana: University of Illinois Press, 1957.

Pleck, J.H. The work-family role system. *Social Problems* 24(4): 417-427, 1977.

Rainwater, L. Mother's contribution to the family economy in Europe and the United States. *Journal of Family History* 4(2):198-211, 1979.

Rapoport, R. and Rapoport, R. *Dual-Career families*. New York: Viking, 1971.

Rapoport, R. and Rapoport, R. *Dual Career families re-examined: New integration of work and family*. New York. Harper and Row, 1976.

Robinson, J.P. *Changes in americans' use of time: 1965-1975. A progress report*. Cleveland, Ohio: Communication Research Center, 1977.

Sanik, M.M. Division of household work: A decade comparison 1967-77. *Home Economics Research Journal* 10: 175-180, 1981.

Scanzoni, J. Social processes and power in families. In W.R. Burr, R. Hill, F.I. Nye and I.L. Reiss (eds.), *Contemporary Theories about the Family*. Vol. 1, New York: Free Press, 1979.

Scheffe, H. A. *The Analysis of variance*. New York: Wiley, 1959.

Sieber, S.D. Toward a theory of role accumulation. *American Sociological Review* 39: 467-478, 1974.

Slater, P. On social regression. *American Sociological Review* 28: 399-364, 1963.

Thoits, P. Multiple identities and psychological well-being: A reformulation and test of the social isolation hypothesis. *American Sociological Review* 48: 174-187, 1983.

Thoits, P. Multiple identities: Examining gender and marital status differences in distress. *American Sociological Review* 51: 259-272, 1986.

Vanek, J. Time spent in housework. *Scientific American* 231 (November): 116-120, 1974.

Verbrugge, L.M. Multiple roles and physical health of women and men. *Journal of Health and Social Behavior* 24: 16-30, 1983.

Voydanoff, P. and Kelly, R.F. Determinants of work-related family problems among employed parents. *Journal of Marriage and the Family* 46(4): 881-892, 1984.

Walker, K. E. and Woods, M.E. Time use: A measure of household production of family good and services. Washington, D.C.: *American Home Economics Association*, 1976.

The Attitudes of Young People
Towards Marriage:
From the Change of Substance
to the Change of Form

Marina Blagojevic

SUMMARY. This paper analyzes young people's attitudes toward marriage. The findings, drawn from the student population of Belgrade, were compiled in 1985. The answers analyzed here are to the question: What do you think about marriage in general and about marriage in our society? Since this is an open-ended question, the answers followed various lines and different frames of reference. The analysis, therefore, will be largely qualitative, rather than quantitative. In view of this, and given the fact that the sample was not representative, the findings suggest hypotheses to be tested by future research.

Views about marriage are an integral part of the consciousness of young people, and analyzing them, like other elements of that consciousness, enables one to detect oncoming changes. A young person's attitude to marriage is shaped by a number of factors, ranging from the characteristics of the global society and prevailing attitudes toward marriage, to the concrete conditions of the person's socialization and the experience within one's own family. But, there is also another specific experience that determines the attitude toward marriage, past and present emotional ties.

Regardless of the factors forming one's attitude toward marriage an examination of these attitudes makes it possible, to a limited degree, to predict future marital behavior. It also draws the "indi-

Marina Blagojevic is a teaching fellow, faculty of Philosophy, Department of Sociology, University of Belgrade, Yugoslavia.

217

vidual marriage'' out of its conceptual cocoon by affirming a consciousness of a certain societal determination of the characteristics
of emotional ties which everyone experiences as something individual and unique, as "the mark of fate.''

GENERAL PICTURE

Given the wide variety of responses, a quantitative analysis was
feasible at the most general level — by classifying the answers into
several groups: those with largely positive opinions about marriage,
those with largely negative ones, and the residual categories of neutral and undefined opinions,* and "no answer.''

As can be seen from Table 1, just over half of the female respondents and just under half of the male respondents take a positive
view of marriage. The differences between the male and female
respondents are much greater when it comes to negative views
about marriage: 18.9% of the men as compared to 8.3% of the
women. This big gap can perhaps be explained by the fact that not
only is a negative attitude toward marriage culturally more acceptable for young men, but also that young women who were less

Table 1:   Opinions of Marriage (and two people living
           together in general)

	W	%	M	%
positive	85	54.1	79	49.6
neutral & undefined	19	12.1	26	16.4
negative	13	8.3	30	18.9
no answer	40	25.5	24	15.1
Total:	157	100%	159	100%

*Included in the category of positive opinions are explicitly positive views
about non-marital unions; included in the category of neutral and undefined views
are those where it was difficult to determine the prevailing attitude to marriage, or
where the attitudes were highly contradictory.

inclined to take a positive view of marriage refrained from answering. Namely, the women showed a marked abstention in giving answers. Although the poll was anonymous, to answer this question required a self-appraisal, the need to be honest with oneself. One easy path was not to answer the question.

On the basis of the given classification of answers one finds that the prevailing attitude of students toward marriage is positive. In view of the specific position of this group of young people in Yugoslavia who are still economically dependent and "preparing" for adulthood and their own independence, it can be assumed that marriage is much more acceptable among other groups of young people who are economically independent.

THE IDEALISTIC DEFINITION OF MARRIAGE

Positive attitudes toward marriage usually include some definition of the "ideal" marriage, with the implicit or explicit assumption that such a marriage is feasible. Young women show somewhat more of an inclination towards such definitions of marriage. The image of an "ideal" marriage is an escape from confronting the reality of marriage in favor of romantic ideas about what marriage "should be like."

The following is a definition of an "ideal" marriage given by several respondents: "Marriage is what true, great love should strive for. A person affirms himself through marriage, he/she gains a fuller understanding of the value of life. He/she is ready to make sacrifices, feels stronger and safer" (F).** The majority of idealistic images of marriage stress the importance of love. Marriage is seen as the logical extension of having a relationship with someone, of being in love, it is seen as the optimum solution for life: "If two people love each other then they simply crown that love with a formal act" (F); "If two people love each other, then marriage is the best solution for their life" (F). Love is the condition for entering into marriage ["I can only marry somebody I love" (F)], and it

---

**(F) and (M) indicate the sex of the respondent.

is also the condition for having a happy marriage ["Marriage is a nice thing only if the husband and wife love each other and get along with each other" (M)].

Note that within the scope of definitions of the "ideal," a given number of answers do not use the term "love." Some examples: "Marriage is . . . a port where a person can always find a refuge" (M); "Marriage is an institution regulated by law, but where a person can find security, protection, happiness" (F). The first answer offers a typically male stereotype of a man "settling down" in marriage and being able to relax at home from the pressures of the outside, hostile world; the second answer offers a typically female stereotype of security, protection and possible happiness.

A number of definitions of the "ideal" marriage treat it as something that makes life easier. For instance: "Life becomes more beautiful and interesting, and life's problems are far easier to bear and resolve" (M), or "I think marriage is a must, if for no other reason than because it is easier to resolve problems when there are two of you" (M). A similar view is the following: "A person needs a mate in life" (M). This rationalization, comes from the young men, not the young women, and indirectly points to the need for a woman's emotional support, which, in turn, means supporting one of the traditional roles of women in patriarchal societies.

Apart from love, which is mentioned the most often in defining the ideal marriage, many answers give variations on the theme of friendship and understanding in marriage: "In order to have a happy marriage, your partner has to be, above all, your friend, sincere and honest" (M). In addition to understanding, mention is also made of "mutual respect," "assistance," "support," "solidarity," "cooperation," and "trust." Idealistic visions usually define marriage as a "union," not an "institution." In a traditional spirit, marriage in quite a few cases is described as "sacred" or as a "holy place," where "peace, respect, and harmony" reign.

In romantic visions, value judgments of marriage are directly reflected through the attitude that "marriage is the most optimum form for two people to live together" (F), that it is a "wonderful institution," or that it is "everything between two people, as long as they live" (M).

Some definitions of marriage resist its instrumentalization. For instance: "Marriage is the best link between two strong emotions of love without a personal interest" (M); "Marriage is for people bound by love, not by advantage" (M). Such definitions become clearer when one analyzes those elements of the responses that refer to the characteristics of marriage or the motives for getting married. Namely, one finds that young people feel that people increasingly enter into marriage in order to satisfy certain interests, which probably refers to material interests. Hence, we can take the aforementioned definitions as reflecting a need to "free" marriage for love, i.e., as a purely romantic vision of marriage.

Marriage implies duties and obligations. Although this aspect of marriage is not frequently mentioned, indicative and interesting are the ways in which it is treated in some of the answers. The contradiction between obligations and pleasure in marriage is expressed in the following views: "Marriage is a union which entails many obligations, but there is such charm to it that most obligations take on a very pleasant overtone" (F), or "Marriage is a happy obligation" (M). In most cases, young people ignore the reality of marriage which is reflected, among other things, in the system of obligations and duties, and they support marriage either explicitly (for example: "I think the most important things are not duties but the emotional relationships in the family") or implicitly as an emotional union. It is interesting, however, that although students were the subject of the poll, none of their answers made any connection between the system of obligations in marriage and the organization of everyday life as a global social phenomenon.

Idealistic definitions of marriage, are relatively widespread and closely tied in with a positive attitude. They also point both to a certain phase in individual development, and to the impossibility of finding within one's immediate surroundings a model, one or several real marriages which would serve as a frame of orientation. This is especially interesting when one sees that most of the respondents live in undivorced families.

The idealistic picture of marriage enables a normative approach. Instead of talking about marriage and what it is, these respondents usually talk about what "it should be": "Marriage should be an ideal union between two people and their offspring" (F), or "Marriage should be a harmony of understanding, love and respect"

(M). This approach maintains a shimmering hope and misty expectations that may easily turn into disappointment and disillusionment. An overly idealistic picture of marriage is certainly one of the deepest causes of broken marriages, especially among young people, which, were the expectations more realistic would have a chance of making it.

THE INDIVIDUALISTIC DEFINITION
OF MARRIAGE

A more realistic approach to marriage is taken by young people who define marriage in terms of the individual characteristics of the persons getting married. Examples: "Marriage is an institution . . . which can be formed by people who have a realistic view of life" (F), or "Marriage should be an equitable union of two equal people" (M). The individual traits mentioned as conditions for marrying and having a successful marriage are: "maturity," stability and independence, "to be able to tie themselves to one person when they no longer want to roam around." There is the need for young people to first discover their own affinities and themselves, and only then to seek out someone "who suits them."

While idealistic definitions treat marriage as a complete entity, a smaller number of young people whose positive attitude to marriage is more reserved indicates the individual needs of the spouses. The attitude that marriage "should be the meeting point of two people who have the same views and the same goals" (M) shows an attempt to resolve the contradiction between individual and marriage goals. Some answers stress the need for the individual to remain free in marriage. Although not numerous, these answers merit attention because they reveal an undoubtedly new consciousness of the importance of individual differences, and of the right to individuality. Here is an example: "I think that what is needed for a successful marriage is equality between the man and the woman, understanding and freedom" (F). The view of marriage as being the result of the marriage partners' individual stands culminates with the view that "one's attitude to one's marriage partner depends on one's attitude to life, i.e., to oneself, others, society" (F). In this response no importance is attached to the influence of the social environment.

The idealistic definition envisions marriage as a stage in the formation of a mature person, as a necessary condition and confirmation of maturity. A more individualistic approach to marriage, on the other hand, stresses the need for mature people in entering into marriage. The latter provides a certain rationalization of the student's own position, a position of non-independence and socially defined nonmaturity, or the prolonged maturing process. At the same time, it internalizes the values of the parents and broader environment which places a high value on achievement at school at the expense of emotional ties ("school first, then love").

What is usually omitted in both the individualistic and the idealistic approach to marriage is the connection between individual growth within marriage and the changing of the marriage itself, which is an omnipresent reality in everyday life. In the time perspective of young people, marriage is seen as a lasting moment. The attitude that "marriage as an institution in general is interesting if the people are sufficiently aware and sufficiently intelligent to organize it without getting bored by it" (M) points, with a certain dose of irony, to the phenomenon of so-called marital monotony. However, in the majority of cases, even when young people talk about marriage as something that should last until the end of one's life, they do not imply by this process a living matter which changes, where people themselves change and go through various phases, but rather a kind of fixed duration in time, marked by the initial enthrallment.

Still, the individualistic approach is also an escape from reality. The attitude that "marriage can be the right thing with the right person" is a relativization of the social characteristics of marriage, reflecting a social consciousness which recognizes the disparity between the ideals of marriage and its actual characteristics. The individual finds a solution in "leaving himself open to fate," "coming upon the right person," wherein success or failure, happiness or unhappiness, does not depend on him/her or on the social circumstances that might influence him/her. This attitude reflects a passive acceptance of social norms, of obvious contradictions and a passive acceptance of oneself.

THE NEGATIVE DEFINITION OF MARRIAGE

Young people take a negative attitude to marriage when they say that marriage is an "obsolete institution," "an institution that is dying," that is "outdated," "outmoded," "senseless" or that it is something that is not "particularly important" because it is "a custom or legacy." The view that "marriage is not necessary today," or that it is a "pure formality," conceals an affirmative attitude to living together out of wedlock, something supported by a large number of the respondents. The negative attitude toward traditional marriage, seen in such formulations as: "I am not in favor of the classical, stereotype kind of marriage" (F), is in contrast to the positive attitude to marriage as such ("it's important that the two people love each other") (F).

The majority of answers that are skeptical about the value, sense and importance of marriage, nonetheless contain an alternative within the frameworks of the existing form of marriage or life out of wedlock. Usually, rejection of marriage, while full of pathos, does not literally mean rejection, but rather searching, by means of negation, for new forms, for new solutions. Hence, the answers themselves are often contradictory. For instance: "I think marriage is an obligation. But, if two people love each other then it simply crowns that love with a formal act" (M), or "I think marriage is still important today, although I am not for strictly classical, institutional marriage, which is good up to a point. I am not for it if it is seen as an obligation, if it is too "suffocating," if it is simply because of the children" (F). Even more radical criticisms of marriage show a reconciliation with the "inevitability" of life in marriage. For instance: "The actual institution of marriage is an insult to a person's individuality and restricts his freedom, but, at today's level of development, marriage is necessary and useful" (M). A similar view is the following: "Marriage is a tiring and exhausting thing which seldom works. Still, it's worth a try" (F).

Negative views of traditional marriage have different footholds. For instance, answers such as: "Nothing for the moment (I'm not thinking of marriage — M.B.), because I sill want to live!!" (M), or "Right now (I think — M.B.) only the best, until I get married" (M), or "As late as possible" (M), reflect classical stereotypes of the man "losing his freedom" when he gets married. At the same time, these answers indicate widely-spread double-standards when it comes to marriage. Namely, it is socially rated high, considered a social obligation, it determines the "normalcy" of the individual, but at the same time is a synonym for "prison," "the end." The ultimate result of the hypocrisy that confused young people discover in their environment is fear. It is well illustrated by the view: "Everybody who's married complains, but everybody still gets married" (M). It is reflected in two almost identical answers by two young men: "I'm afraid of marriage because it is "the end" and "I'm afraid of marriage as "the end."

The second starting-point of criticism of marriage and a negative, or at least reserved attitude toward it, is realism. Those who base their views of marriage on the experience of everyday life are not prone to see it as something "lofty." Some simply perceive the disparity between the ideal and reality. "What I can say about marriage is that it isn't what it should be" (F). Others are somewhat less lenient. "I think many marriages are an absolute mistake" (M) — says one young man, concisely expressing the results of his experience as an observer. Still "harsher" is the view of a young woman: "As something I encounter every day — I'm very disappointed. I do not think it meets its objectives, I think it makes people unhappy." It is interesting to note a definition given by a young woman, obviously on the basis of her negative view of marriage: "Marriage is a legal institution which should regulate disturbed relations between people who live together." How much truth is there in that?

With some young people, albeit a small number, a negative attitude stems from their perception of the changes that take place in marriage with time. They are ready, with a certain dose of irony, to point out that "love melts like ice in the sun" (M) or that marriage is "a good thing as long as people love each other and do not still know each other that well" (F). Or, as one young man put it metaphorically: "Just a glass of honey, the rest is bile."

Marriage is also criticized in terms of threatening the individuality, integrity and freedom of the individual. Here it seems to be unclear to young people whether it is at all possible to have a marriage that does not hamper the individual: "Personally, I'm for marriage if it does not impede the freedom of the man and the woman. If that's impossible, then I think it is better to live together out of wedlock" (F). Affirmation of individual needs culminates in the following view: "I think that one can live and love and create outside of marriage" (F).

The majority of young people who are critical of marriage, nonetheless accept it. Examples: "Marriage is a necessary evil without which one can't do" (F), and "Marriage is a stupid, but necessary institution" (M). It is hard to say whether here it is a case of realism or passivism.

The most radical view against marriage is certainly the following: "Marriage is just a tie and I think it is pointless to tie yourself to one person for your whole life" (M). This attitude, while insufficiently elaborated and isolated, nonetheless indicates the emergence of a new awareness of possible new forms of emotional ties.

LIVING TOGETHER OUT OF WEDLOCK: A CORRELATE OR ALTERNATIVE?

Given the relatively wide-spread view that marriage is a "formality" and that one should not insist on form but rather that emotional ties between people are important, among young people there is a positive attitude to living together out of wedlock. It must be stressed, however, that this is seen not only as an alternative to marriage (such attitudes are fewer in number), but primarily as correlates, as something that exists parallel with marriage. Living together usually comes first, before the couple has children. Hence, there are few views that living together out of wedlock jeopardizes marriage: "I think that liberalizing marriage leads to the opposite of what it is. Living together out of wedlock is not marriage" (M). Therefore, greater tolerance towards living together out of wedlock does not necessarily mean rejecting marriage. "I have nothing against living together out of wedlock, but marriage is something more elevated" (F).

A smaller number of answers see such an informal relationship as living together out of wedlock as a way out of the existing crisis of marriage. There are views that it is only in life together out of wedlock that full sexual equality can be achieved, i.e., that the domination of the male can be avoided.

Some of the respondents see life together out of wedlock as a step in the development of marriage: "I personally believe that marriage is slowly losing its institutional frameworks, that it is turning into a free relationship" (M). In contrast to this view are those that consider life together out of wedlock as a pure negation of marriage or as an essentially marital relationship.

Among the advantages of living together out of wedlock are its modernity ("Marriage is an obsolete institution"), spontaneity, freedom, and independence. All the same, an ample dose of romanticism appears to exist in defining life together out of wedlock, which is seen as a means to avoid "marital obligations."

Young peoples' high tolerance for living together out of wedlock leads them to call for giving the same legal treatment to marital and non-marital unions: "It is up to the individual whether he wants to formalize the relationship on paper or not" (F). However, there are also those who think that giving the same legal treatment to the one and the other brings into question the essence of "the freedom of relationships."

Living together out of wedlock is largely treated as a premarital union. Namely, having and raising children is connected with marriage. Children are also the most frequently mentioned motive, apart from love, for getting married and for the existence of marriage.

CHILDREN AND MARRIAGE

An integral part of idealistic definitions of marriage is the view of the necessity of marriage because of children. Children justify marriage, they make it meaningful and necessary. Marriage, in the opinion of some, only assumes its full meaning if there are children. Consequently, "marriage is a necessary institution primarily because of children, and also because of the marriage partners themselves" (M). Love for one's children, in the view of some of the respondents, overgrows and overpowers love between the marriage partners and overshadows it: "Love for the children, first of all, and also, of course, between the parents" (F). Marriage is necessary for the children, but children are necessary for the marriage. Character-istic, in this respect, is the following view: "In today's society, marriage is much less consolidated than before . . . Children should be the plaster that brings together the partners" (M). In some of their answers, young men see marriage as a condition for "continu-ing the species."

The instrumentalization of marriage because of children culmi-nates in the stand: "I think that with age all love is transferred to the offspring and that one lives for them" (F). Here marriage is defi-nitely not seen as a union between two people, but as an instrument for reproduction of "the labor force and builders of a society" (F). Personal happiness becomes irrelevant, while the individual's sacri-fice for his children, and indirectly for society, is put on the highest pedestal of moral values. Love, here, is separate from one's duty to the community. What remains is the satisfaction of performing one's duty, which replaces happiness.

Marriage is considered necessary for the development of the child's personality, for its normal and socially desirable develop-ment. The parents should be "stable" so that their children "can identify with them." The family is necessary because it must make it possible to "raise and develop children, as physically and men-tally healthy people" (F). Marriage is treated as the condition for both parents to give their love. Love in the family as an essential condition for socialization appears in the view: "The only precondi-tion for love to govern the world (utopia) is for the individual to learn to love and be loved from birth, and here I think the family plays the primary role" (M). This "utopia" hints at the possible emancipatory role of the family, by forming an individual who will not be captive to egotism. Here, then, the family appears as an active factor of possible social change, an attitude that is otherwise extremely rare among young people. At the same time, it points to the potentially very important direction of emancipatory trends: from the family to society, not the reverse. While isolated, this way of thinking is in consonance with current trends of the changing distribution of authority in the family and family roles.

Young people who are prone to favor life together out of wedlock feel that marriage is "a more suitable form for organizing a family"

(F). With a good deal of realism they see that "children from marriages and those from non-marital relationships receive different treatment in society" (F). The result of this hypocrisy in the treatment of children can include exclusive acceptance of a non-marital relationship, but without children, i.e., giving up parenthood so as to remain in a non-marital relationship and use the advantages of "free relationships."

Rare are such views as the following: "I am not in support of marriage. It would be much better for the parents to take equal care of the children, and not for the children to determine their life together, if it doesn't make both of them happy" (F). Such views observe without the slightest hypocrisy the conflict between the interests of the parents and the interests of the children. They condemn enslaving parents with children, and as a solution propose joint, genuine rather than formal care for the children, which would probably go beyond the obligations of customary forms of child support. Another alternative to marriage, when children are in question, is reflected in the following view: "Long live free love; we will all love children and raise them together in a commune." Although isolated, this view of a young man whose parents are divorced points to the need for finding new forms of ties between people, forms that are more suitable to the modern individual, forms that would free his emotions and not repress and functionalize them in terms of the survival of a repressive society.

The following opinion shows that marriage often does not fulfill the role of an optimum agent for the child's development: "It's sad that in most cases children do not have a real father or a real mother, yet live in a 'harmonious' marriage" (M). As opposed to the group of young people who feel that marriage is essential for the normal development of a child, here we have a group that feels marriage should not be maintained at any cost. An example is the following: "I think that there would no longer be any point to a marriage if the marriage partners ceased having any understanding for one another, even if they have children" (F). Even more exclusive is the view: "I'm against it (marriage — M.B.), if it is taken as an obligation, if it is too "suffocating," if people stay married only because of the children."

THE POLARIZATION OF ATTITUDES
TOWARDS MARRIAGE:
CRISIS AND FUTURE

Attitudes to marriage in Yugoslav society are largely polarized. The majority of respondents, especially those that are traditionally oriented, feel that marriage in Yugoslavian society is "in a crisis." Some think it is in a "special crisis," others that "as an institution it has fallen into a crisis," that "marriage in our society is a failure as an institution." Some think that it is in a "big" and others that it is in a "minor" crisis. Others claim that marriage is "degraded," and still others believe that it is in a "moral crisis." One interesting view is that "marriage in our society is at a low level, because we are backward" (M). This is probably a projection of the problems of the social structure onto the status of marriage. Divorce is usually taken as an indicator of the crisis of marriage. Other causes of the instability of marriage, include the economic crisis and women's emancipation ("everybody lives for himself/herself"). Some young people talk about the crisis of marriage in terms of their own generation's experience. They do not see a possibility for entering into marriage themselves, given the existing economic and social situation in Yugoslavia.

An interesting explanation of the crisis of marriage in Yugoslavian society is given in the following answer: "Marriage is in a crisis in our society: one-time forms are dying out, but new ones are not emerging" (M). This sociologically highly relevant explanation touches the very crux of the problem of the dying out of old and creation of new family forms suitable to changed conditions. A similar view is that "the development itself of society is making certain stands change, and today certain old patriarchal and newer, freer ideas are in conflict" (F). These two views of the crisis of marriage do not take a traditional stand, but rather perceive the need for change that would include marriage as well. Nonetheless, in the majority of cases the respondents seem to take a traditional stance in their view of the crisis of marriage. Marriage is said to be in a crisis because it does not correspond with idealistic and romantic pictures of marriage. The instability of marriage is proclaimed as negative, instead of treating instability as the emergence of individual choice, including divorce.

Young people see one of the causes of the instability of marriage as the pressure exerted by the environment to marry. They talk about the "unfair" attitude taken toward unmarried people, which "pushes people into bad marriages" (F), or say that in Yugoslavian society "a young person who has finished school and got a job is then expected to get married" (F). The same respondent observes, however, that "more and more young people are following their own instincts with regard to marriage or living together." Another important cause of the instability of marriage is identified with "bourgeois ideas which stress material advantage over harmony" (F). Marriage is threatened in the wake of the economic crisis because "society is unable to provide young people with jobs or apartments, which are the basics for life" (M).

A large number of young people do not feel that marriage in Yugoslavian society is in a crisis, but rather that it is traditional or patriarchal and as such sufficiently "resilient." There is a polarization between those who talk about the crisis of marriage, most often from a traditional viewpoint, and those who talk about patriarchal and traditional marriage in Yugoslavian society, usually from the viewpoint of the need to change existing marital forms. Some, however, reconcile themselves to marriage feeling that it is necessary on the certain level of the development of a global Yugoslavian society: "Marriage is an obsolete institution, but in our conditions it is necessary." (F).

A small number of respondents connects the crisis of marriage with a negative concept of tradition. "In our society, the institution of marriage is still based on strong patriarchal foundations which often creates various frustrations and disagreements. And the woman is often overburdened" (F). The following view also discusses the position of women in marriage: "The position of women in marriage has not changed much, and I think that because of the economic crisis that position has even deteriorated" (F). This is an isolated view and contrary to those that blame the crisis of marriage on "emancipated women." In any event, it points to the possible strengthening of traditional forms at times of crisis, determined by not changed values but also by reality. Survival is the responsibility of the family, and therefore, indirectly, of women.

Young people see that there are major variations in marriages in terms of different parts of society. The majority perceive this for certain geographic, and even social segments, which is understandable given the fact that in most cases the students are actually migrants, coming to Belgrade from smaller towns. Although isolated, the following opinion on the class division of marriages in Yugoslavian society is worth noting: "In our society there are bourgeois and there are workers' marriages. All they have in common is that both have barely one child, but the causes of this similarity are absolutely different and well-known" (M).

One of the causes given for the instability of marriages is that "in our society people are mostly too young when they get married," some because they are inhibited by the tradition that anyone who "does not get married by around 30 is too old" (F). A similar view is that "there are many rash and failed marriages between immature people" (F), and that people "easily get married" (M).

The most critical of marriage in Yugoslavian society are those who observe marriage simply: "I think that in our society there are very few happy marriages because of the absence of love and trust" (F).

The following criticism is also radical: "In our society marriage is a strongly bourgeois, inviolable institution which desperately hides all the failings it unquestionably has" (M). But, the most extreme is the following: "Marriage in our society is slavery for one's own existence and that of one's offspring" (M).

CONCLUSION

Young people certainly realize that marriage is changing. Some shut their eyes to the changes, claiming that they are temporary, others are prone to escape into romantic visions, and others still are simply open to change. Some are afraid of the changes, for they have no real alternatives, while others accept them along with the risks. Still, most young people do not see either themselves or their generation as being the vehicles of change, as those who should change marriage, rather than just accept it as a given, inviolable institution. The majority are passive, even when they perceive all the shortcomings of marriage, even when they are realistic, they submit to marriage as the only solution. The existing form of marriage is considered to be propagated by tradition as more than it actually is, than it deserves. Namely, marriage in terms of traditional marriage is only itself a historical form that inevitably changes.

Given the omnipresent passivism of young people, it is not surprising that they accept marriage. Rare are such answers as: "A lot needs to be changed" (F), or marriage "should be modernized." Young people see life together out of wedlock as a possibility, but it often bears the mark of escape, because "marriage without a signature," contrary to what one respondent thinks, does not mean "marriage without obligations." Paradoxically, maybe increased freedom also increases obligations.

Is the solution serial monogamy offered as a "prescription" by one young man: "One should get married several times"? Is the answer to the crisis of marriage a return to the traditional dignity of marriage or to "free love"? Will the future really bring a solution, as one respondent believes, because "this institution as such is collapsing"? But, young people are more prone to passive acceptance than to asking too many questions. Nevertheless, the acceptance of marriage as a form of life together may mean a tendency towards a change in the content of marriage, primarily towards a change of sexual roles.

A qualitative analysis of attitudes toward marriage in general and in Yugoslavia in particular made it possible to do a typology of attitudes, one that is hypothetical in character and would need to be checked by additional, more complex research. The underlying criterion in this typology is the similarity or divergence of attitudes toward marriage in terms of traditionalism versus modernism.

At the next, more concrete level, types are differentiated on the basis of 7 elements: (1) the way in which marriage is defined (realistic as opposed to idealistic definitions of marriage and definitions of marriage as an institution as opposed to marriage as life together); (2) attitudes on the permanence and unchangeability of marriage as a social creation; (3) attitudes on the relationship between the individual and marriage (subordinating the interests of the individual to those of two-some, or vice versa); (4) attitudes on the roles of the sexes (egalitarianism or preference for a hierarchy); (5) attitudes toward divorce; (6) attitudes toward parenthood; (7) attitudes toward living out of wedlock and other alternative forms of living together. By excluding rare, unlikely combinations, 5 basic, "ideal" types were arrived at.

1. The Conservative-Traditional Type

Young people belonging to this type are distinguished by a realistic, almost utilitarian attitude toward marriage. Marriage is treated as the only possible framework of the individual's social life, as the most important aspect of a person's sociability, the basic criterion of a person's "normalness." One marries because "one should," because "others expect it," because "life is easier when there are two of you." Marriage is a social obligation, mostly because it is the framework for biological reproduction, because it enables the "continuation of the species." Children are the purpose and goal of marriage, parents "sacrifice" themselves for children, but they expect "repayment" in their old age. Harmony is more important than love for a good marriage. Harmony is ensured by the order that comes from the hierarchy between husband and wife, parents and children. Sexual and generational roles are clearly differentiated. The interests of the individual in marriage and the family are subordinated to those of the whole. Individualism is rejected, and hence so are individual differences. Therefore, forms of joint life other than marriage are rejected (forms other than formal or customary, heterosexual, monogamous). Marriage is primarily treated as a lasting, unchangeable institution. Divorce is rejected for reasons of conformity, and because of the fact that marriage is above all an economic institution, a community of interests. Realistic expectations substantially reduce the possibility of disappointment. The instability of modern marriages in Yugoslavia is seen as more or less a passing "crisis" of marriage as an institution, caused by various external factors (the social and economic crisis, unemployment, housing problems . . .).

2. The Idealistic-Traditional Type

It is characteristic for young people who belong to this type that within the framework of traditional forms of marriage they incline towards change in the content of inter-personal relations in the direction of modernism. In this they are assisted by an idealistic, romantic point of view concerning the sense and purpose of the existence of marriage. In the essence of their definition of marriage is love, which is accompanied by friendship, understanding and respect. Marriage is looked on as the condition for the happiness of the individual, his essential fulfillment. Children are the "crown of love" and the point of living. Love can and should endure for a lifetime, hence the disinclination towards divorce. Divorce is unacceptable because of the children. Similarly, living out of wedlock is not acceptable — because of the children. Like a "magic wand" love solves the problem of sexual roles. The members of this type, namely, believe that love generates cooperation, and cooperation — equality. They see men and women not as bearers of different social roles, but exclusively as people with different individual characteristics. A romanticised picture of the marital relationship prevents them from surmising the possible conflict between the interests of the individual and the interests of the marital union. Also in a romantic vision, marriage is not viewed as a social institution which has certain socially determined characteristics but as a separate relationship whose quality is determined by emotions and fate. Marriage is seen as an a-historical institution, something that exists regardless of time and space, as the relationship of two people in love.

3. The Modern-Idealistic Type

Young people who belong to this type consider that there can also be changes in the form and in the content of marriage. They support the idea of living out of wedlock, and even consider that it has certain advantages over marriage. Nevertheless, they accept marriage as inevitable when there are children. Although they believe that in the essence of every relationship and even marriage, there should be love, young people who belong to this type show a greater degree of realism than the young people from the previous type. They are less inclined to believe in "everlasting love" and accept divorce more frequently. They see divorce as a means of resolving the conflict between individual goals and the goals of the marital union. A successful marriage is only one that harmonizes these goals. Their stands are clearly defined regarding the equality of the marital partners, solidarity and cooperation. They treat parenthood as a separate and independent quality. They do not link parenthood exclusively to marriage, nor marriage exclusively to parenthood.

4. The Liberal-Individualistic Type

Young people who belong to this type consider that the happiness of the individual is what is most essential. Individual development is the criterion for the sense and success of a relationship. Durability is unimportant. Therefore, they are more tolerant towards different forms of life together. They have substituted traditional moralism with realism and utilitarianism ("what is pleasing — is good"). They are inclined to a negative definition of marriage. They accept marriage out of conformism and not out of principle. They do not seek their fulfillment solely in emotional or quasi-emotional relations, but also in work. They regard parenthood as an option: children are not an aim in themselves, nor are they the aim of a relationship.

5. The Radical-Alternative Type

The young people belonging to this type see themselves as the bearers of change, as those who should create new forms of family relations, "a new sensibility." They reject marriage as a form. For the most part humanistically oriented and nonconformist, they have strong utopistic opinions, in the positive meaning, in their views of the individual, marriage and society. In the main, they do not define change, they sense it. Their creed is the release of emotionality. They aspire to attaining a harmony between the aims of the individual, primary groups and society.

One can put forward as a general hypothesis, that the distribution of each type among young people in Yugoslavia follows a so-called normal curve, whose peak is in the third type. However, besides this hypothesis, several more specific ones are also possible. Since the proposed typology has a dynamic as well as a structural character one can assume that in time distribution changes so that more and more of young people's attitudes belong to the third, fourth and fifth type. Apart from that, it may be assumed that there is a connection between the class or stratal structure of society and distribution of certain types. Thus, with the improvement of the social origin of the individual the probability grows that the attitudes will belong to a "higher" group. The assumption would be similar regarding the level of development of each region of Yugoslavia. One should, for instance, expect that the first type would be the most common among young people from a poorer social background in the under-developed parts of the country, whereas, the fourth and fifth type would be most common among young people belonging to the highest social strata in the more developed areas of the country. Apart from that, the social crisis in Yugoslavia which accentuates the individual's return to primary groups, first of all to the family, will, in all likelihood, influence an increase in positive attitudes towards marriage and a traditional acceptance of marriage.

Nevertheless, since attitudes towards marriage are dependent not only on social conditions, individual characteristics such as personal character, personal experience regarding the parental family as well as the individual's emotional experience can influence the inclusion of the attitudes of individuals in a specific type and the distribution of thereof. Besides, one may assume that there is a clearer distinction between types on the level of real behavior than on the level of attitudes. It is also probable that all types are not equally firmly structured and that extreme types are the most distinct in comparison to other types.

SELECTED BIBLIOGRAPHY

Milic, A. Teorijske preliminarije uz odnos krize porodice i drustvene krize, Marksisticka misao. Beograd, MC CKSKS, March 1985.

Milic A., Berkovic E., and Petrovic R.; Domacinstvo, porodica i brak u Jugoslaviji, Beograd. Institut za socioloska istrazivanja Filozofskog fakulteta u Beogradu, 1981.

Mlada, generacija danas, collection of articles, Beograd. NIRO "Mladost," 1982.

Omladina i drustvene krize, collection of articles, Beograd. Srbostampa, 1983.

Reis, I. L. Some Observations on Ideology and Sexuality in America, *Journal of Marriage and the Family*, 43, 2, May 1981.

Rener, T. Strategija krize: porodica, Marksisticka misao, Beograd, MC CKSKS, March 1985.

Spanier, G. B. Married and Unmarried Cohabitation in the United States: 1980, *Journal of Marriage and the Family*, 45, 2, May 1983.

Wilkie, J. R. The Trend Toward Delayed Parenthood, *Journal of Marriage and the Family*, 43, 3, August 1981.

Childless Marriages

Rosemarie Nave-Herz

SUMMARY. This article reports about an empirical research project concerning childless marriages in the Federal Republic of Germany. The following thesis was verified: Temporary childlessness seems to be chosen as a "way out" when a decision has to be made between divergent value orientations: work-orientation and the traditional mother-role acceptance. It is not a matter of the work-orientation of the woman alone but rather the combination of this with a particular concept of motherhood. Temporary childlessness arises only from the combination of these two things.

INTRODUCTION:
REASONS AND AIMS OF THE STUDY

The following is a report on an empirical research project which addresses the question why an increasing number of marriages in the Federal Republic of Germany remain childless.

When one looks at the literature on the subject of childlessness one finds that very many investigations of childlessness have been carried out in the USA and Canada. As early as 1979 the journal *Marriage and Family Review* published a survey of this question in an article based on more than 200 pieces of academic work on voluntary childlessness and 40 on related themes (Veevers, 1979). In 1986 Sharon K. Houseknecht wrote in her article on childlessness, "For a decade now, there has been an accelerating accumulation of research on this topic, especially since 1975" (1986:369). Yet both writers point out that despite the increased number of publications

---

Rosemarie Nave-Herz is Professor at the Institut für Soziologie, Universitat Oldenberg, Denmark.

the results to date have been of a more exploratory and descriptive character and are still unsatisfactory.

In the Federal Republic of Germany this topic has been completely neglected by researchers of the sociology of the family and demography. Until now childlessness has been treated as a medical or psychosomatic problem. It has also been the subject of cultural commentaries, one example appearing as early as 1926. This essay by H. Stieve with the evocative title "Infertility resulting from an unnatural way of life" does not present any empirically proved facts but confines itself to general moral observations.

The concept "childless marriages" is not even mentioned in German handbooks, anthologies and introductory texts on the sociology of the family (see Nave-Herz, 1987).

The lack of sociological studies of childlessness in the Federal Republic of Germany is remarkable in view of the fact that a large number of empirical investigations of attitudes to having children have been carried out since the further fall in the birth-rate in 1964. The Federal Republic of Germany has the lowest reproduction rate in the world (1984 = 1.3) and the West German population has been decreasing constantly since 1974 (Höhn and Otto 1985: 457, 481; Höpflinger 1987). The Ministries have supported research projects investigating the causes of the fall in the birth-rate in the Federal Republic of Germany and the future consequences of this reduction in population (see e.g., Mackensen and Umbach, 1986). But all the investigations of the changed German attitudes to having children only raise the question why parents want to have children and why they limit the number of children they have. They do not ask why they do not have or wish to have any children. And yet the percentage of childless couples in Germany has risen constantly since the end of the last century (see Table 1).

In model projections of the possible development of the numbers of children by the year 2000 the proportion of childless marriages in the Federal Republic of Germany is estimated at 20%. This would be twice the percentage of families with three children (see Table 2).

Some commentators, particularly women, interpret the increased number of childless marriages as a sign of a rejection of children and an increase in alternative life-styles. They assume, then, that

Table No. 1:

Year of marriage	percentage of marriages which remained childless
1899 and earlier	8·4
1900	9·7
1903	8·9
1906 (Prussia)	9·6
1909	10·3
1912	12·0
1913	12·3
1946 – 1950	13·0
1951 – 1955	13·0
1958 – 1962	13·0
1963 – 1967	14·0
1968 – 1972	17·0
1973 – 1977	18·0

Sources: Statistik des Deutschen Reiches, 1920: 11 ff.;
Bundesinstitut fur Bevölkerungsforschung, 1984: 356.

241

Table No. 2:

Number of children	Percentage of marriages
0	20
1	30
2	35
3	10
4 or more	5
Total:	100

Source: Deutscher Bundestag, 1985: 30

more and more women are now making a conscious choice to remain childless throughout their lives.

On the other hand, the medical profession and those taking a psychosomatic approach claim that the increase in childlessness is due to medical or psychosomatic causes. To confirm their claim they point to the statistics of gynecological clinics and advisory services specifically for childless couples, which report an increased number of parents seeking advice (Stauber: 1979). However, this statistical increase could also simply be the expression of an increased need nowadays to seek help from a doctor or an adviser when there are problems with conception.

The validity of these two contradictory interpretations of the conditions which have caused the increase in childless couples in the Federal Republic is the subject of an empirical investigation. The first results of which are reported below.

METHODOLOGY

This research project was divided into two sections: In the first phase open narrative interviews were conducted. 10 childless couples who had married in the year 1950, 10 in the year 1970, and 10 in the year 1980 (30 couples in all) were interviewed. In the second phase 163 semi-standardised oral interviews were conducted, 103 of them with women and 60 with men. The partners of the interviewees were mostly present; but the questions were presented to one partner only. Also, no data could be included for those who had married in 1950 since an appropriate sample could not be found. This is because the number of longer childless marriages was lower in 1950 than today. In addition, many of these marriages have since ended in divorce. For the divorce rate among childless marriages in the Federal Republic of Germany is very high (Höhn and Otto, 1985).

The interviews were conducted in the summer of 1986. The open narrative interviews proved particularly useful obtaining differences in social reality and the processes by which decisions for or against children were reached. For this reason the following report concentrates more on this first phase of our project.

REASONS FOR CHILDLESSNESS

Attitudes to Having Children
Given by Those Questioned

Types of childlessness should be distinguished (see also Houseknecht, 1986: 369 ff.). There is involuntary childlessness (that is childlessness due to medical or psychosomatic causes) and childlessness which was the result of a conscious decision by the couples. A further distinction is between a decision in favour of life-long childessness and one in favour of childessness for a limited period. Finally there is the category of temporary childlessness which has now reached the stage where the parents wish to terminate it, whether consciously or without any particular urgency.

In this investigation we have tried to take these different types of childlessness into account. Table 3 shows a relatively even distribution of the different reasons for present childlessness and thus proves the existing heterogeneity of social groups which are hidden behind the common label of "childless marriages."

We also asked our interviewees what their intentions regarding children had been immediately after marriage, in order to discover changes in the way couples had planned their lives. The quantitative distribution in Table 4 is not so even as in the previous one, thus showing that childlessness is a process which goes through different

Table No. 3: Attitudes to "having children"

- in % -

I should like to have children	19	
it makes no difference to me	9	28
I want to wait	14	
I don't ever want any children	18	32
It is impossible on medical or psychosomatic grounds	37	
no reply	3	
	100	
	(163)	

stages. The majority of couples who are childless today wanted children when they married, but wanted to wait first (= 50%). In about 6% of cases however the result of this "waiting period" was that they decided not to have children at all. Others discovered that the realisation of their desire to have children was either no longer possible or had in fact been impossible from the outset. These different stages were clearly described in the narrative interviews. Thus, some couples reported that their involuntary childlessness had turned into an involuntary one not only on grounds of age but also because of other changes such as accident or illness. Other couples had discovered only after deciding to terminate the period of temporary childlessness. From the start there had been a physiological barrier to their having children, they never had a choice. These two factors probably account for the high proportion of medically-caused childlessness (see Table 3).

Medical research has thus on the one hand increased the possibility of planning the realization of the desire to have children, but on the other hand it has also increased the incidence of unawareness of medically-caused childlessness.

The attitudes of the couples with regard to their involuntary childlessness varied widely between the marriage cohorts. The couples who had married in 1950 defined their childlessness as fate. Their statements on the subject are very short and simple. For in-

Table No. 4: Attitudes to "having children" immediately after marriage

– in % –

I should like to have children	20	⎤ 26
it makes no difference to me	6	⎦
I want to wait	50	⎤ 65
I don't ever want any children	15	⎦
It is impossible on medical or psychosomatic grounds	7	
no answer	3	
	100	
	(163)	

stance, "there was nothing we could do, we just had to accept it", or "that was just the way it was, that's all there is to it." Often they hadn't even consulted a doctor. Couples who had married in 1970 had actively fought against their involuntary childlessness. They had attended a variety of clinics. They had undergone various medical treatments, but without success. Listening to their recounting all the things they had gone through in order to have a child, one has the impression that they saw in the child something like a Messiah.

Reasons Given for Conscious
Voluntary Childlessness

In order to find out whether today's voluntarily childless marriages in the Federal Republic of Germany are the expression of a consciously chosen alternative life-style, the couples were asked about the reasons for their decision against having children. They were presented with a total of 37 statements and asked to say whether they agreed or disagreed with them. Table 5 gives a distribution of the answers.

The statements which indicate the desire for an alternative life-style were grouped in Table 5 in the two categories: "Reasons having to do with partners" and "Reasons having to do with own personality." Only 23% of all answers fall into these categories. There is no great difference between temporary and life-long childlessness.

On the other hand work-related reasons are most frequently given for the decision not to have children. This confirms the increased work-orientation of many young women today which has also been established in other investigations with different methodological procedures (see I. Sommerkorn's secondary analysis, 1987). In the qualitative interviews the women's description of this work-orientation included the wish not to have to give up working, whether because of strong commitment to the job, material reasons, or because they were aiming at a professional qualification or promotion. They were mainly supported by their husbands in their attitudes to work.

The results may therefore be summarized as follows: The increased work-orientation of women, while inhibiting the fulfillment

Table No. 5: Reasons for consciously-chosen childlessness at the beginning
of the marriage

- as a % of all replies -

	temporary childlessness	life-long childlessness	total
Reasons related to work	28	22	26
Financial reasons	16	10	13
Rejection of or negative attitude to children	15	25	20
Reasons having to do with partners	12	15	13
Reasons having to do with own personality	11	9	10
Age (too young or too old)	10	8	9
Other reasons	7	11	9
	100 (549)	100 (200)	100 (749)

(It was possible to give more than one reason)

of the desire for children, still has a strong influence on decisions in favour of childlessness in the Federal Republic of Germany. In contrast to this the conscious choice of an alternative life-style is seldom given as the reason.

It is also interesting that so many of those who plan never to have any children have a negative attitude to children or reject them altogether. Even their decisions, then, are largely characterized by the negation of something and not only by the positive advocacy of a particular life-style.

Concepts of Motherhood and Reasons for Voluntary Childlessness

In analyzing the narrative interviews we noticed that childless women had very varied concepts of the mother-role and that there seemed to be a link with the reasons for their childlessness. A content-analysis of the narrative interviews was conducted. The methodological problems of this procedure cannot be discussed in this short article.

We identified three different concepts of motherhood: Some estimated very highly the value of children for their own lives. This group gave the mother-child relationship precedence over the relationship between the parents. For them the child should be looked after only by the parents while it was still a baby. We called this attitude a *traditional conception of the mother-role*.

Some women said that they estimated the value of children for their own life was very high, but the husband-wife relationship was equally important to them as the mother-child relationship. They did not think that the care of the young baby could only be undertaken by the parents. We called this view: an *altered mother-role acceptance*. Less frequent in our sample was a *non-acceptance of the mother-role*. These women completely rejected the mother-role for themselves.

The next question was whether there was a connection between this "mother-typology" and the reasons given for the childlessness of their marriages. We found that temporary childlessness often coincided with a traditional view of the mother-role and at the same time with strong work-orientation of the wife. This last result at first seems contradictory because one might suppose that a traditional mother-role acceptance would not result in childlessness. But on the other hand this result is very clear. For these two orientations cannot be combined with regard to the profession and to the traditional mother-role. They are mutually exclusive. Some couples try to solve this conflict by postponing having children in the hope of removing the conflict at a later date. But for some couples this problem will solve itself involuntarily later on. They will find that it is too late, time has run out for them.

Temporary childlessness seems to be chosen as a "way out" when a decision has to be made between divergent value orientations: work-orientation and the traditional mother-role acceptance. It is not a matter of the work-orientation of the woman alone but rather the combination of this with a particular concept of motherhood. Temporary childlessness arises only from the combination of these two things.

Our thesis was verified by the questionnaires. Seventy-three percent of our interviewees who postpone their desire to get a child think that a "good mother" can only be a mother who has no professional activity. We can say that voluntary childlessness is often due to the sub-systems having changed by varying degrees. Changes in education and in the working system for women have been considerable, but changes in the family system have been few. Therefore, from a macrosociological perspective, voluntary childlessness can often be identified as a cultural lag.

REFERENCES

Calhoun, L. G. & Selby, J. W.: Voluntary Childlessness, Involuntary Childlessness, and Having Children: A Study of Social Perceptions; *Family Relations*, 1980, 29, 181-183.
Callan, J.: The Voluntary Childless and Their Perceptions of Parenthood and Childlessness, *Journal of Comparative Family Studies*, XIV, 1, 87-96.
Höhn, C. & Otto, J.: Bericht über die demographische Lage in der Bundesrepublik und über die Weltbevölkerungstrends, Zeitschrift f. Bevölkerungswissenschaft, 1984, 4, 445-518.
Höpflinger, F.: Wandel der Familienbildung in Westeuropa, Frankfurt: Campus Verlag, 1987.
Houseknecht, S. K.: Voluntary Childlessness; *Handbook of Marriage and the*

Family; M.B. Sussman & S.K. Steinmetz, (eds.) New York: Plenum Press, 1987, 369-395.

Mackensen, R. & Umbach, E.: Auswirkungen eines Bevölkerungsrückgangs auf die Lebensbedingungen in der Bundesrepublik Deutschland — Szenarie bis 2040, Berlin: Institut für Soziologie der Tu, 1986.

Nave-Herz, R. (ed.): Wandel und Kontinuität der Familie in der Bundesrepublik Deutschland, Stuttgart: Enke Verlag, 1988.

Ramu, G. N. and Tavuchis, N.: The Valuation of Children and Parenthood Among the Voluntarily Childless and Parental couples in Canada; *Journal of Comparative Family Studies*, XVII, No. 1, 1986, 99-116.

Sommerkorn, I.: Die erwerbstätige Mutter in der Bundesrepublik Deutschland — und Problemveränderungen; in: R. Nave-Herz, Hg., Wandel und Kontinuität der Familie in der Bundesrepublik Deutschland, Stuttgart: Enke Verlag, 1988.

Stauber, M.: Psychosomatik der sterilen Ehe, Berlin 1979.

Stieve, H.: Unfruchtbarkeit als Folge unnatürlicher Lebensweise, München 1926.

Veevers, J. E.: Voluntary Childlessness: A Review of Issues and Evidence; *Marriage and Family Review*, 1979, 2, 1, 3-26.

Veevers, J. E.: Childless by Choice, Toronto: Butterworths, 1980.

Veevers, J. E.: Voluntary Childlessness. A Critical Assessment of the Research, in: E. D. Macklin u. R. H. Rubin, Hg., Contemporary Families and Alternative Lifestyles, Beverly Hills, California: Sage Publications, 1983, 75-96.

Nuclear and Extended Family Attitudes of Jordanian Arabs

Kapur S. Ahlawat
Ali S. Zaghal

SUMMARY. Using a sample of 419 families from the northern region of Jordan, people's attitudes toward extended and nuclear family types were measured on two separate attitude scales. Each scale consisted of 42 Likert-type items. The alpha coefficients were .93 and .94 for extended family and nuclear family attitude scales, respectively. The effects of sex, level of education, area of residence, age, and marital status on the two attitudes were investigated. Appropriate statistical analyses of the data revealed that Education and Marital Status had significant effects on the extended family attitude but not on the nuclear family attitude. Sex, and Area of Residence, in contrast, had significant effects on the nuclear family attitude but not on the extended family attitude. The age factor, however, had significant similar effects on both attitudes. The two attitudes were found to be rather independent of than complementary to each other.

Sociologists generally recognize the family as the primary social institution and the basic unit of society. Family structure, therefore, has been one of the major preoccupations of sociological research over the past few decades. Research has mainly focused on the phenomenon of change in family structure and the causes and consequences of transition from joint family to nuclear family. Various theories attributing changes in family structure to forces of social change such as industrialization, modernization, urbanization, eco-

Kapur S. Ahlawat is Associate Professor (Psychometrics), Faculty of Education and Fine Arts, Yarmouk University, Irbid, Jordan. Ali S. Zaghal is Associate Professor (Sociology), Faculty of Arts, Humanities, and Social Sciences, Yarmouk University, Irbid, Jordan.

251

nomic development, ideological and cultural factors, and evolution of the family itself have been promulgated and examined by sociologists (Burner, 1961; Degler, 1980; Goode, 1970, 1982; Hareven, 1982, 1987; Kahl, 1960; Khairy, 1984, 1985; Ottoman, 1986; Stone, 1977).

In the context of Arab family, social scientists using different sources of data and writing from different perspectives have reached diverse conclusions about the nature of extended and nuclear family structures.

One group of researchers has described the traditional Arab family as extended, patrilineal, patrilocal, patriarchal, endogamous, and occasionally polygynous in which marriages were typically arranged by parents and divorce was easy to achieve for men but not so easy for women (Nasir, 1965; Patai, 1952, 1962; Williams and Williams, 1965).

The second group has adopted a two-pronged position and described the Arab family in terms of rural/urban dichotomy, extended family being predominant among the rural communities and the nuclear family widely gaining ground in urban communities especially among educated classes (Baer, 1964; Berger, 1962; Daghestani, 1953; Nahas, 1956).

The third group of researchers, in contrast with the previous two, has concluded, mainly on the basis of survey data, that the nuclear family is the basic pattern in Egypt, Jordan, Kuwait, Lebanon, Palestine, and Saudi Arabia (Antoun, 1972; Asad and Khalifa, 1977; Farsoun, 1970; Goode, 1970; Khairy, 1984, 1985; Khuri, 1975; Peterson, 1968; Prothro and Diab, 1974; Thakeb, 1981). Goode (1970) goes to the extent to state that the extended family never was the general norm among Arabs in the twentieth century mainly for economic and demographic reasons. He further adds that describing the Arab family as extended is a description of the ideal but not of the factual state of affairs (Goode 1970, pp.123-4). Peterson (1968, pp.536-7) after reviewing statistics and surveys concludes that the extended family of three generations living together under one roof is an unfamiliar phenomenon in rural and urban Egypt since the beginning of this century at least. Antoun (1972, pp.50-2) reports that 62% of the families in the villages in north Jordan were living as nuclear families. Prothro and Diab (1974) investigated the family patterns of couples who married during the sixties in Jordan (Amman), Syria (Damascus) and Lebanon (Beirut, Tripoli and Bourij Village) and found a significant majority of them living as nuclear families.

Regarding the extent of transition from extended family to nuclear family in Jordan, Asad and Khalifa (1977) report that during the period 1972 to 1976 the trend toward the nuclear family existed in all sectors of Jordanian society. According to Asad and Khalifa (1977), 75% of the people working in the urban areas lived in nuclear families. In semi-urban areas 72% lived in nuclear families and even in rural areas 69% of the people lived in nuclear families.

Despite the strong tendency towards urbanization and nuclearization of the family structure in Jordan the ties between members of the nuclear family and their extended kith and kin are strong. The emergence of the nuclear family in Arab society has not severed the umbilical cord with the kinship which has been a vital aspect of Arab society. Even those who live in nuclear families do not become isolated; they retain their emotional bonds with their extended relatives and take pride in fulfilling their traditional obligations and commitments towards them. In this sense, the kinship ties in the Arab world have remained basically unchanged (Farsoun, 1970; Khairy, 1984; Khuli, 1974; Shukri, 1979; Thakeb, 1982; Ottoman, 1986). As Ottoman (1986) has recently concluded, the visits, and financial and traditional responsibilities between the nuclear family and their parents as well as other relations based on kinship and neighbourhood are still strong.

Almost all the studies referred to above have derived their conclusions from the respondents' answers to factual questions or census-type data. The psychological or latent dimensions underlying the phenomenon of nuclear and joint family structure seem to have escaped the researchers' attention.

Attitude theory enjoys a prominent position in social psychology, sociology, and social sciences in general. One good thing about attitudes is that they stem from people's deep rooted values and accumulated experiences. But the primary virtue of attitudes lies in their functional utility for guiding human behavior and predicting peoples' likely course of action. From this viewpoint the knowledge of attitudes of different communities towards the nuclear and joint family is crucial not only for the better understanding of the process of change in family structure but also (and perhaps more importantly) for providing much needed perspective of the change for the social planners and policymakers.

PURPOSE

The research in this field, referred to earlier, has documented the nature and extent of the process of change in the Arabic family structure but has not touched upon people's attitudes and feelings about the change or toward either type of family structure. Transition in the way of living and family structure provides for reappraisal of the traditional values and reshaping of the old attitudes. Refreshed attitudes, in turn, depending upon their direction, may either facilitate further evolution or cause friction in the process of social change. In view of the above, the intention of this attempt was to provide for the information lacking in the area of attitude toward the family structure.

In general, the purpose of this study was to explore the attitudes of different groups of Jordanian peoples toward nuclear and extended family systems. More specifically the study intended to investigate:

A. the differences in the attitudes of males and females, town-dwellers and village-dwellers, married and unmarried, people with different levels of education, and different age groups;
B. the differences between the attitudes of each group toward the nuclear family and the extended family.

METHOD

Population groups were defined in terms of their *residence* (whether they live in villages or city), *sex* (male or female), *age* (16 to 21 years, 22 to 40 years, or 41 years and above), *education* (elementary/no education, secondary education, college/university), and *marital status* (married or unmarried). Irbid, the largest city in the northern region of Jordan, and six villages in the Irbid district were selected for the study of judgmental basis.

Subjects

Two hundred and twenty families belonging to the above forty years age group (110 from the city and 110 from the villages) were selected from the census records. One girls' school and one boys' school was randomly selected from all the high schools in the city. Then one 11th grade class was randomly selected from each school. The same procedure was adopted to select one girls' and one boys' section from the villages. Also two classes from girls' community colleges and two from boys' community colleges were randomly selected. Two community colleges (one boys and one girls) were taken from the villages area and two from the city. Also 31 teachers coming from different schools studying part-time for their master's degree in education were included in the sample.

Sample

The total sample consisted of 419 usable questionnaires. However, each specific analysis employed a slightly different sample size (which was never less than 404) because cases with missing information were deleted from the analyses. The sampling distribution of the 404 complete cases according to the vital characteristics of the study is as follows: (a) On the basis of sex, 245 were males and 159 females; (b) On the basis of marital status, 212 married and 192 unmarried; (c) On the basis of area residence, 256 lived in villages and 148 in city; According to age, 185 were from 16 to 21 years, 143 from 22 to 40, and 76 from 41 to 88. The actual numbers used for each analysis and reported in the tables are slightly more than these.

Instrumentation

Separate attitude scales were constructed for measuring attitudes toward the extended family and the nuclear family. Thurstonian procedures were applied to collect basic information regarding the referents, extended family and nuclear family. Information covered various aspects of attitude toward the nuclear family and extended family. The facets of attitude included economic or financial security, care for children, care for elderly, education, personal privacy, individual freedom, alienation from family, emotional ties, conjugal harmony, social mobility, etc. Out of large pools of items, 56 items were selected for each scale after careful scrutiny. All the selected items met the criteria usually prescribed for constructing good attitudinal items. Items were designed to be rated on a 5-point Likert scale (From Strongly Disagree to Strongly Agree). After data collection items were subjected to usual classical test theory based item-analysis procedures. On the basis of item-remainder correlations and varimax rotated common factor loadings, 42 items were finally selected for each attitude scale. The Cronbach's alpha reliability coefficients for 42 item extended family and nuclear family attitude scales were .93 and .94 respectively. These high alpha coefficients provide ample evidence of the homogeneity for both attitude scales. The details of the development procedures and psychometric properties of the scales are being reported in a separate article.

Data Collection

The data were collected from the students during their normal classroom periods but householders were interviewed by trained interviewers in their own homes. Educated subjects filled in the attitude questionnaire themselves, the responses of illiterate subjects were recorded by the interviewers.

RESULTS

Since the purpose of the study was an exploratory one and the survey sample was selected on judgmental basis, the data were analysed using unequal cell-size unbalanced survey design techniques of statistical analyses.

To start with simple gross effects of variables; level of education, and age on the attitude toward the extended family and nuclear family were explored via separate oneway analyses of variance. Information on education was collected in terms of years of study and highest level of examination passed or certificate obtained. For

ANOVA purposes education factor was categorized into three levels: elementary education, i.e., grade 9 or less as low; secondary education, i.e., grade 12 as medium; and college or university education as high level of education. Likewise the continuous variable age was trichotomized: 16 through 21 years as youth; 22 through 40 as adulthood; and 41 through 88 years as old age.

The means, standard deviations, the results of oneway ANOVAs and Scheffe's multiple comparison tests are presented in Tables 1a and 1b.

Education and Attitude

On the basis of education the sample was divided into three groups: Low, Moderate, and High. The 95% confidence intervals for means in Table 1a and the tests of statistical significance in Table 1b show that education is a significant factor in shaping peoples attitudes towards extended family. People with high (i.e., col-

TABLE 1a

Means, Standard Deviation, and 95% Confidence Intervals of the Low, Moderate, and High Education Groups on the Extended Family

and Nuclear Family Attitude Scales (N=412)

Scale	Group 1	N	Mean	SD	95% CI for Mean		
Extended Family	L	75	121.45	27.84	115.05	To	127.86
	M	233	121.67	25.65	118.36	To	124.98
	H	104	131.62	24.17	126.91	To	136.32
Nuclear Family	L	75	107.05	28.28	100.55	To	113.56
	M	232	105.89	24.92	102.67	To	109.12
	H	103	104.50	31.89	98.27	To	110.74

TABLE 1b

ANOVA Table for Education Level Effects on the Extended
and Nuclear Family Attitude Scales

Extended Family Attitude by Education Level

Source	DF	MS	F	P. of F
Between	2	3887.54	5.88	.003
Within	409	660.68		

Scheffe's Multiple Range Test (= .05) $\overline{X}H > (\overline{X}M = \overline{X}L)$

. . . .

Nuclear Family Attitude by Education Level

Source	DF	MS	F	P. of F.
Between	2	145.88	0.19	0.82
Within	407	752.77		

lege or university) education tend to have more favourable attitude towards extended family, whereas there is no difference in the attitude of people with no education, elementary education or secondary education. However, there are no statistically significant differences among the three education groups in their attitude towards the nuclear family.

The lack of significant differences in the nuclear family attitude scores of groups of people with different levels of education causes some concern because of two reasons. First, education has been commonly identified as one of the crucial determinants of attitudes. Second, this result seems to be contrary to the conclusion reached by Thakeb (1976) in Kuwait, Quraitem (1981) in Saudi Arabia (Jeddah), and more importantly by Zaghal (1988) in Jordan (Irbid).

All three studies cited above reported that a large proportion of their educated samples preferred the nuclear family over extended family. However, a closer inspection of the studies referred to reveals that none of them investigated the attitude which is a more complex entity, generally measured by a well constructed scale, than a simple preference assessed on the basis of a single question. It is a fact, supported by several surveys, that larger proportions of high education groups actually live and, therefore, indicate their preference for the nuclear family, and comparatively smaller proportions of less educated live as a nuclear family due to a multitude of reasons and circumstances and yet the two groups may hold a similar general attitude toward the nuclear family as they share so many other values and beliefs in common. This seems more likely to be happening here.

Age and Attitude

Age or generation gap, besides education, is commonly asserted to be another important influence on peoples' attitudes toward extended and nuclear family structures. To investigate this influence, the sample was split into three age groups, young, middle, and old, presented as Age-1, Age-2, and Age-3 respectively, in Tables 2a and 2b. Table 2a shows the means, standard deviations, and 95% confidence intervals for the means of the three groups for their attitudes toward extended and nuclear family systems. Differences due to age are statistically significant ($p < .000$) for the extended family, and ($p < .025$) for the nuclear family on both attitudes. On both attitudes the middle age group (22 years to 40 years) manifested more favourable attitudes than the younger generation group (16 years to 21 years). However, in either case, the attitudes of the older generation did not differ significantly at alpha $= .05$ level from those of the two younger age groups.

Sex, Rural/Urban Environment, Marital Status, and Attitudes

Sex, rural and urban living experiences, and marriage experience seem to be obvious factors that might play substantive roles in moulding people's attitudes toward extended and nuclear family systems. Differences in attitudes due to these factors were examined separately for each factor on each attitude scale via independent sample t-tests. The results of the t-tests are reported in Table 3.

Regarding the extended family, there are no statistically significant differences in the attitudes of males and females, but there are highly significant differences (p < .001) in their attitude toward the nuclear family. It seems that men show more positive attitudes toward the nuclear family than women do.

On the rural/urban dimension also, there is no difference at all between the means of the two groups on the extended family attitude scale, whereas, on the nuclear family attitude scale there is statistically significant difference (p < .011) between the attitudes of rural and urban people; urban residents show a substantially more positive attitude toward the nuclear family than the people who live in villages. This finding concerns the actual practice reported by several survey studies referred to earlier that nuclear family living is practiced more widely in urban areas than in the rural or bedouin settings. Zaghal (1988) on the basis of the Yarmouk University's

TABLE 2a

Means, Standard Deviations, and 95% Confidence Intervals for the Means of the Three Age Groups on the Extended and Nuclear Family Attitude Scales (N = 413)

Scale	Group	N	Mean	SD	95% CI for Mean		
Extended Family	Age 1	186	118.49	24.54	114.92	To	122.04
	Age 2	146	130.92	24.89	126.85	To	134.99
	Age 3	81	124.89	28.28	118.63	To	131.14
Nuclear Family	Age 1	186	102.69	19.37	99.89	To	105.50
	Age 2	144	110.78	34.51	105.10	To	116.47
	Age 3	81	104.44	28.25	98.19	To	110.69

TABLE 2b

ANOVA Table for Age Effects on the Extended and Nuclear

Family Attitude Scales

Extended Family by Age Groups

Source	DF	MS	F	P. of F
Between	2	6352.60	9.82	.000
Within	410	647.04		

Scheffe's Multiple Range Test (= .05) $\overline{X}_2 > \overline{X}_1$
....

Nuclear Family by Age Groups

Source	DF	MS	F	P. of F.
Between	2	2756.60	3.70	.025
Within	408	744.05		

Scheffe's Multiple Range Test (= .05) $\overline{X}_2 > \overline{X}_1$

---

evening students sample from Jordan, Quraitem (1981) on the basis of the Jeddah sample from Saudi Arabia, and Thakeb (1976) on the basis of the Kuwaiti sample from Kuwait have reported similar results. The proportion of people indicating their preference for nuclear family was significantly higher in the urban residents than in the rural ones. It seems to be a common finding of most Arabic family studies that urban, educated, upper socio-economic classes, by far, prefer the nuclear family to the extended family.

In contrast, along the married/unmarried dimension, there is no statistically significant difference in their attitudes toward the nuclear family but a highly significant difference (p < .001) in their attitude toward extended family; married people show a more fa-

TABLE 3

Means, SDs, Separate Variance Estimated Two-Tailed T-Values,
Significance of T between Sex, Urbanity, and Marital Status
Groups on the Extended and Nuclear Family Attitude
Scales

		N	Mean	SD	T-Value	DF	2-Tail P
	Male	251	123.75	26.23			
Extended					-0.27	348.67	0.785
	Female	161	124.46	35.46			
....							
	Male	250	109.42	26.42			
Nuclear					3.40	325.33	0.001
	Female	160	100.01	27.91			
	Rural	261	123.45	26.51			
Extended					-0.57	326.66	0.567
	Urban	150	124.95	24.92			
....							
	Rural	262	103.13	26.58			
Nuclear					-2.55	285.45	0.011
	Urban	147	110.43	28.48			
	Married	217	128.16	25.99			
Extended					3.28	404.67	0.001
	Unmarried	192	119.91	24.80			
....							
	Married	215	107.23	32.27			
Nuclear					1.34	364.05	0.180
	Unmarried	192	103.69	20.16			

vourable attitude toward the extended family than their unmarried counterparts.

The above results indicate the gross influence of each variable on the attitudes of people. Social psychologists know it very well that in natural community settings, determinant factors seldom act in isolation. Usually, in complex social environments these factors act and counteract upon each other, thus, the so-called independent variables are seldom independent of the influence of other variables.

Effect of Each Variable Adjusted for All Other Variables

In order to assess the influence of each variable having controlled for the effects of all other variables in the study, the data were analysed by factorial analysis of variance using the regression or unique sum of squares method. Particularly, the proportion of partial variance in the attitude scores due to each individual factor, sex, marital status, residence, and generation was investigated with the education (years of study) factor as the covariate. The results of the factorial ANCOVAs are given in Table 4.

Extended Family Attitude

From the extended family attitude portion of Table 4 it is clear that only the age factor has a statistically significant contribution to the variance in extended family attitude scores when the influence of all other variables including education has been partialled out. However, when the gross effects of these variables were tested, the marital status was a significant discriminator (p < .001, See Table 3) of attitude toward the extended family between married and unmarried groups of people. Also, differences due to education were significant (See Table 1b) at that time but now education's net effect on attitude toward the extended family is not statistically significant. From this perspective, age seems to be the most powerful singlehanded contributor to the variation in attitude toward the extended family.

TABLE 4

Regression (SSTYPE UNIQUE) Method Based Factorial Analyses of Covariance on Extended Family and Nuclear Family Attitude Scales' Scores

Source of Variation	Extended Family Attitude				Nuclear Family Attitude			
	DF	MS	F	Sig	DF	MS	F	Sig
Covariate Yrs of Education	1	1120.058	1.753	.186	1	992.180	1.448	.230
Main Effects	5	2514.203	3.934	.002	5	3588.516	5.238	.000
Sex	1	74.007	.116	.734	1	7513.670	10.967	.001
Marital	1	331.217	.518	.472	1	.004	.000	.998
Rural/Urban	1	254.076	.398	.529	1	2645.406	3.861	.048
Age	2	2429.770	3.802	.023	2	3504.360	5.115	.006
Explained	6	2238.258	3.502	.002	6	3024.785	4.415	.000
Residual	397	639.057			394	685.128		
Total	403	662.866			400	720.223		

Nuclear Family Attitude

An examination of the portion of Table 4 subheaded "nuclear family attitude" tells an entire different story of the potency of each factor shorn of the invisible influence of the other concomitants.

All the variables have significant contributions to the variation in attitude toward the nuclear family, except years of education and marital status which were not significant when their gross effects were tested via oneway ANOVA, and t-test, respectively. Sex and age effects are highly significant with ($p < .001$) and ($p < .006$) respectively, rural/urban permanent residence factor is also significant at the $p < .05$ level.

Relationship Between the Two Attitudes

The preceding results of the various analyses of the data reveal that the nuclear family attitude and the extended family attitude are not explained by the same factors. More specifically, sex and residence factors explained the attitude toward the nuclear family but not the attitude toward the extended family. Contrarily, education and marital status explained the variability in attitude toward the extended family but not toward the nuclear family. Only age factor accounted for significant variance in both attitudes. Yet another revelation from the data was that means of the extended family attitude scores were consistently higher than those of the nuclear family attitude scores in all the groups of people. Could it mean that the two attitudes are quite different constructs independent of each other? Although one would naturally assume the two attitudes to be complimentary, the results of this study cast strong doubts on the complimentarity hypothesis.

In order to investigate independence hypothesis, product moment correlations between the two attitude scales' scores were computed for different groups of people. Also, paired sample t-tests were conducted on the two sets of scores for each group. The results of the correlation and paired t-test analyses are presented in Table 5.

The column headed "Corr" in Table 5 records extremely low, near zero, negative correlations between the two attitudes among all the groups. Only in the rural male and all male subsamples the correlation reached statistical significance at 0.01, and 0.05 levels

TABLE 5

Means, SDs, Correlations and Paired t-Tests between Extended and Nuclear Family Attitude
Scales' Scores of Different Groups

| Group | N | Extended Family Attitude | | Nuclear Family Attitude | | Corr. | t-Value | Prof. |
		Mean	SD	Mean	SD			
Male	247	123.55	26.15	108.79	25.89	-0.14*	5.89	.000
Female	160	124.54	25.52	100.01	27.91	-0.14	7.70	.000
Rural Male	134	123.84	26.21	105.30	25.83	-0.04	5.71	.000
Urban Male	111	122.66	25.96	112.64	25.58	-0.28**	2.56	.012
Rural Female	124	122.85	26.85	98.95	25.35	-0.16	6.68	.000
Urban Female	36	130.39	19.44	103.64	35.55	-0.12	3.77	.001

* = significant at alpha < .05

** = significant at alpha < .01

respectively. Even though statistically significant, the observed degree of relationship is quite negligible and insubstantial for practical considerations. The correlations between the two attitude scores were not statistically different from zero at the 5% level of significance. The paired sample differences between the two attitude scores are highly significant in all the groups. The mean attitude scores on the extended family scale were invariably higher than those on the nuclear family scale in all the analyses. This seems to confirm the supposition that the two attitudes are conceptually different from each other.

DISCUSSION AND CONCLUSIONS

The findings of this study lead to the following conclusions:

1. People with college and university education tend to have a more favourable attitude toward the extended family structure than people with less than college education or no education at all but there are no significant differences on this attitude between people with secondary education and those with elementary education or no formal schooling at all. However, education seems to make no difference in people's attitudes toward the nuclear family structure, i.e., irrespective of the level of education people feel the same way toward the nuclear family.

2. There are no significant differences in the attitudes of males and females toward the extended family but males tend to view the nuclear family structure more favourably than do the females.

3. The areas of permanent residence (i.e., the rural and urban community environments) seem to have no differential influence on the attitude toward extended family but quite a significant ($p < .01$) impact on people's attitude toward the nuclear family. City people show a significantly more positive attitude toward the nuclear family than do the village people.

4. There are no significant differences in the attitude of married and unmarried groups toward the nuclear family, however, the two groups show highly statistically significant differences in

their attitudes toward the extended family structure. Married people are inclined to appreciate the virtues of the extended family system more than the unmarried ones.

5. Middle age (22 years to 40 years) appears to sensitize the attitudes of people toward both family structures. This age group scored statistically significantly higher than both older and younger age groups on both the attitude scales. The differences between young and old age groups on both the attitude scales were not statistically significant at the 5% level.

6. All the people, in general, have a more positive attitude and feeling towards the traditional extended family structure than they have toward the rather modern nuclear family in spite of the fact that most of them have reported that they have been living in nuclear families.

7. The nuclear family attitude and the extended family attitude are two almost independent and distinct concepts, not the complementary dimensions of a single composite construct, the attitude toward family structure.

Discussion

Recent studies focusing on the emerging popularity of the nuclear family structure in the Arab world have asserted that education has played a crucial role in accelerating the process of transition from the traditional extended family to the modern nuclear family structure (Khairy, 1985; Ottoman, 1986). Sociologists proffer compelling arguments as well as empirical data to derive the causal relationship between education and transition to the nuclear family. Particularly, in Jordan, over the past two decades, the rapid progress in education and the proliferation of the nuclear family have gone hand-in-hand. From such observations it is rather tantalizing to hypothesize that the "higher the level of education the more favourable the attitude toward the nuclear family, and conversely, the less favourable the attitude toward the extended family." The results from the data of this study contradict both hypotheses. No differences were found in the nuclear family attitudes among the three groups with low, medium, and high levels of education. On the other hand, college or university educated groups showed a significantly more favourable attitude toward the extended family. This poses a dilemma. It may be correct that progress in education along with other developments has led to the changes in family structure but it seems plausible that education has also enhanced people's appreciation of their cultural values and traditions, in this case, the Arab tradition of extended family structure. It is quite possible that forced by circumstances people have to live in the nuclear families and yet cherish for the benefits the traditional extended family system had provided through the age. Home-made goodies is still providing in the form of free baby-sitter, or a helping hand for the wife in the house in the time of need, or getting some social, emotional and economic help occasionally. Perhaps its more than appreciation, it could be one way of expressing loyalty and identity to one's long cherished system associated in their mind with Arab-Islamic culture.

From this point of view, the findings of this study, actually, lend support to the observations of Farsoun (1970) and Khairy (1984) that weakening of the extended family structure has not loosened the strong emotional ties of kinship in the Jordanian society. The consistently higher scores on the extended family attitude scale among all the groups provide further evidence in support of this suggestion. When other factors were controlled, the effect of education vanished from both attitudes, but the age factor had significant impact on both the attitudes. In particular, the middle age group (22 to 40 years) scored significantly higher on both attitude scales than the younger and older age groups. Moreover, this factor retained its impact on both attitudes even when the effects of all other factors had been partialled out. Perhaps family attitudes are not one of the primary concerns at the young age (16 to 21 years) because young people are likely to be busy in their high school requirements, and seriously thinking of getting their university education, the draft system, and securing a job in the workplace as the most important priorities at this age level, and the attitude and feelings of the older people (above 40 years) have been mellowed down. It is the age of twenties and thirties during which people in Jordan establish their families. They have to make active choices and learn to live with the consequences — usually a mixed bag. In the absence of any hard evidence, one may be reasonably tempted to surmise that, in this age group, new life experiences and family responsibilities and turmoils of adjustments to changing life style are likely to accentuate their family related attitudes for getting the benefits of both systems.

The extended family institution due to its traditional, cultural, and sentimental values has been idealized, therefore, there were no significant differences in extended family attitude due to either sex or area of residence. However, there were highly significant differences due to sex and area of residence in peoples' attitude toward the nuclear family. Males superceded the females and urban people superceded the village people on this attitude. Area differences are understandable because almost everywhere urban people are more susceptible to changes than the rural people but reasons for males harbouring a more favourable attitude toward the nuclear family than females are not so conspicuous. Judiciously designed studies are needed to unravel the intricacies of reasons for such differences.

Regarding marital status there were no significant differences on the nuclear family attitude but on the extended family attitude married persons outscored the unmarried ones. However, when variance due to other factors were adjusted for, this difference vanished.

One observation made by some sociologists in the United States is that with increasing industrialization, urbanization, and occupational complexity there did not occur a wholesale transition from the kin to the nuclear family structure (Sussman and Burchinal, 1962; Sussman, 1970, 1972). Rather, nuclear and kin families as well as other forms such as single parent existed side-by-side in pre-industrial times.

No evolutionary process was operating whereby kin families became nuclear in structure as a consequence of industrial development. There may have been generational shifts from kin to nuclear and nuclear to kin structure dependent on economic, social, and political circumstances and conditions of migrating and non-migrating populations. Kin members have remained supportive of one another and even today, among the poor and minority populations, survival is dependent upon the help of one's kin. The pages of history are full of stories of kin assisting one another even though they may not share the same household in an urban environment. Separate households may meet the desire for privacy and intimacy while still enabling the kin network to function over generational time.

Limitations

The limitations of this study stem from the sample of the study which was limited to Irbid city and its surrounding villages. Also the sampling procedures were mainly judgmental and therefore the sample cannot be called truly representative of the total population even in that area. The characteristics of the people in the southern desert areas or in the capital city Amman may be different from those of the population of this study. Nevertheless, the fundamental values of the people do not vary so much, and, since the conclusions of the study are based upon the response data and not on the frequency counts, the sampling efficiency may not pose a real threat to the validity of results. Finally, it was only a preliminary exploration and in spite of its sampling deficiency it has yielded quite interesting and illuminating results which can serve as valuable hypotheses for further well planned investigations into this intricate field of family structure related attitudes. However, the findings of this study must be treated as tentative rather than conclusive.

REFERENCES

Antoun, R. *Arab village: A social structural study of Jordanian peasant community*. Bloomington: Indiana University Press, 1972.

Asad, S., and Khalifa, A. *Family structure in relation to fertility in Jordan*. Amman: Jordan Department of Statistics Press, 1977.

Baer, G. *Population and society in the Arab East*. London: Routledge and Kegan Paul, 1964.

Berger, M. *The Arab World to-day*. Garden City: New York: Doubleday, 1962.

Burner, E.L. Urbanization and ethnic identity in north Sumatra. *American Anthropologist*, Vol. 63, 508-514, 1961.

Daghestani, K. The evaluation of the Moslem family in Middle East countries. *International Social Science Bulletin*, Vol. V, 681-693, 1953.

Degler, C. *At odds: Women and the family in America from the revolution to the present*. New York: Oxford University Press, 1980.

Farsoun, S. Family structure and society in modern Lebanon. (Ch.9). In L.E. Sweet (Ed.), *People and cultures of the Middle East*. Vol. II. New York: Natural History Press, 1970.

Goode, W. *World revolution and family patterns*. London: The Free Press, Macmillan Publishing Co., 1970.

Goode, W. *The family*. New Jersey: Prentice Hall (p.7), 1982.

Hareven, T. *Family time and industrial time*. New York: Cambridge University Press, 1982.

Hareven, T. Family history at the crossroads. *Journal of Family History*, Vol. 12, Nos. 1-3, ix-xxiii, 1987.

Kahl, J.A. Some social concomitants of industrialization and urbanization. *Human Organization*, Vol. 18, No. 2, 1959-1960.

Khairy, M. Patterns of relations among some nuclear families and kins in Amman City/Jordan. *Dirasat (Social Sciences and Education)*. (The University of Jordan Journal), Vol. 11 No. 6, 43-74. (In Arabic), 1984.

Khairy, M. *Social relationship among some Jordanian nuclear families*. Amman: Cooperative Press. (In Arabic), 1985.

Khuli, S. *Family in a changing world*. Cairo: Egyptian Institute for Books. (In Arabic), 1974.

Khuri, F.I. *From village to suburb: Order and change in greater Beirut*. Chicago: University of Chicago Press, 1975.

Nahas, M.K. The family in the Arab world. *Marriage and Family Living*, Vol. 16, 294-300, 1956.

Nasir, M. The family and social welfare in Iraq. Unpublished paper, Kuwait. (In Arabic), 1965.

Ottoman, I. Changes in the urban family in Jordan. *Social Studies Journal*, Vol. 14, No. 3, 153-177. (In Arabic), 1986.

Patai, R. The Middle East as a culture area. *The Middle East Journal*, Vol. 6, 1-21, 1952.

Patai, R. *Golden river to golden road: Society, culture and change in the Middle East*. Philadelphia: University of Pennsylvania Press, 1962.

Peterson, K.K. Demographic conditions and extended family households: Egyptian data. *Social Forces*, Vol. 46, 531-537, 1968.

Prothro, E., and Diab, L. *Changing family patterns in the Arab East*. Beirut: American University of Beirut, 1974.

Quraitim, A. et al. *The Saudi family: Role and change and their effect in decision making*. Jeddah: King Abdul Aziz University. (In Arabic), 1981.

Shukri, A. *Modern attitudes of family study*. Cairo: House of Knowledge. (In Arabic), 1979.

Stone, L. *The family, sex, and marriage in England 1500-1800*. New York: Harper and Row, 1977.

Sussman, M.B. and Burchinal, L. Kin family network unheralded structure in current conceptualization of family functioning. *Marriage and Family Living*, 24: 231-240, 1962.

Sussman, M.B. The urban kin network in the formulation of family theory. In R. Hill and R. Koenig (eds.) *Families in East and West: Socialization Processes and Kinship ties*. Paris, France, Monton, 481-503, 1970.

Sussman, M.B. Family, kinship and bureaucracy. In A. Campbell and P. Converse (eds.) *Social Change and Human Change*. New York: Russell Sage Foundation, 127-158, 1972.

Thakeb, F. Attitudes of the Kuwaitis from size and structure of the family. Kuwait: *Journal of the College of Arts*, Vol. 9, 135-1465. (In Arabic), 1976.

Thakeb, F. Size and Composition of the Arab family: *Census and survey data. International Journal of Sociology of the Family*, Vol. 11, 171-178, 1981.

Thakeb, F. Family-kinship ties in modern Kuwaiti society. *Annals of Arts Faculty*, Kuwait: Kuwait University, Vol. 3, 1982, 23-44. (In Arabic), 1982.

Williams, H., and Williams, J. The extended family as a vehicle of culture change. *Human Organization*, Vol. 24, 59-64, 1965.

Zaghal, A.S. Attitudes of Yarmouk University evening students towards issues related to woman: *Damascus University Journal* (in press). (In Arabic), 1988.

Partnership Cultures

Kris Jeter

INTRODUCTION

Mythologists and scientists agree about the history of the world. *Once upon a time there was chaos. Then, three and a half billion years ago, a star and a planet mated and their gasses intermingled. Cell by cell, life formed, fish, amphibians, reptiles, mammals, and humans with the most sophisticated brain of all. Chaos reappeared in the form of sibling rivalry and turf wars.*

Deep within, we remember the time when, we, like the fish in the original cosmic sea, were gently, serenely rocked within the uterine sea of unity. We mourn and hope, knowing that somewhere, there is conscious community, consensus, partnership and vision. We yearn and seek, knowing that sometimes, there is mindful empathy, harmony, unity, and action.

Elaine Pagels, in her research on *The Gnostic Gospels*, has stated that the history of the world has been authored by the winners, and so a review of the literature may not provide an accurate picture of how partnership cultures are born and sustained.

However, buried, layered beneath Mother Earth is a gold mine of information, albeit not written words, which can provide a more holistic view of world history. This mining activity, carried out both below water and land, requires the interdisciplinary skills of anthropologists, archaeologists, architects, artists, botanists, chemists, climatologists, engineers, geologists, historians, mythologists, paleontologists, social scientists, and zoologists working together

Kris Jeter is Associate Director of Mentor and Learner Relationships for the Jean Houston Human Capacities Training Program and Director of Programs and Communications for The Possible Society. Address correspondence to: 800 Paper Mill Road, Newark, DE 19711.

in partnership. As we look at an excavation and are told a historical story, we may ask, "How do they know that?" Interdisciplinary teams of scholars carefully place pieces of information into mosaics of meaning, not unlike Persephone and Cinderella, patiently sorting the seeds of knowledge into a pattern. This methodology could be discussed at another time.

Archaeology has defined a chronology of three major ages in accordance to the primary used resource for tools to extend human capabilities. These are the Stone, Bronze, and Iron Ages. We will be discussing the lessons that we may learn about partnership cultures from two Stone Age communities. Therefore, quickly reviewed are this age's subdivisions.

a. Eolithic—The stage where very crudely chipped flints are used for hunting and food gathering;

b. Paleolithic—The stage where rough or chipped stone implements are used for hunting and food gathering;

c. Mesolithic—The stage where polished instruments are used for the final stage of intensified food gathering and hunting;

d. Proto-Neolithic—The movement from food-gathering and hunting to food producing is well under way;

e. Neolithic—The stage were farming and stock breeding are well established; and

f. Ae-neolithic—The stage where copper is introduced into the construction of household utensils, jewelry, and weaponry.

These stages cannot be universally time dated because lands that have been ice free longer and those which have more natural resources often move from the Stone to the Bronze to the Iron Age at an earlier time than other lands. Anthropologists and archaeologists are discovering that the precise stages are inadequate to describe cultures because cultures consist of beings and varied forms of organizational structures and geographic areas.

Groups of individuals may be in various archaeological ages or in transition from one to another. Even in this Computer Age, neolithic communities are quite prominent. Populations still struggle for survival; they still strain and toil for clothing, food, and shelter.

Marija Gimbutas in her book, *The Goddesses and Gods of Old*

Europe: Myths and Cult Images has synthesized the gleanings of over 160 archaeological excavations to document her theory about the existence of a matrilineal era in Old Europe between 6500 and 3500 B.C.E.

In *The Chalice and the Blade*, Rian Eisler, has explicated Gimbutas' history into the future. Eisler has described societies as being patterned on a continuum between chalice and blade cultures. The chalice cultures worship the generation of life and nurture the powers of the universe. They are models of partnership. The blade cultures establish and enforce domination.

In this paper, I shall investigate the connection between Partnership Cultures and the Human Spirit. I shall explore the concept and metaphors of partnership as exhibited in two archaeological excavations referred to by Gimbutas: Lepenski Vir, Yugoslavia and Catal Huyuk, Turkey. In September 1988, I visited the remains of both sites.

I am defining partnership as the conscious, empathetic, purposeful, gender free, and less hierarchical connection of humans with all life. Lepenski Vir and Catal Huyuk yield viable, unique, and valuable lessons on partnership cultures of importance to us today. The majority of residents of both excavations were gifted artists and inventors who while co-creating the world conducted their lives in partnership with each other and with the spirit.

LEPENSKI VIR

Lepenski Vir, a town in eastern Yugoslavia, was discovered in 1960 during the planning stage for building a hydro-electric dam on the Danube River. From 1965 to 1969, archaeologist Dragoslav Srejovic led a comprehensive excavation of the site. Important artifacts of these ancient beings have been moved to higher ground before flooding occurred. Other artifacts are on display in the Belgrade National Museum, and the remainder of the excavation is underwater.

Between ten and seven thousand years ago, when the ice was melting, the earth was slowly warming, and the mammoth was becoming extinct, the hunter who had till now migrated from cave to cave for shelter while following the large herds of herbivorous mammoths, had to develop a new life style.

At least two hunters, Cro-Magnon individuals of erect, sturdy, tall stature, large faces and heads, and deep-set eyes arrived at a bend of the Danube River to find a virtual Garden of Eden. Their sunny canyoned sanctuary 170 meters long and 50 meters wide was bounded closely by the swift river with a foreboding whirlpool and steep cliffs of a mountain range. The mild, almost oceanic climate allowed humans to live outside of caves. The earth was covered with fruit and nut trees. The mammoths of the Ice Age were replaced by more dispersed, less plentiful, and more nimble animals. Carp and catfish were drawn into the river's whirlpool and the humans needed only walk into a shallow riverbed before the whirlpool, and pick out the catch of the day for dinner.

During the Post-Glacial Age, Lepenski Vir was one of the first known communities to evolve extemporaneously, without assistance from earlier developed communities in the Near East. In this paper, I shall discuss the stages of development of Lepenski Vir, observing how the architecture, sculpture, engravings, and altars reflected the community as it attempted unsuccessfully to transit from the Mesolithic to the Neolithic Ages, a Revolution of Ages.

At first, during the Proto Lepenski Vir (5800-5600 B.C.E.) culture, twenty individuals, members of three or four biological families, utilized nature's resources for the maintenance of the group. Each adult had equal birthrights and equal tasks and worked diligently to survive. There were no vestiges of status or prestige for the living or dead. The Proto Lepenski Vir level of the dig is similar to that of concurrent levels of other digs.

However, as the population of this community, isolated and bound within natural frontiers, increased after approximately two hundred years from twenty to one hundred, the community had to make conscious and to actualize their values. The resident's mindful choice and co-creation of a new cultural, economic, and social system based on partnership and quality of life has made Lepenski Vir a unique excavation from which we can learn.

Dragoslav Srejovic found several graves of eighty year old individuals who were buried with status items and has proposed a theory. He believes that at the first critical point of the population explosion, these wise spiritual elders planned the physical layout of the town so that each family had space and the community lived in partnership with the environment. Middle Eastern traditions embellished by linguistic modes have associated the architect and carpenter with the magician. These professions are believed to hold knowledge of the mysteries. The planner of Lepenski Vir knew the mysteries of architecture, astronomy, engineering, and geometry; it was their magic and myth.

There was one central sanctuary and below it, down the incline and toward the water was the marketplace. As each home was to be built, the wise spiritual elders would carefully lay out and bless a plan for the foundation of a trapezoidal shaped home where there was direct diagonal access to the market place and to the river. The spirit was acknowledged; each home contained an altar.

During Lepenski Vir Ib (5400-5150 B.C.E.), this town plan was respected and carefully followed for generations, even during rebuilding and renovation, when land of varied heights was appropriately terraced into the plan. Added to the interior's sacred center area was a stone table and two sandstone sculptures. Sculpture appeared for the first time. Next to each fireplace stood a huge carved rock boulder.

During Lepenski Vir Ic (5150-5050 B.C.E.), after 450 years of ordered living, a division occurred. Lepenski Vir Ic appears to be two towns, each with their central sanctuary and marketplace. Sculptures of animal and fish heads were amplified with fish bodies. Artists recognized that the skin is an obvious veneer which covers arteries and muscles, the carrier of blood and the potency of the body. Heads appear to have brains. On one altar, a burgundy colored stone portrays the vulva at the specific time of giving birth. The curved line now makes blossoms, braids, clovers, eyes, figures-of-eight, fossils, hearts, spirals, and wheels.

During Lepenski Vir Id (5050-5000 B.C.E.), the living space in the home's interior was expanded and the scared area was crowded together. Red triangular shaped stones, thought to represent ancestors or, perhaps vulvas, were arranged as if in a mosaic and added to the sacred area. Less stones are sculpted. The few that were worked have the appearance of two dimensional, rather than three dimensional rocks. The curved lines look warped and swerved. This period lasted fifty years.

During Lepenski Vir Ie (5000-4950 B.C.E.), there was an attempt to return to the basic town plan of Lepenski Vir Ia. The entire community was built on fragile step terraces away from the river. The access ways were perpendicular and zigzag. Foundations were geometrically imperfect. Construction was hurried and haphazard. Building materials were frail. It was as if the town was weighted down. After fifty years, an unknown event changed the course of the community. Every dwelling was destroyed.

Lepenski Vir II (4950-4850 B.C.E.) was built upon the fragile step-terraces with only a dim memory of its heritage. Retaining walls were collectively built in an attempt to prevent landslides. Upon the foundations of Lepenski I, the residents built defective dwellings with flimsy floors not in consonance with the landscape.

The art of Lepenski Vir II is unparalleled. The sculpture entitled, The Deer in the Forest, has varied designs placed in an unusual way on a two-dimensional surface. The sculpted figures have snarled trunks, piercing eyes, and traumatic frowns. The head of one figure is larger than that of a human, an unprecedented sculpture for its time. Are these figures suggesting an inconceivable aversion, an unnerving duress, or forecasting a portentous catastrophe? A sense of premonition and trepidation is voiced by the sculpture. Indeed, Lepenski Vir II had only a one hundred year history.

In comparison to the architecture of Late Palaeolithic and Early Neolithic sites, Lepenski Vir was exceptional and unrivaled. Dwellings had definitive, solid foundations that met meticulous geometric ratios. Perhaps, Lepenski Vir living between perilous cliffs and a whirlpool and crowded by kin developed an introverted personality which was mirrored in the community sanctuary and the private shrines in each home. The trapezoid was the shape of the home as well as the available land. The town was a microcosm of the macrocosm. Each morning, the rising sun pierced the entrances of each home, bathing the altar with warmth.

Each nuance of the environment was studied so that the humans could live in harmony with nature. They extended the capabilities of the hand by transforming stones into tools. Survival, however, depended more on the community's sensual accurateness and innate instinct with physical dexterity and force. Small dogs were domesticated to be hunting companions.

Over time, labor was divided into roles and individuals became specialists with unique talents. The skeletons of both women and men are quite sturdy and sexual identity is difficult to determine. It is assumed, however, that the division of labor was not sex differentiated. Yet, rugged individualism was not adequate for life at Lepenski Vir. The hunting of game and the acquisition of stone for building, sculpture, and tools required that specialists consolidate and merge their talents into one effort. Together, they would leave their refuge, climb steep cliffs, travel through dense forest for a day, track and capture game, loosen and carry huge boulders, and deliver themselves and the goods back to their community. Banishment from the community meant doom. Between the sheer rock cliffs, the rapidly moving river, and the thick wild forest, an exposed individual became weak and helpless.

All work was dedicated to the life of the community. The individual primarily was in service to the group rather than the group existing solely for the benefit of the individual. Existence demanded partnership. Each individual became a partner with every other individual observing the rituals of the collective cosmology.

CATAL HUYUK

Catal Huyuk, a city in central Turkey, was discovered by British archaeologist James Mellaart in 1951 when he was working under a small grant to apply field survey techniques to the discovery of historic cultural sites of Anatolia. Mellaart proved that discipline, persistence, and time rather than money can be the best research tool. He persevered in walking and horseback riding to travel the length and breadth of Anatolia. His arduous task to prepare distribution maps and reports of the various sites and a severe attack of a viral dissentary prevented him from returning to Catal Huyuk until 1961. In four seasons, Mellaart uncovered one thirtieth of the archaeological site. Intrigue and politics far more colorful than those exhibited in the classic movie, *The Orient Express*, halted the excavations. Today, there are two large openings in the ground overgrown with bushes and grass at the site. The artifacts of this ancient civilization are in the Anatolia Museum in Ankara.

Catal Huyuk, a city with a population of 5000 to 6000, was occupied from 7100 to 6300 B.C.E. Catal Huyuk, Jericho of Syria-Palestine, and Jarmo of Mesopotamia, are the largest known Near East Neolithic sites of this era. Catal Huyuk and Jericho are the oldest known cities in the world.

Catal Huyuk is situated at the convergence of a river and a lush place for wheat fields, animals, and humans. To the south and west, are the Taurus or Bull Mountains, the fountainhead of the river. At that time, the Taurus Mountains were the home for bear, deer, and leopards. To the north, were salt marshes, and to the east and west were rich grasslands, home of cattle, gazelles, lions, and wild asses.

The foundation of the city's economy was progressive agriculture, animal breeding, hunting, commerce, and crafts. The residents had the most well balanced diet of all Neolithic peoples in the Near East. Ninety per-cent of the meat consumption was beef.

The residents of Catal Huyuk consisted of three races. Sixty percent were hardy Eurafrican, twenty-four percent were circular-headed Alpines, and seventeen percent were thin, delicate-boned Mediterraneans. This community readily welcomed emigrants. This acceptance of peoples from outside of the community resulted in the creation and dissemination of creative art, crafts, philosophy, language, and technical practices throughout Anatolia.

Fourteen consecutive levels of buildings have been dug. The city did experience occasional devastating fires. Otherwise, in its 800 year history, Catal Huyuk lived in abundance, peace, and tranquility, without experiencing war—a record in the history of the world. There were no city ramparts or walls. The city was constructed of houses and cattle enclosures, arranged detached, side by side in large blocks without formal streets. Perhaps, Catal Huyuk was the first city to have what we call today the mother-in-law apartments or granny annex! As a family grew, another house was added to the chain. This architectural plan was faithfully followed throughout the city's history.

Each dwelling was a 25 square meter rectangular room built with mud-brick placed upon a rock foundation and topped with a flat room. This room had a half attic assembled of lumber and plaster. At least two walls had high upper windows cut directly underneath the eaves. To the side of the large room was a small storage area constructed out of mud-brick placed directly upon the soil without a foundation. The only entrance to this dwelling was through a wooden ladder placed against the south wall of the larger room.

Catal Huyuk was the trendsetter of Neolithic technology. Only bone, clay, obsidian, reeds, and wood were readily available. All other materials were obtained through extensive trade. Over the years, more and more pottery was used and its texture was refined. Boxes with fitted lids, plates, and vessels of all sizes were carved of wood. Animal hair and wool were woven into the first known textile in the world.

The first known mirrors in the world were made in Catal Huyuk with the black, glass-like obsidian gathered from a nearby volcano. The mirrors were employed to reflect personal beauty and spiritual beings. Obsidian was also employed to make arrow-heads, blades, sickles, and spear-heads. Awls, beads, drills, jewelry, and knick-knacks were constructed of copper and lead.

The bodies of the dead were laid bare so that vultures could clean the bones. The skulls were then colored and adorned and the entire skeletons buried under the home's sleeping-platforms. Homes were often reconstructed on their original structures and generations of a family would be layered upon each other. Some males were laid to rest with burnished rock weapons. Some females had jewelry placed with them.

Between every three or four homes was a memorial shrine. It was highly embellished with animal heads and horns, figurines, reliefs, stalactites, and statues. The dead buried within were surrounded with lavish items and weapons.

The statues were most often of females ranging in age from adolescent to crone. The Goddess was dual-headed with the sensibilities of both the virgin and the mother. She would often stand behind a leopard or was supported by two leopards while giving birth. Modern day Christians are astounded by the similarity between their kretch and the Catal Huyuk arrangement of a goddess mother and baby within a cave, perhaps, with her consort.

The walls contained bold reliefs of females either dancing with horizontal arms, or birthing children with vertical arms and legs. The leopard was depicted alone or with a partner and is thought to symbolize the female. There were no reliefs of males. The heads of bulls and sometimes rams and stags were cast within the plaster along with their antlers and horns. These animal parts are thought to symbolize the male.

Bricks were the length of three human hands and the width of one hand. The shrine walls were painted in monochromatic ochre panels or entirely in many colors. Designs included simple and complex patterns plus human hands. Today, in the village neighboring the dig, the depth memory of Catal Huyuk survives through the presence of human hands painted on the walls of homes and partitions.

Catal Huyuk shrines contained the first known landscape paintings in the world. The city and a volcano erupting were pictured in one painting. In another painting, deer were being hunted by men with weapons. Rituals were depicted in two shrines in which males bearing weapons yank at the tails and tongues and try to apprehend wild bears, boars, bulls, deer, and lions. Because killing was not shown, we hypothesize that these pictures tell the story of animal domestication or a myth. A common theme of the paintings was death.

After 800 years of peaceful living, Catal Huyuk was deserted. It was rebuilt on the opposite side of the river and Catal Huyuk West had an 800 year history. The reason for this move is not known to us today and Catal Huyuk West lies unexcavated by any archaeological team.

Catal Huyuk, although progressive in advancing the Neolithic culture, still hunted in the rich Plain of Konya and maintained many customs of its Upper Palaeolithic heritage. Catal Huyuk conserved Upper Palaeolithic practices more than any other Neolithic site. These artistic practices, indeed rituals, included macaroni, meander, and spiral designs; natural images of animals, deities, and humans; ochre painted skeletons and burial bowls; plaster reliefs; stone tools; sea shell and tooth jewelry; replications of the ritual hunting and injuring of animals; wall-paintings; and talismans of the bird-woman deity. The remembering of the past while progressing into the future seemed to be an important component in their long history.

CONCLUSION

In this analytic essay, I have been investigating the connection between Partnership Cultures and the Human Spirit, utilizing archaeology as a metaphor. In both Lepenski Vir and Catal Huyuk, there are similar and different stories which extend over time which the archaeological record allows us to see. Marija Gimbutas after examination of over 160 archaeological excavations in Old Europe has theorized that there was a 3000 year matrilineal era when there was no warfare. Riane Eisler has explicated Gimbutas' history, indicating that the history of the world has had matrilineal and patrilineal periods. I believe that neither one is a perfect system.

Today, we can make choices about our future. By the mercy of the universe, we have paleolithic excavations plus paleolithic aboriginals who have survived and are living reminders of how to live in concert with animal and human life, the landscape, and the solar system. We can harvest Pangaia as we make conscious choices about our future.

I am defining partnership as the dynamic interrelationship in which each human has a part in co-creating the world. Partnership is the unity of the transpersonal self with fundamental human qualities, working in consonance with the solar system. Thus, in partnership, humans who recognize their transcendent powers of consciousness and are motivated by broader and less selfish impulses than physical needs and egoistic emotions ponder and act on ultimate questions—meaning, purpose, and value of human life.

The basic vision of preliterate and literate societies is to survive in the face of hazards and dangers endemic in nature and humankind. Survival depends on living the paradigm of partnership: sharing, cooperation, and empowering within a communal system of individuals, related to one another by blood, marriage, or extended kinship.

Partnerships among community members are required in order to develop a partnership with nature and the deities. Individuals by themselves can not survive or attune to the spiritual life demanded by their deities unless they work and worship in union. Trying to obtain a superordinate goal and survival requires individuals to often subordinate personal desires, wishes, and behaviors in deference to the group norms and practices.

Activities around a superordinate goal, one which cannot be achieved without the involved cooperation of others encourages co-partnering—while reducing tension, rejection, and intolerance among community members. Early socialization into co-operative and partnership patterns provides for a modus operandi in later life, attuned to the spirit and the demands of nature and the deity.

Lepenski Vir and Catal Huyuk inhabitants had both emerged from the early Paleolithic Ages where the goal of life was "To Kill, or Be Killed" by the mammoths to later Paleolithic Ages where they could begin to address, "To Be, or Not To Be." Oswald Spengler wrote, "Man is the only being that knows death; all others become old, but with a consciousness wholly limited to the moment, which must seem to them eternal. They see death, not knowing anything about it." Humans leaped into consciousness upon their recognition of the spiraling cycle of life. These humans respected and ingested the powers of their ancestors, deities, and totems. In the grand cycle of life, the humans then presented the ingested powers back to the universe and solar system in empathy, service, and unity.

Dragoslav Srejovic, Yugoslav excavator of Lepenski Vir wrote,

> . . . one thing is certain: the first farming and stock-breeding communities, including those that built the Lepenski Vir IIIa and IIIb settlement emerged after the achievements in the domestication of animals and cultivation of plants had been taken out of their original ritual context. However, once they became common skills, available to all, the traditional social relations were abolished, the monumental art disappeared, the old myth became extinct, and the entire Lepenski Vir culture collapsed.

The Revolution of the Ages was and continues to be a dramatic life-altering spiral which requires partnership with tradition, art, and myth.

I would like to propose a theory. For the past thirty years, professionals in business, development, education, medicine and social services have applied Abraham Maslow's hierarchy of needs to the work with individuals. I, myself, taught nurses in the early 1970s how to evaluate the status of a client using Maslow's hierarchy. To briefly review Maslow's Theory, individuals must satisfy one level of needs before they can satisfy the next level.

There are five levels of need. The first level includes the basic needs of food, water, and reproductive sex. The second need is shelter. The third need is love and belongingness. The fourth need is self-esteem. The highest need is self-actualization, realization of unity with all life. Maslow believed that individuals satisfied waves of needs. For instance, an individual would be working on obtaining of food, water, and reproductive sex primarily and also working on finding shelter. In the past several years, it has been vogue for individuals to speak of themselves as self-actualized. Actually, Maslow felt that only a few individuals ever achieved self-actualization, such persons as Ghandi, Albert Schweitzer, Mother Theresa, and Harriet Tubman.

Acknowledging Maslow for his very positive contribution to the humanization of our world and begging his forgiveness for tampering with his theory, I would like to propose an addition to his theory. I propose that we transform the one hierarchical pyramid into two interlocked pyramids, a symbol which mythologists call King Solomon's Seal and the Star of David. As we look at the aboriginal arts and cultures, we see that the survival of the world depends upon the incorporation of the spirit of unity, the concept of self-actualization within every act of life. The acts of obtaining food, water, and reproductive sex plus shelter need to be interposed with the spirit of thankfulness, celebration, and unity.

As I look at the international views of 1988, I am encouraged by the recognition of the value of partnership by nations. During the past two generations, there have been 120 wars. The United States and the U.S.S.R. together spend 600 billion dollars on defense. The nations of the world are evaluating the economic and human costs of war. After a nine year occupation, Vietnam is talking about removing itself from Cambodia. The tragedy of the American ship mistakingly shooting down a civilian plane caused Iran and Iraq to look at the costs of their eight-year war. The USSR, with its first class defense and its third class economy, has reevaluated the costs of their war in Afghanistan. This long war has required many expensive soldiers, guns, helicopters, and planes and has been an economic disaster. Soviet withdrawal has started from Afghanistan. The utter, ultimate economics of war may be the primary motivator for nations to become partners in peace.

I am most heartened by the partnership we witnessed regarding the California gray whales stranded in a hole in the ice near Point Barrow, Alaska. This partnership occurred between groups who around some issues have been adversaries. The Native Americans wish to harvest animals within the prescribed rituals of their heritage. As partners with our ancestors, the Post-Glacial Age Hunters of the Mammoth, they do not slaughter trapped young whales. As partners with their totem, they ingest and embody the powers of the whale. As partners with all life, they are empathetic with trapped youth. The Native Americans informed federal authorities of the situation. They did not have to, they could have killed the whales and informed the Department of Interior about the extenuating circumstances and the necessary killing to rationalize the exceeding of their quota by three.

The Native American's demonstration of partnership with their ancestors, their totems, nature, each other, adversaries, and strangers has been a testament to the world. News services told the world of the whales. The telephone company hired extra operators to field the calls from as far across the world as Australia and Madagascar.

The Native Americans, patiently with axe, shovel, and chain saw chipped away at the ice to maintain and construct breathing holes for the whales. Folk from the mainland provided whirlpools to keep the holes from freezing over. Individuals from all over the world stood in the freezing cold to bear witness, and encourage the animals to swim through the narrow waters, from air hole to air hole, five miles to the open sea. Daily in school, the Eskimo children drew pictures, sang songs, and enacted skits praising the strength and endurance of the whales. Environmental advocacy groups, federal agencies, and oil conglomerates provided expertise. Russian ice breakers smashed a path through 30 foot high ridges of ice. The two young whales were released to make their first annual migration to California. Japanese whalers have even promised not to kill these two whales!

Mythologists and social artists can co-create the history of the world. One day it will be told like this.

Once upon a time there was chaos. Then a star and a planet mated and their gasses intermingled. Cell by cell, life formed, fish, amphibians, reptiles, mammals, and humans with the most sophisticated brain of all. Chaos reappeared in the form of sibling rivalry and turf wars. Gradually, humans outgrew the stage of sibling rivalry, realizing that all humans are brothers and sisters, partners with each other and the resources of the world. The true adjustment is within the human heart.

We dance, sing, and express ourselves in art and drama, knowing that conscious community, consensus, partnership exist within our hearts. We rejoice and celebrate, knowing that mindful empathy, harmony, unity are available to us all. Ab-original life, underground literally and figuratively, can be remembered. We can co-create the future of conscious, empathetic partnership with our ancestors, the powers of spirit and nature we incorporate within ourselves, our neighbors circling the planet.

REFERENCES

A Guide to Catalhoyuk. Translated from the Turkish by Hasan Inal. Konya, Turkey: Directory of the Konya Museum, 1983.

Akurgal, E. "The Prehistoric Period." *Ancient Civilizations and Ruins of Turkey: From Prehistoric Times until the End of the Roman Empire*. Translated from Turkish by John Whybrow. Sixth Edition. Istanbul, Turkey: Haset Kitabevi, 1985.

Eisler, R. *The Chalice and the Blade: Our History, Our Future*. San Francisco, CA: Harper and Row, 1987.

Gimbutas, M. *The Goddesses and Gods of Old Europe 6500-3500 BC: Myths and Cult Images*. New and Updated Edition. Berkeley, CA: University of California Press, 1982.

Gimbutas, M. Personal Communication. Los Angeles, CA: 8 August 1988.

Hayes, F. Personal Communication. Menlo Park, CA: 10 December 1988.

Mellaart, J. *Catalhoyuk*. New York, NY: McGraw-Hill, 1967.

Rothenberger, E. Personal Communication. Oxtepec, Mexico: 21 November 1988.

Srejovic, D. *Lepenski Vir*. London, England: Thames and Hudson, 1968.

Srejovic, D. *Lepenski Vir*. Belgrade, Yugoslavia: National Museum, 1979.